AMERICA'S BUSINESS

By the same author

AMERICAN MYTH, AMERICAN REALITY

NO THIRD CHOICE:
Progressives in National Republican Politics, 1916–1921

AMERICA'S BUSINESS

James Oliver Robertson

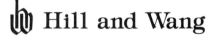

Hill and Wang
A division of Farrar, Straus and Giroux
NEW YORK

Printed in the United States of America
Published simultaneously in Canada by Collins Publishers, Toronto
Designed by Tere LoPrete
First printing, 1985

Library of Congress Cataloging in Publication
Robertson, James Oliver.
America's business.
Bibliography: p.
1. Business enterprises—United States—History.
2. Businessmen—United States—History. I. Title.
HD2785.R55 1985 338.7'4'0973 84-22429

TO

Haney Morgan Robertson

and

Frances Elizabeth Courtney Hensel Robertson

who

gave me much more than a start in the business of life

and who

introduced me to the rewards of contrary thinking

Acknowledgments

No one ever writes a work of history alone, and in this general interpretation I have been particularly dependent on the work of others. In the bibliography I have tried to acknowledge my great debt. But it is necessary to say, at the beginning, that I would never have dared to proceed without the ideas, research, and interpretations in the works of Thomas C. Cochran and Alfred D. Chandler, Jr., and in Sigmund Diamond's *The Reputation of the American Businessman.*

There are a great many people who, over many years, have helped me learn about America's business. I am indebted and grateful to Richard F. Samson and Anne Y. Samson, whose knowledge and encouragement have always been there; Jerry Davidoff and Denise T. Davidoff, who have helped me learn about the law, advertising, marketing, and the corporate world; Moses P. Epstein, who found a fascinating research job for a graduate student and introduced me to the textile business; R. E. Ostby, Jr., and Leila F. Ostby, who have shown me entrepreneurship and management; James W. Rodriguez, who has taught me about small business and communities; C. F. Sornberger, who has guided me in the ways of the market and the world of finance; Steven J. Stadler, who has revealed to me the complexities and joys of public corporations, modern management, and finance; Ethan C. Tolman, who has kept me alive to the human beings in business; and Arthur W. Wang, whose constant encouragement and great skills have taught me much about business—mine, his, and America's.

There are many others who have been particularly helpful: Fannie S. Cohen (who should always head such a list), Mercer Field, John A. Light, Walter Plotch, Lillian Poses, S. Bruce Smart, Jr., David J. and Sally Steinberg, and both Rachel M. and Jonathan M. Robertson, who have let me learn something of their business, and who have been of immense help to mine.

I have had generous support from a variety of institutions in the research and writing of this book. I am particularly grateful to the University of Connecticut, especially Dean Julius Elias of the College of Liberal Arts and Sciences, the Research Foundation, Assistant Dean Ann Huckenbeck of the School of Business, Professor Edmund H. Wehrle, Head of the History Department, and Norman Stevens of the Babbidge Library. I am also very grateful to the Master (then Professor Sir William Hawthorne) and Fellows of Churchill College, Cambridge University; to the Business History Conference; and to the libraries of Harvard University, Cambridge University, and the University of London.

Colleagues and students have listened to my ideas on America's business and its history and have helped considerably with challenges, ideas, and suggestions as well as patience. I am very much in the debt of Fred Carstensen, Diane Cox, Marvin Cox, Richard O. Curry, Irene Q. Brown, Richard D. Brown, Joel Kupperman, Karen O. Kupperman, Lawrence Langer, Robert Lougee, James McKelvey, Kent Newmyer, Thomas Paterson, and Harry Stout—all from the vicinity of the University of Connecticut; Richard Fry, of Illinois College; Robert Gross, of Amherst College; Rupert Wilkinson, of Sussex University; Jonathan Zeitlin, of Cambridge University (who let me sit in on his first course of lectures); Charlotte Erickson, Mark Kaplanoff, Bettye Wood, David Reynolds, John Thompson, and the members of the American Studies Seminar of the History Faculty, Cambridge University, in 1982–83; J. R. Pole and the members of his seminar at Oxford; Jonathan Steinberg and Sandra Rabin of Trinity Hall, Cambridge University, as well as David Platt; and Gordon Wood, of Brown University.

There have been many others—friends, colleagues, students, and business people—who have contributed to my education about America's business, who cannot all be named here, and to whom I am grateful. Finally, this whole book is much more Janet's business than she planned.

J.O.R.

Contents

AMERICA'S BUSINESS

What Is America's Business?

Books and articles about business—how to do it big, what's right about management, what's wrong about it, why the Japanese are better at it than we are, what must be done to do better business and more of it, and how we can produce better entrepreneurs—are legion. There are dozens of magazines devoted to the practice, the techniques and technology, and the success of American business. We all assume business to be an important part of life (for better or worse). The questions we ask about business are how to do it, or how to control it. Not where did it come from, or why do we have it.

Until I had lived outside the United States and tried to explain my country to others, I had not realized how much the language, attitudes, and assumptions of business permeate American life and make it different from the lives and cultures of other peoples in other nations. Like most Americans, I had grown up believing that business and "free enterprise" and "capitalism" were part of human nature, not peculiar to America.

What others see, and we often do not, is that business has an unusually powerful influence on the behavior, the attitudes, the beliefs, and the perceptions of all Americans. Business is central to our lives. We have an extensive business mythology: businesses, business people, and the fortunes made from business figure largely in the stories we tell of American heroes and heroines. Business has a central role in our interpretations of our national past—we all know something of the importance of corporations and plantations, merchants, fur traders, stockbrokers, colonizing companies, railroad land grants, robber barons, and mass production.

Why? Where did all this come from? How did business become so important to Americans? Has it always been the way it is now, or has it changed over the years? The answers are not altogether what I expected.

I have sketched the development of American business in (roughly) chronological order because the world-as-it-is, which everyone accepts and challenges, tries to succeed in, and tries to change, comes out of time past. Such a reconstruction has made some very important patterns clear.

First, it becomes obvious that what we today call "business"—the production and movement of goods to markets for profitable sale—was much more important and pervasive in the daily lives of the English, Spanish, French, Dutch, and other European colonists in America than it was in the nations from which those colonists came. The early English colonies were business corporations. Second, business developed into a revolutionary force. Unusually widespread business activity in America subverted the strong beliefs in class and a class-structured society which were (and still are) characteristic of Europeans and their societies. In America, people who acquired wealth through successful business "rose" to positions of social and political power in their own lifetimes as a result of their business success, not because of their class, birth, or inheritance.

The political and social ideals of the American Revolution—independence, equality, democracy, and individualism—were inextricably connected to business activity. For many Americans after 1776, seeking profit in the marketplace, acquiring the possession and use of land and other property brought individual independence, social equality and mobility, and proved the right of the individual to participate in government and exercise political power.

The corporation began to be used by American business people immediately after the Revolution. By the beginning of the twentieth century it had become characteristic of American business (but not of businesses in other rich, industrializing nations). The corporation became popular because it provided a solution to conflicts peculiar to America—between community control and individual freedom, between government regulation and business independence, and between the business use of public powers and the ideal of private property.

Powerful ideals of community and commonwealth have existed since the Revolution in constant conflict with the American ideals of individual freedom and independence. For two hundred years, fierce conflicts over the control and regulation of business, as well as over the close and advantageous relations of businesses to governments have been characteristic. What has significantly changed has been the size and nature of the businesses and their relation to the governments involved—as well as popular beliefs about the relations of business to democracy.

The connection between the labor essential to agriculture and manufacturing and the business activity of seeking markets and profits has been unusually close and long-lasting in America. Slavery, machine manufacturing, integrated factories, interchangeable parts, assembly lines, and automated production have all developed or been elaborated as part of a business drive to produce and market more goods with as little work as possible.

Big business corporations—with their bureaucracies, armies of workers, and nationwide scope—were created by American business nationalists in the late nineteenth and throughout the twentieth century. They revolutionalized the nature of the marketplace—establishing a single national market and destroying local and regional markets—transformed production, and achieved a measure of control of markets, resources, work, and money never before possible to businesses. Big business corporations also restructured American federalism, destroyed much of the power of local and state governments, and helped create a stronger, more centralized national government.

American big business brought the development of the modern consumer society. The twentieth-century American practices of mass production, mass marketing, and mass consumption have been exported and (particularly since World War II) emulated by other advanced, industrial nations. American big businesses have become multinational giants, the American people have become remarkably affluent, and new questions about the nature of America's business have arisen.

There has been, in the twentieth century, a gradual loss among Americans of a sense of individual participation in business. When, in the 1920's, Calvin Coolidge said that "the business of America is business" he seemed to mean big business, not struggling individual entrepreneurs. Most Americans today think big business is real business.

The millions of small shops, stores, and entrepreneurs in America, the "everyday" activity of making and taking goods and services to a marketplace and trying to sell them for a profit, the entrepreneurial work of creating marketable products and companies (from local crafts to the newest kinds of computers)—that isn't "business" to most Americans. It is simply common sense, natural, what any free and sensible human being does. We are not surprised to find entrepreneurial activity in other countries, even in countries opposed to "capitalism," because we assume such activity is inherent in human nature, not something peculiar to Americans.

The majority of working Americans today are the employees of business companies. They spend their working lives participating in the marketplace, profit-seeking activities of their firms and companies. But they do not think of themselves as "in business," or as "business people." They are, they will insist, employees, or workers, or professionals, or managers, or administrators; and if they *are* involved in business, they are not in business for themselves (which, in American logic, makes them less involved in business).

It is a mistake—which many foreigners make—to think that all Americans *like* business, or approve of big business, or think that "what's good for General Motors is good for America." Far from it. There are today, and there long have been, many who have devoted their lives and their energies to doing battle against business in all its forms. The possibility of "opting out" of business, business behavior, and business "life-style" has, for at least three centuries, been available to Americans (but the option has always been out of the predominant mode, which says something important about the influence of business). One successful New York businessman insisted, in an interview for this book, that businesses were vast, corrupt and corrupting, faceless, powerful corporations. They had, he said, been hand-in-hand with government ever since the Constitution was written in Philadelphia in 1787. They were so powerful today, he said, that he doubted that Americans could use the government to protect themselves from them. Most Americans, he contended, had opposed business most of the time, fought against businesses, and hated businesses and business people. "Besides," he concluded, "American business has failed. Look at the steel companies—or the car companies. They're losing out to the Germans and the Japanese. Can't even make a car that will sell." Even successful American business people have strong and serious doubts about America's business.

But all Americans find it necessary to be concerned about business, whether they consider it successful or a failure, good or evil, freeing or corrupting. Americans from an early age are told of the fascinations, the possibilities, the stories and myths, the profit motive and market behaviors, the dazzling expectations, and the potential rewards attributed to business enterprise. There is a peculiarly American relationship to business. What it is, where it came from, and how it has been transformed is what this book describes.

I have focused on the development and change over time of American business attitudes, institutions, people, and behavior. This is not an economic history concerned with growth, "welfare," money, GNP, or other statistical abstractions. While it touches on public policy as well as economic "forces" and systems, it is not a history of those things. The word "capitalism" does not appear in the rest of the book. As we use that term, it carries so great a load of judgment and prejudice it is difficult to explain anything by it. It was given its enormous load of meaning by the classical economists and by Karl Marx. Marx's analysis of the development of industrial culture in Western Europe is brilliant and enduring, but his theories of history and social development do not apply, so far as I can see, to the history, structure, or development of American society. It is impossible to discuss capitalism without using the analytical categories Marx created and elaborated. I have tried to avoid the ideological baggage—classical, Marxist, present-day Keynesian, and conservative—that a discussion of capitalism requires.

I have included short profiles of successful businessmen in the narrative. There are problems in using these. Apologists for American business believe that its leaders epitomize its virtues, and that wealth and success are the result of the application of "business principles," hard work, and "the American system." Critics have called business leaders "robber barons" (and worse), and while some critics would agree that they are products of the system, few argue that their behavior was virtuous or should be emulated. But people who made great fortunes in business did indeed exist, and many

Americans believe that they are—for better or worse—typical. They must be explained, because they represent what others aspired to and what the society both permitted and encouraged, and because American business has produced more great fortunes than business in any other nation. I have used as examples people who were thought of as eminently successful by their contemporaries, because the nature of their success defined the limits of what was popularly acceptable business behavior in their generations. And I have used men as examples because they were, until recently, the sex most involved in markets and most visibly pushing the limits of business behavior (and I have depended heavily on the research and writings of others in this book, and there is, unfortunately, very little literature on women in American business).

Finally, a warning. Most Americans today believe that change is a rapid, revolutionizing process; that technological and economic change is more or less automatic and progressive (each change based upon and better than the last). Yet the changes which have created today's American business have come slowly. The mere introduction of a new idea, practice, invention, or technology has not brought immediate or widespread use or acceptance. Robert Fulton built an operating steamboat in 1807, but it was not until 1893—eighty-six years later—that the tonnage of ships using steam first exceeded the tonnage of sailing ships. The Wright brothers flew their first plane in 1903, but it was thirty years before commercial aviation began to attract many passengers, and even after sixty years of flight, fewer than five percent of all Americans had been in an airplane.

There has never been a guarantee that the world will buy a better mousetrap—or want a better explanation or accept a new idea. There is always opposition to novelty. People in general are committed to things as they are; they like to hang on to what "works." Those who introduce new ideas, technologies, or ways of doing business have to sell them—

they become advocates to convince others. They attack the established order. And the established order fights back. Change is often neither rapid nor automatic—and not always for the better.

The course of America's business has been marked by change, but only rarely and exceptionally has that change been welcomed by those already in business, or encouraged by interests already vested, or advocated by the established order. It is only after the fact, not in the midst of doing business, that change, uncertainty, and competition have ever seemed good. American business people have sought to control their world, predict their futures, and eliminate the chaos and uncertainty of competition. Those involved in America's business have, like everyone else, always looked to the past, to "tried and true ways."

Creating American Business 1565-1776

For more than two centuries before the minutemen fought the British at Lexington and Concord in April 1775, before the Congress in Philadelphia declared the united American states independent in July 1776, large numbers of Europeans and Africans settled in colonies in America. During those two centuries, many of those colonists had become engaged in trade—with the Indians, with each other, with Great Britain, and with other people in the world. But while there was trade, there was not, as the American Revolution began, anything which could be defined as particularly and peculiarly American business. The idea that commerce, trade, and shopkeeping for profit were business, and that there was anything uniquely American about it, developed after the Revolution.

There were few in 1776 who used the word "business" to denote trade or commerce. Most thought of business simply as "activities" (the state of being busy) or as a person's particular affairs ("what he does is his business"). The more modern American definition of business as the *activities connected with the production, movement, acquisition, and exchange of goods and services in a market for profit* gained currency very slowly. Even now that meaning of the word "business" is the twenty-first meaning listed in the *Oxford English Dictionary* (published in England in 1933), the sixth meaning listed in *Merriam Webster's New International Dictionary* (second edition, published in America in 1943), and the second meaning in the *American Heritage Dictionary* (published in America in 1969).

Nevertheless, some of the attitudes later associated with American business, and some of the practices and assumptions which we today believe are characteristic of American business, developed during the two hundred years of colonial life before the American Revolution. The Revolution and later generations of Americans who have tried to realize its ideals created a social fabric which might be called a business civilization. But that fabric was woven out of fibers and threads of colonial experience.

The first of those threads was widespread engagement in trade among the colonists. By 1776, business activity was not confined to a particular class, social group, or occupation. It had become the preoccupation of the majority of American households—a significant difference from the norms of European society.

Second, agriculture—the primary productive occupation—was a business. It was oriented toward the quick exploitation of land and resources for market and profit. The majority of colonial farmers by 1776 hoped that every crop was a cash crop. There were, of course, some who lived on the land and did not produce for the marketplace (who did not farm, as the word was understood in the eighteenth century). Such people were considered shiftless, lazy, dirty, and poor; they were called squatters, backwoodsmen, swamp yankees, crackers, poor whites, and trash by the majority of farmers, who were in the business of raising goods and trying to get them to market and sold at a profit.

Third, before 1776, in America, land had become a commodity. There was widespread speculation in land, but even those who did not speculate commonly bought, sold, and exchanged land for profit. Land was widely owned (in contrast to Europe, where the ownership of land was limited to a small minority of the population). The majority of free American families owned land; most farmers worked their own (not some landlord's) land.

Fourth, by 1776, social prestige, political power, and high position could be earned in America, achieved by successful business activity. Power, prestige, and position were not, as all knew, simply the result of birth or inheritance, noble blood or gentle forebears (although such "advantages" of class did still bring those traditional rewards). A person could acquire wealth, and with it leisure, position, and power. Trade could lead, in American life, to the status of gentleman; success permitted one's children to claim the privileges and power which in Europe belonged exclusively to the governing classes, the gentry, and the nobility.

Fifth, slavery was widespread by 1776. Slaves were the basis of the commercial production and profitable international marketing of several major American crops. The importing, buying, and selling of slaves had become one of the largest of colonial businesses (even larger and more important in the West Indian colonies than in North America). The demand for human labor in the nonmechanized, commercial-agricultural, relatively unpopulated American colonies was great, so that traffic in non-African, indentured (or "bond") servants was also very large.

Sixth, finding, exploiting, and controlling markets for American goods was a universal concern—not by any means the only concern of Americans, but a very important one.

Finally, increasing numbers of colonists believed, by 1776, that business activity—the production, transport, acquisition, and exchange of goods or services in a market for profit—was morally virtuous and socially useful. Belief in the morality of trade was, furthermore, not limited to the class who were called merchants and tradesmen.

The Old World Transplanted

The Europeans who migrated to the New World intended to make *some* changes in the circumstances of their lives, and they believed America offered that opportunity. But most of them did not intend to alter what they thought of as the God-given social order in which civilized human beings lived their lives, just as they did not intend to alter the kind of food they ate, the houses they lived in, or the ways they acquired food, clothing, shelter, warmth, and the conveniences of life.

Little about life in America was as they expected. Everything brought to the New World—including the ideas in people's minds and what they believed to be real—underwent "a sea-change into something rich and strange" (as Shakespeare put it in *The Tempest*—a play written about the New World). Altered beliefs, subtly changed expectations, and new practices grew and developed in America. But the transplanted Europeans continued to think in the same terms and tried to operate in the same institutions as they had in the Old World. The very idea of deliberately adapting one's habits and one's "life-style" to altered external circumstances was considered shocking and unpleasantly revolutionary (even as late as 1719, when Daniel Defoe published *Robinson Crusoe* in England. Crusoe, it should be noted, had a servant, Friday, who did a lot of the adjusting for him). Since it was impossible for most Americans to compare their own beliefs and practices with those of Europe, the differences that developed remained invisible, and most of the inhabitants of the British North American colonies thought of themselves as good "Englishmen" right up to the American Revolution.

The circumstances of the American colonies were different from Europe. The North American colonies were, without exception, established for the development of trade or for the exploitation of available resources. In North America, distances were vast, and the distance of the colonies from Europe—in time as well as miles—was very great. There was no extensive existing agriculture in America, and the crops that were grown by the natives were strange to Europeans. There were no available sources of gold, silver, precious stones, pearls, or other concentrated sources of what Europeans recognized as available wealth. There were no large populations of natives producing food or goods; therefore, little possibility of trade or exploitation of labor. There was an unimaginable extent of wilderness—what most early English settlers thought of as "desert" (countryside which was neither inhabited by civilized human beings nor recognizable as useful arable land). There was a climate of extremes of heat and cold completely unfamiliar to Europeans. It is little wonder that European ideas, perceptions, and behavior changed under such unexpected and different circumstances; but it is important to remember that, for generations, the European colonists resisted changes and tenaciously clung to what they believed was right, proper, civilized, Christian, and real.

The first two permanent European settlements in what would become the United States were established by Spain at St. Augustine, Florida, in 1565, and in New Mexico a few years later. Both were intended for the development of trade. In the first two decades of the seventeenth century, the English established two permanent settlements after several unsuccessful tries—at Jamestown in 1607 and at Plymouth in 1620—and the Spanish established one or two more. More than a century after Columbus's first voyage in 1492, the European invasion of North America began.

The New World was still a new idea in Europe at the beginning of the seventeenth century. Only a few thousand Spaniards, some Portuguese, a scattering of Italians, French, English, Dutch, and Scandinavians had migrated to the New World and begun to conquer the native Americans and spread Christianity. Large native civilizations had fallen under the control of the Spanish government and its Church, and the fabulous wealth of "the Indies" had become a permanent part of the European perception of America. It was the dream of acquiring such wealth that led Spanish, French, and English adventurers to North America.

Their success in large part depended on the willingness of their governments and the ruling classes back home to accept the idea, the possibility, that trade—the acquisition, transportation, and sale of goods for profit—was a legitimate, valuable activity for a Christian nation. Success also depended upon finding, supporting, and controlling a class of people who were willing to engage in trade. Since the value of trade, and the willingness of people to participate in it, seems so obvious to Americans today, it is difficult to imagine people not motivated by what we think is rational economic self-interest and who did not believe in the national value of trade. Yet the majority of Spaniards, for example, both in the Old and the New Worlds, believed in conquest, believed in Christian crusades against the heathen, believed that Christians who conquered and converted heathens were entitled to the tribute, taxes, surpluses, and valuable metals produced by those peoples— but they did not believe that Christian gentlemen or Christian nations engaged in trade. Merchants (who were decidedly not gentlemen) were allowed to engage in trade in order to provide luxuries desired by those who ruled—in the New World as the Old—but their trade was restricted and controlled, and their profits regulated, taxed, and periodically confiscated, seized, or forcibly "loaned" to rulers and government.

In England, by the seventeenth century, merchants had gained considerable freedom to govern their own affairs, and guilds of merchants (often called merchant companies) were chartered by the government, granted certain liberties, and frequently controlled the governments of cities (as they did in London). Merchants were producers of manufactured (literally "hand-made") goods as well as traders. In England, they were, as a class, considered beneath all gentlemen, knights, and noblemen (who controlled all the land and its produce).

Most goods in Europe moved from the primary producers (those who worked the land, the peasants, yeomen, and husbandmen) to the landowners by way of dues, rents, taxes, and tribute—not through buying and selling. Markets for goods were few, they could be held only with permission of the governing classes, and all market activity was regulated and controlled. While England was, by the seventeenth century, much engaged in trade, the number and influence of her merchants (her businessmen) was far outweighed by those whose wealth and power came directly from dues, rents, and produce of the land.

Not even those who belonged to the merchant class believed that business activities were moral or socially useful. Late in the sixteenth century, John Browne, a London merchant, wrote *The Marchants Avizo*, a handbook for young merchants traveling to Spain or Portugal. He advised them to conduct themselves humbly and religiously. He admonished them to observe and conform to the habits of the country they were in, and he insisted that they carefully carry out their instructions and commissions. When Browne's book was published in 1607, it contained models of letters for young merchants to write to their master, of accounts to be kept, and of bills of lading to be issued and accepted. It also contained tables of foreign weights, measures, and monies, with English equivalents. And there were parables and fables for young merchants to study during their travels. What is striking about the book, for a twentieth-century American, is its lack of economic information. There is nothing about markets, nothing about money (except some brief exchange information) or credit, nothing about sales, nothing about goods. What mattered to the merchant writing, and to the young merchants he was advising, was their *conduct*, in religion most particularly, in regard to their masters, in their commissions, and in relation to the customs of the countries to which they might travel. Trade was important, but Browne did not see it as separate from proper conduct, the maintenance of the proper relationships between masters and men, and careful, conscious adherence to proper religious practices and beliefs.

There were many in England and on the Continent in the seventeenth century who opposed colonizing the New World, who believed that colonies (they were often called "plantations") were socially destructive, were in the interests neither of the "nation" (the king and the ruling classes) nor of society. Those who argued for the establishment of colonies (and the literature advocating plantations increased rapidly in early-seventeenth-century England) couched their arguments in terms their readers could understand and approve. The "one proper, and principall end of Plantations, is, or should be," Richard Eburne wrote in 1624 in *Plaine Pathway to Plantations*, "the enlargement of Christ's Church on Earth; and the publishing of his Gospel to the Sons of Men." The stated purpose for the chartering and founding of virtually every English colony was the establishment of the Church and the expansion of Christianity.

Eburne's second argument was that colonies increased the dominion of the king, who was the representative of God's authority on earth, upon whom every person and family in the kingdom depended for position, security, and prosperity. An increase in the dominion of the king brought new territories, lands, and treasures available to those who inhabited the society over which the king ruled. Englishmen willing to "transplant" themselves to colonies, Eburne wrote, might exchange "for their bad cottages, good houses; for their little gardens, great grounds; and for their small backsides [back yards or back lots] large fields, pastures, meadows, woods, and other like plenty to live upon." Wealth, power, and honor flowed from the ownership of land under the king's dominion, in Eburne's world—not, as we might see it today, from each person exploiting his own land, or from manufacturing and producing goods and selling them.

There was trade in Eburne's world, and, he said, if everyone understood as English merchants did, how much trade would be increased by plantations, then everyone would want plantations. But there were many merchants and potential investors who argued that there was no profit in plantations—and they could cite many attempts by Spanish, French, and English merchants and adventurers to establish trading posts in North America which had collapsed, despite being well financed and supported. Sir Walter Raleigh's Roanoke settlement, for example, had disappeared. The people at a well-established post called Sagadahoc (in what is now the state of Maine) had been taken off and the post abandoned just the year after the Virginia Company established a post at Jamestown. In 1624, the year Eburne published his book, there were few in England who believed that the settlers remaining in Virginia after seventeen years of intensive effort and expensive investment would survive, much less produce any profitable trade.

Eburne countered by arguing that no one had tried plantations long enough:

> It is not one year's work or two, to get a good state in lands. . . . They that go over to such a business [i.e., activity] have many things to do first, before they can have time to gather wealth about them: as to build, to rid their grounds, to make fences, to destroy wild and hurtful beasts, to get over good and profitable cattle, to plant and sow their grounds, and the like: All which be matters of great labor, time, and expense. . . . It is well if seven, or ten, or twenty year's hence, haply in the next generation, men can attain unto riches. It is enough for the fathers to take in the grounds, and settle the lands and livings for them and theirs against the time to come. . . .

Eburne and his contemporaries saw plantations in the context of a social world established by God and ruled by a king in which wealth, profit, and territories were sought in order to provide estates, livings for families over many generations. Each class had a fixed place in the social, economic, and political pyramid. The king was at the top, and below him were the ranks of nobles, knights, and gentlemen, yeomen and husbandmen, merchants and artisans, and at the bottom, cottagers, laborers, and servants. Land and the right to use or profit from it was the basis of wealth and of social and political position. Land was the only *real estate* upon which anyone could depend for continued existence.

The family was assumed to be the fundamental unit of economic activity, of social position, and of political power. The family and its household, high or low on the social scale, was the context in which most people lived their lives. Families were nuclear, focused upon the father and mother, and for all members of a household—children, dependent relatives, apprentices, servants of all kinds and levels of skill and age, retainers and other employees and hangers-on—the father was the master who stood *in loco parentis* in law and custom for all, and was responsible for the care, feeding, housing, clothing, warmth, training, education, morals, and continuing prosperity of the household. The relationships within that extended family were moral, not economic. (Even apprentices, servants, and journeymen paid by the day, who seem to our modern eyes to have had exclusively economic relationships to their masters, were believed to owe their masters the same honor, loyalty, filial duty, and labor that children owed parents; the masters owed them the same responsible care and nurture they owed children.) This family structure for the organization of productive work lasted well into the nineteenth century.

The colonies in America grew and developed in such a hierarchical society, governed by the royal household and the king's servants. In that society, merchants were a limited class—the people who engaged in trade. The lower orders worked—to produce necessary and useful goods. The upper orders were the people who counted—they maintained the king's dominion, and God's, by directing and managing the king's court and the royal government, the Church, the army, and local government and defense.

Widespread Trade

The Pilgrims who came to Plymouth in 1620 intended to establish a religious community. And they did. But they required backing—investors willing to pay for the *Mayflower*, supply ships, tools, equipment, and manufactured goods from England. The settlers continued to require food and additional supplies for years. The backers had to be repaid, and the colony had to produce in order to trade for the goods it could not make itself. In November 1621, barely a year after Plymouth was first settled, the *Fortune* arrived, carrying new settlers and bringing provisions from England. When it sailed back to England in December, it was loaded, according to William Bradford's account *Of Plymouth Plantation*, with

> good clapboard as full as she could stow, and two hogsheads of beaver and otter skins which they [the Pilgrims] got with a few trifling commodities brought with them at first, being altogether unprovided for trade. Neither was there any amongst them that ever saw a beaver skin till they came here and were informed by Squanto. The freight was estimated to be worth near £500.

The people in the Plymouth settlement who were "unprovided for trade" and ignorant of the most valuable of commodities—furs—which could be found for trade were not unusual. Migrants to America often came from rural areas and from lower classes in Europe. For such people to produce or acquire goods in order to trade required that they change their assumptions about agriculture, about the activities appropriate to different social classes, and about what they were put on earth to do.

In Plymouth, community leaders formed a merchant syndicate to do the trading for the whole colony, and thus the colonists learned how to trade. By 1626, Bradford recorded that the Pilgrims, "finding their corn (what they could spare from their necessities) to be a commodity (for they sold it at 6s. a bushel) used great diligence in planting the same." With furs and fish and clapboard, "and their corn after harvest," Bradford wrote, "they got good store of trade, so as they were enabled to pay their engagements . . . and to get some clothing for the people, and had some commodities beforehand." For more than a century, the Plymouth colonists were in strenuous competition with other colonies, companies, and merchants, producing and shipping goods along the coast of Massachusetts to trade for profit and the commodities they continued to need.

The merchants, underwriters, and "proprietors" of colonies and settlements, towns and trading posts throughout the English colonies from the beginning of the seventeenth to the last quarter of the eighteenth century created a constant pressure on every productive adult to engage in trade. The English underwriters of the Massachusetts Bay Company (another religiously motivated foundation) retained a monopoly of half the beaver trade, all the salt trade, the transportation of all goods and people to the colony, and the retailing of goods to all the colonists. Those monopolies were potentially very valuable, since more than ten thousand immigrants poured into the Massachusetts Bay Colony in the 1630's, and Massachusetts continued for a century and a half to be one of the largest and most populous of all the English colonies.

Massachusetts was founded by a chartered merchant company and the presence of merchant values and beliefs was maintained by the very institutions through which the colony was governed. To be a "free man" of the company and the colony meant, initially, to be a stockholder. The free man of a New England town was one of its proprietors. Merchant companies were ordinarily governed by quarterly stockholders meetings, called Great and General Courts, held in the headquarters city of the company. The Massachusetts leaders brought their company charter with them to Boston, and so the Court met in Boston (the Commonwealth of Massachusetts is still governed by a legislature called the Great and General Court). A governor and a board of assistants were appointed by the General Court to conduct the day-to-day affairs of the company between meetings of the General Court. So the Massachusetts colony was governed—as were many of the colonies—by bodies which owed their institutional forms to merchant companies.

Those who survived and prospered in the American colonies acquired an active interest in trade or production for trade. People who could adapt to life in the strange American "wilderness" and adapt to the necessity of trade (or could be forced to adapt, as slaves, indentured servants, and impoverished young people were) were the survivors. They lived in plantations, settlements, and towns, and they found themselves (many very reluctantly) engaged in trade.

The Business of Agriculture

A farmer, in seventeenth- and eighteenth-century England, was ordinarily a person who paid a fixed amount of money that permitted him to exploit an economic privilege. There had long been farmers of taxes in Europe, and farmers of state monopolies (salt and tobacco in France, for instance), who paid their governments fixed sums for the right to collect taxes, or sell salt or tobacco. A farm could also mean "a tract of land held on lease for the purpose of cultivation." But ordinarily people engaged in agriculture were peasants, or yeomen, or husbandmen, not "farmers."

In America, by the eighteenth century, a farmer was anyone (other than slaves, servants, and hired laborers) who tilled the soil. The label reflected the American reality. The American tiller of the soil produced not merely for subsistence and to pay rent or dues, but for market and profit.

The European peasant, in most cases, did not own land, had little need for goods not already available to him, and owed most of his surplus to his landlord. By 1650, however, as Darrett Rutman pointed out in "Governor Winthrop's Garden Crop" (an article in the *William and Mary Quarterly*, 1963), there were "some 15,000 people, perhaps 3,000 families" in Massachusetts.

> If averages hold good, each family held between twenty and thirty acres, of which between ten and twenty were in cultivation, probably three or four planted in grain earmarked to be sold and ultimately exported. These three or four acres would yield sixty to 100 bushels of wheat, or twelve to twenty pounds sterling in English goods per year. . . . This constituted probably the greater part of the annual income (discounting the home consumption of farm products) of the Bay family.

Americans became farmers, and the farmers found themselves behaving like merchants in search of profitable markets.

Whatever class they came from in the Old World, the circumstances of the New World—the scarcity of manufactured goods, the unavailability of local markets, the scarcity of people with needed skills or proper social position—seemed inexorably to push Americans toward trade (thus began the process of changing the class structure in colonial society). In the mid-seventeenth century, William Pynchon founded Springfield, Massachusetts, as a fur-trading post in the Connecticut River valley. As Bernard Bailyn wrote in *The New England Merchants of the Seventeenth Century*, Pynchon did not think of himself as merely a merchant.

> In England he had been a landed gentleman with large holdings . . . and he succeeded in transferring that status to the clearing on the Connecticut River. As chief magistrate, main landowner, and employer of almost every settler in Springfield, he could rightly have considered his role that of a manorial lord. His day books and journals . . . from 1645, show him

> during the best years of the fur trade deeply involved in supplying goods and equipment to the neighboring farmers as well as in buying and marketing their crops. . . . His trading posts became branch retail stores and there he collected the local crops for transshipment to the coast for sale.

Pynchon was unusual among early Americans, in that he left large holdings and his status as a landed gentleman behind; from being one among many landed gentlemen in England, he became a "manorial lord" in the Springfield settlement. Yet in order to achieve that high and successful status in America, he had become deeply engaged in trade, retailing, buying, seeking markets, and selling furs and produce. In short, a gentleman, in America, had to be a merchant in order to retain his high status: a confusing, topsy-turvy world for the thousands who emigrated to America, and for the tens of thousands who were born in America and tried to reconcile the realities of their lives to their beliefs.

They believed that "being in trade" was déclassé for gentlefolk. They believed that a merchant's status was class status, acquired by birth and long apprenticeship, fixed, and separate from the higher classes of gentry and nobility. Above all, they believed that the husbanding of the soil was the God-given lot of the vast majority of mankind, from which families could earn their daily bread and provide for those who owned the land and governed society. But, in America, even merchants and gentlemen had to cultivate their own soil in order to produce any goods, and anyone who desired an income beyond mere subsistence had to engage in trade.

Land as a Commodity

Abundance of land was a fact of American life. From it flowed, in what seems in hindsight a naturally and inexorably logical progression, the clearing and cultivation of that land by ever-increasing numbers of people, the marketing of the produce of the land, the "land-office business" of buying and selling land, and speculation in land. From the abundance of land, and the labor of thousands and then millions on it, came the profits, the savings, and the growing capital upon which later industrialization, economic development, and the ultimate wealth of America depends.

The "logic" of the American land's productivity, and of progressively increasing wealth based on its abundance, was not at all clear to the colonists. In the first place, the geography of North America (which we know) was only partially known to them. In 1705, Robert Beverley said, in his *History and Present State of Virginia*, that Virginia

> is bounded on the South by North *Carolina*; on the North by *Patowmeck* River, which divides it from *Maryland*; on the East by the main Ocean, called the *Virginia* Seas; and on the West and North-West by the *California* Sea, whenever the Settlements shall be extended so far.

It was a century later, in 1804, that another Virginian, Thomas Jefferson, sent the first official American exploring party (commanded by two more Virginians, Meriwether Lewis and William Clark) from the Mississippi River to the "California Sea" to find, among other things, just how far it was and whether the land was good for anything. They reported that it wasn't, it was the Great American Desert.

Most of the abundant land of North America was "desert" in the eyes of the colonists, uncultivated savage wilderness unfit for human habitation. "Wilderness skills" were not part of the upbringing or training (or expectations) of people imbued with seventeenth- and eighteenth-century European ideas about society, family, agriculture, and proper Christian behavior. Such people wanted to husband the soil, live in proper cottages and houses, and grow crops, as their ancestors had. Cutting trees, removing stumps, breaking new ground, planting unfamiliar crops and tending them were not part of their traditions—only reluctantly would they do those things. It is difficult for us to believe today that they expected "land" to be *real estate* (what later Americans called "improved" land), made up of fields and pastures, fenced, hedged, well defined, well used, husbanded, and cultivated; they expected roads and bridges, cottages and villages. They did not want to give up their expectations, or the tried-and-true ways of tilling the soil and making it productive, even when they found themselves unable to use those ways in America. And although it was the ones who did adapt, and did take up new ways, who survived, they nevertheless taught their former ways and old expectations to their children and grandchildren in the New World. For centuries the perception has lived on in America that wilderness is the *unfortunate* and typical state of American land, and that the land needs to be "civilized" and "improved" by the unproductive labor of clearing it and "opening" it to proper cultivation and production.

Yet land has continued to carry its European definition as the basis of civilized society, the ultimate source of individual and national wealth and success. Ownership of land gave a person a stake in society, a right to belong, a place, a position—even an "independency." So the American abundance of land remained a magnet, a strong temptation to people who believed that the possession and use of land was both symbol and substance of power, status, wealth, family security, and estate.

The only way to make the abundant wilderness into the productive real estate of European dreams was to bring people to it, to settle, cultivate, and trade. There were no great Indian populations with extensive agriculture such as the Spanish had found in Mexico. Clearing and cultivation required extensive, intensive human labor. Africans and a stream of Europeans of the poorer sort were forced to migrate to America and forced to work on clearing the wilderness and cultivating it. But the easiest and least expensive way to attract free labor to North America was to distribute land in return for population and labor. The king and the royal government of England, the merchant companies, the great proprietors, and the colonial governments all granted land in America in large and small quantities to people who seemed likely to "take up" the wilderness, clear it, work it, or attract other people who would. The land was granted in "fee simple" or in "free and common socage," which made it heritable, transferable by sale, devisable by will, free of all the old feudal obligations and dues, and subject at most to a small "quit rent" or "ground rent" to the grantor.

As a result of the abundance of land and the willingness to distribute it with minimal social, political, or economic obligations, population was attracted and land ownership became very widespread. By 1776, a majority of the families in the colonies owned and cultivated their own land—a remarkable difference from European reality. The social and economic independence that Europeans associated with ownership of the land was commonly available to the free and able-bodied in America.

Land had also gradually become a marketable commodity in colonial America, in part because of its abundance and widespread distribution. While many continued to view the land they cultivated as the family estate, to be husbanded, preserved, and passed on intact to succeeding generations, they had also begun to believe that some land—land that was still wilderness, land not needed for cultivation, or land which was separated from that under cultivation—could be bought and sold with a view to making a profit in the transaction. Such land came to be viewed as a commodity, like grain or other crops, not as real estate. People created markets in land. Even those who farmed were often willing to sell their farm for a profit (with the view to buying another, better place).

Land speculation and development (the purchase, division

into smaller plots, and resale of large tracts) was, by early in the eighteenth century, another indication that Americans commonly thought of land as a commodity. Dealers in land could become wealthy speculating in it, and because it was land they were marketing and profiting from, they could be considered gentlemen rather than successful tradesmen—an important difference in a society that still believed that wealth and power belonged to class (not that class status was earned by the acquisition of wealth).

For example, Daniel Dulany, the younger son of an Irish gentleman, arrived with his two brothers in Maryland in 1703. All were indentured and sold. Daniel, eighteen, had attended the University of Dublin, and he was bought by George Plater, a planter-lawyer-businessman, who used him as a law clerk and plantation accountant. By 1709, Dulany was free and began the practice of law. He married, acquired a plantation, lost his wife, remarried, increased his practice, bought other plantations, acquired minor offices, and by 1715 was being called a "gentleman." He became a banker, with several thousand pounds sterling lent at interest to planters, farmers, tobacco merchants, artisans, and tradesmen. He joined others in single-venture partnerships—in 1729, for example, he and others sold "a cargo of two hundred choice Negroes worth £4000 sterling." He was frequently the partner of Charles Carroll of Annapolis, one of Maryland's most successful merchants, and in 1731, with Carroll and others, formed the Baltimore Company, which became the largest iron producer in the English colonies. (When Dulany died in 1753, the company shares, worth £700 when the partnership was formed, were worth between five and ten thousand pounds sterling, and the company owned "several furnaces, three forges, 150 slaves, and 30,000 acres of land.")

Dulany's principal equity, however, was in land. He owned and ran producing tobacco plantations; he bought and rented plantations to tenants; he bought, sold, and used slaves and indentures; he bought warrants for land grants from the

Maryland proprietor, and speculated in land warrants for a total of 55,000 acres during his lifetime. He located and surveyed unclaimed lands and laid out plantations and settlements which he sold to settlers and from which ground rents were collected. The largest of his speculative settlements was the town of Frederick.

Speculators like Dulany—and by the time of the Revolution it was difficult to find a large landowner or merchant in America who was not involved in similar schemes—brought the widespread surveying, division, and distribution of land, encouraged immigration and the development of trade, and made land a marketable, profitable, exchangeable commodity. Land remained a symbol of many deep and important social functions and ideals, but it had acquired a new meaning. It was possible for Americans to be in the land business.

Trade and Success

William Fitzhugh (1651–1701) was born in England, the younger son of a woolen-draper, and migrated to Virginia when he was about twenty. Like many younger sons of urban merchants, he was provided with a grammar-school education in the classics and probably with an apprenticeship in the law, before he joined his older sister and her husband in Virginia to seek his fortune. He practiced law there and found opportunities through his practice and connections to acquire land, property, and profit. Within three years, he married the eleven-year-old daughter of an established Virginia family, receiving with his bride a Negro man and woman, three cows, six ewes and a ram, several hogs, a bay gelding, a necklace of pearls, and dishes, furniture, and kitchen equipment sufficient for housekeeping. Three years later, Fitzhugh and his wife settled along the Potomac in Stafford County, Virginia. In 1677, at the age of twenty-six, he was elected to the House of Burgesses.

Throughout the thirty years he lived in Virginia, Fitzhugh called himself, indiscriminately, "gentleman" and "merchant"—labels which were, for most of English society, descriptive of two distinct social and economic positions. A gentleman in England was of gentle birth and landed wealth, a man of "leisure" who governed his society. An English merchant, on the other hand, was a man who sought profitable markets for goods and services. He might be as wealthy as a gentleman, but not of such high birth or station, not leisured; he was engaged in trade rather than in government. In America, Fitzhugh found it possible to be both. He was, in the first place, a planter, engaged in the large-scale production and marketing of tobacco and other cash crops. He was also an aggressive, versatile merchant, engaged in trade, banking, speculation, crop buying, shipping, and rent collecting. And he was a gentleman as well, a landowner, attorney, lobbyist, lawmaker, and government administrator.

In America, throughout the colonial years, there were very few noblemen and not many gentlemen. High positions went to those who could claim the visible trappings (in the American context) of landed wealth, experience with government, and capable handling of public affairs. The restrictions which applied in English society, reinforced by powerful vested interests, were neither strong nor well established in colonial America. As a result, Fitzhugh was able to become a merchant, a farmer, and a gentleman member of the Virginia ruling class.

By the time he was thirty-five, Fitzhugh thought he had succeeded. He described his plantation to his brother-in-law in England. It contained, he wrote,

> a thousand Acres, at least 700 Acres of it being rich thicket, the remainder good hearty plantable land, without any waste either by Marshes or great Swamps. . . . upon it there is three Quarters well furnished, with all necessary houses, ground & fencing, together with a choice crew of Negros at each plan-

> tation, most of them this Country born, the remainder as likely as most in Virginia, there being twenty nine in all, with Stocks of cattle & hogs at each Quarter, upon the same land is my own Dwelling house, furnished with all accomodations for a comfortable & gentile living, as a very good dwelling house, with 13 Rooms in it, four of the best of them hung, nine of them plentifully furnished with all things necessary & convenient, & all houses for use well furnished with brick Chimneys, four good Cellars, a Dairy, Dovecote, Stable, Barn, Hen house Kitchen & all other conveniencys, & all in a manner new, a large Orchard of about 2500 Apple trees most grafted, well fenced with a Locust fence, which is as durable as most brick walls, a Garden a hundred foot square, well pailed in, a Yeard wherein is most of the forsaid necessary houses, pallizado'd in with locust Punchens, which is as good as if it were walled in, & more lasting than any of our bricks, together with a good Stock of Cattle hogs horses, Mares, sheep &c, & necessary servants belonging to it, for the supply and support thereof. About a mile & half distance a good water Grist miln, whose tole I find sufficient to find my own family with wheat & Indian corn for our necessitys & occasions. Up the River in this Country three tracts of land more, one of them contains 21996 Acres another 500 acres, & one other 1000 Acres, all good convenient & commodious Seats, & wch. in a few years will yield a considerable annual Income. A stock of Tobo. with the Crops & good debts lying out of about 250000lb. besides sufficient of almost all sorts of goods, to supply the familys & the Quarter's occasions for two if not three years.

He calculated his income, from the sale of tobacco, grain, and meat beyond what was needed to feed and clothe everyone on the Plantation, at 60,000 pounds of tobacco, or £300, per year, a generous income at the time.

Fitzhugh was quite conscious of the need for capital, a labor supply, good management, and good markets, for the successful operation of his ventures. In 1690, he wrote his formula for success to a Bedfordshire acquaintance who intended to "settle" one of his sons in Virginia. "The best method for such a settlement," Fitzhugh wrote,

> is by lodging in some Merchants hand in London 150 or 200£ for the buying, a good convenient seat of land, which upon so much ready money some may in a short time be purchased, & then about such another sum lodged in the hands of some of the Royall African Company who for that will engage to deliver Negroes here at 16 or 18 or to be sure £20 per head, which purchase so made of Land & Negroes, the dependences upon a Settlement, as horses Cattle, hogs &c. are easily purchased here to begin with, & continually raised for a future support. . . . A Settlement thus made, will make a handsom gentile & sure subsistence. . . . Whereas if he should have three times the sums above mention'd, its certain it will yield him a great deal of Tobo., but if either neglect carelessness or unskilfullness should happen its all brought to nought, & if the best husbandry & the greatest forecast & skill were used, yet ill luck at Sea, a fall of a Market, or twenty other accidents may ruin & overthrow the best Industry.

For all his success, high social position, and political power, Fitzhugh remained a believer—as did most colonial Americans even at the time of the Revolution—in that social pyramid in which men possessed power, wealth, land, and the right to govern because they were gentlemen (not because they had been financially successful). In his old age—between age thirty-seven and his death at fifty—Fitzhugh devoted an increasing amount of time and effort to securing his position as a gentleman. "For now with my buildings finished, my plantations well settled, & largely stocked with Slaves," he wrote to his principal London merchants, "I esteem it well politic as reputable, to furnish my self with an handsom Cupboard of plate." A cupboard of silver dishes and implements, prominently displayed in one of his better rooms, with a coat of arms engraved upon it (he went to some lengths to establish his right to a coat of arms, the essential right of a gentleman), would, as Fitzhugh was aware, not only "give my self the present use & Credit," provide his children with "a certain portion" when he died, but also convince all who beheld or knew of such a display that its owner was a man of high station and leisure, a gentleman rather than a merchant or a man of business. Over the years, he increased his collection of "plate" and acquired an English carriage and a great variety of other goods calculated to reinforce his visible status as a gentleman.

Fitzhugh is an outstanding example of the possibilities America offered to those who engaged in trade: high status in local society, and the power associated with the status. An individual could become a gentleman in his own lifetime. Landless, laboring servants could acquire land. Toiling farmers could profitably market their produce, buy and sell land, and be somebody. Successful colonists could acquire position, influence, and station in society—by acquiring wealth. The significance of class was undermined—a development which underlay the importance of business to Americans in the centuries after William Fitzhugh (merchant, gentleman) died.

Work and Slavery

Human labor—work, and the people who did work—had become an actively traded commodity in America by the time of the Revolution. Not only were free workers mobile and actively sought by employers, but large numbers of workers—Africans who were slaves, Europeans who were indentured or bonded servants—were bought and sold in markets both for their labor and for profit. In Europe, by contrast, those who worked were ordinarily bound to their places and trades by law and custom.

Human labor was essential in the production of crops. Animals contributed little to the work of agriculture, and labor-saving machines did not become available until the nineteenth century. The work of clearing land, cutting trees, making lumber, plowing, planting, cultivating, harvesting, building, manufacturing, and most of the labor of transportation was done by people (often using hand tools). In America the effort to turn the abundant land into production required ever-increasing numbers of people. The pressing demand for human labor brought—as Edmund S. Morgan has brilliantly demonstrated in *American Slavery, American Freedom*—the creation and expansion of slavery, drastic changes in the conditions and expectations of all service and employment, and fundamental revisions in traditions, beliefs, and behavior regarding work.

In the traditional English pyramid of social classes, specific duties and responsibilities were assigned to each class. Government, politics, the arts, and public affairs belonged to the gentry and nobility, who were distinguished by their wealth, ostentation, and leisure. Work belonged to the lower orders; it was their God-given lot in life. For some, like the merchants, and the yeomen, husbandmen, and small freeholders, work had become a characteristic moral virtue of their class. For others, the very lowest classes of the poor, the landless, the unemployed, and the unfree, work was a necessity to which they had to be driven by their masters and betters.

Three kinds of lower-class workers were available in colonial America: freemen, servants, and slaves. Freemen were generally assumed to work on their own land, at least as much as necessary to get food, but as the colonies became more settled and populated (and as their populations of free-roaming horses, hogs, and cattle also increased), it was not difficult for a freeman with a gun (which most male colonists had) to eat and live without doing much work. The free who aspired to improve their estates, to farm land for profit, to acquire wealth and social and political position, did so by controlling the work and production of others. The small freeholder, who worked his own land, often had to sell his produce to a larger, more affluent neighbor (and thus turn over most of his profit to that neighbor) in order to get his produce to market. The free could also control the work of those who were not free.

Servants—persons bound by contract or custom to labor in a master's household for a term of years—had long been a primary source of labor in English society. Many poor migrants to America paid for their passage by "bonding" or "indenturing" themselves into servitude. As servants, they were provided food, clothing, and shelter, and in return they worked for their masters for a given term of years. Their bonds or contracts could be bought or sold in America, without consulting the servants. Ship captains sometimes auctioned off indentured servants to the highest bidders at dockside, and gangs of indentured servants were sometimes marched from one town to another and sold as buyers presented themselves. There were laws, customs, and traditions in England which gave a servant some control over his or her life. But in the colonies pressures on masters to get as much work as possible from a servant made the lives of servants more degraded than in England. Masters increasingly established greater control over the work of their servants. A servant in America, as Edmund Morgan has written, became "a thing, a commodity with a price." A servant in Virginia by the late seventeenth century was, according to Morgan, "a machine to make tobacco for somebody else." Laws concerning recalcitrant and runaway servants in the colonies became progressively more harsh.

But servants were a valuable form of property. They usually emigrated to the colonies voluntarily. Though they were of the very lowest order of society, they were still Christian. Their status may have been low, in their own and their masters' eyes, but they ultimately became free, entitled to land and status.

Africans, on the other hand, were enslaved before they came to the colonies, forced by those who captured them to come to America. They were, furthermore, heathen pagans. Strange as it seems to us today, slavery did not exist in English law. Throughout the seventeenth century, Africans were treated much as servants were, but their status as slaves—unfree persons, bound to their masters for life, their labor and their children the property of their masters—developed rapidly in colonial law and practice. It was not until the eighteenth century that large numbers of Africans were brought to the North American colonies and the plantations of the Southern colonies used slave labor exclusively (the African, unfree population of the "sugar" islands of the West Indies exceeded the North American population of blacks until late in the eighteenth century). By that time, many wealthy colonists realized that with slave labor they could, in Morgan's words, "exceed all their previous efforts to maximise productivity."

Slave productivity was greater than that of servants or paid free laborers. Slaves had time in the work year to raise their own food, clear and cultivate new land, and produce children to replace the superannuated. But slaves were expensive. They required, as Fitzhugh early pointed out, investment equal to, and often greater than, the investment in land; so it was only the wealthy who could afford them. For the eighteenth-century entrepreneur who desired the maximum control over the product of his lands, and who of necessity required intensive human labor to make the land productive, slaves were the most productive available machines.

But slavery developed and spread in America well before people became fascinated with machines. The willingness to use slaves, the willingness to treat people as things, developed slowly out of several elements in colonial life: first, from the powerful desire to control the labor of others in order to make profits, acquire wealth, and secure high social position visibly based on the number and quality of one's dependents;

second, from the duty of Christian gentlefolk to discipline the indigent, pagan behavior of the poor and the non-European into some semblance of proper, Christian industry; and, finally, from the responsibility of every master, every head of household, to make the most advantageous use of the labor of all in his household for his family's security and independence, the improved dominion of the king, and the greater glory of God.

The rise of slavery in America, as Morgan has pointed out, occurred at the same time that new attitudes about the poor were spreading in England justifying the necessity of forced labor (in workhouses) in order to discipline them. The spread of such attitudes may well have accompanied the spread of the "Protestant work ethic" in the years after the collapse of the Puritan commonwealth in England. But what more and more Englishmen were saying about the poor, more and more Americans were saying about their servants and about slaves. Africans were "a brutish sort of people." They, like servants and the poor, were "shiftless, irresponsible, unfaithful, ungrateful, dishonest; they got drunk whenever possible; they did not work hard enough or regularly enough." The solution was not to free these people or to eliminate their poverty. "Everyone but an idiot knows," one Englishman said, "that the lower classes must be kept poor, or they will never be industrious." The solution was to compel the poor, the servants, and in America the slaves as well, to work—for the wealth and profit of those who owned them or their services.

To Market, to Market

The majority of free families in America, by the time of the Revolution, owned and worked their own land. On a large or small scale, nearly all of them produced goods which they intended to sell or exchange in order to acquire goods they needed or wanted. They sought markets in which to exchange goods for profit.

Throughout the colonial years, natural waterways served as the fastest, most efficient highways to move bulk goods to markets. The technology of water transportation and ocean navigation largely determined what markets could be reached, where entrepôts could be established, which markets would flourish, as well as the possibilities of commercial activity and success. Roads were expensive to build (because of geography, climate, sparse population, and unavailable labor) and difficult to maintain, so there were few, they were short, and none provided easy or extensive movement of goods. Those who were not near a waterway found transportation expensive—sometimes prohibitively so—communication extremely slow, and the possibility of commerce or profit much reduced.

The principal markets and towns in colonial America were located where there was convenient access to the sea (bitterness and resentment developed immediately between the townspeople, who could be actively involved in commerce and whose wealth grew as a result, and the "rural folk," who were blocked from direct participation and who, perforce, had to make do with traditional values and subsistence instead of profit). Furs, tobacco, lumber, grains, rice, dyestuffs, naval stores, meat, hides, and iron were the products traded and exchanged in the port towns (Boston, Newport, New York, Philadelphia, and Charleston were the largest by 1750) and shipped overseas to markets where they were sold. Local merchants in America who had access to quantities of marketable products and to the sea, whether or not they were located in a town—Southern planters like William Fitzhugh or George Washington, for example—could collect shiploads in their own warehouses and ship to overseas markets from their own docks. The major markets for American goods were in English ports—London and Bristol were the favorites. They also provided the goods Americans wanted (wines, teas, cloth, silver, tools, porcelain, manufactured goods of all kinds, and servants). The English Caribbean colonies (the "West Indies") were nearly as important. Foodstuffs and barrel staves (barrels were the universal "packaging" for goods shipped by land or sea) were exchanged in the Caribbean for sugar and molasses (from which rum was manufactured) and slaves. To a lesser extent, Americans traded in markets scattered along the edges of Europe, in the Azores and Canaries, in Africa, and in French, Dutch, and Spanish colonies in the Caribbean.

The experience of the English colonists in America, living widely separated from other families or settlements on the edge of the known world thousands of miles and many weeks from England and other well-populated places, led many to think of "markets" as remote, impersonal abstractions (as some of their contemporaries, philosophers now called "economists," were beginning to do). When William Fitzhugh used the phrase "a fall of a Market" to describe one of the hazards of the tobacco trade, he was possibly thinking of an abstract market much as a modern American would. But for most colonists, and for most English and Europeans until well into the nineteenth century, a market was a specific place where, at specified times, real people dealt in goods which were physically present. (Abstract economic thought only slowly became part of popular discourse: when Adam Smith, in *The Wealth of Nations* in 1776, wrote about "the higgling and bargaining of the market" and the "propensity in human nature . . . to truck, barter, and exchange one thing for another," he was still drawing on the widespread experience of a market as an actual place.)

By ancient tradition, and in common law, markets were created by governments and regulated by local magistrates. The gradual spread of the ideals of commonwealth, and of republican virtue, in English and American life in the eighteenth century, brought renewed life to the strong custom of the regulation and control of markets. The legislatures of colonies, and the leading men of towns and parishes throughout the colonies, made laws which carefully regulated the hours, days, and places of markets, the weights and measures to be used, the quality (and sometimes quantity) of goods to be sold, and the obligations of purveyors. Smiths, for example, were required by law to repair firearms; the ingredients and measures of bread and beer sold in markets were established by law; prices for goods and services, for inns and taverns, for hauling and cartage and ferries, were matters of legislation. All public sales or exchanges of goods, all auctions, all trade with the Indians, were subject to careful regulation and enforcement. Fair prices, fair wages, and reasonable profits were generally agreed to be matters too important to the commonwealth to be allowed to be decided by individuals.

Local leaders and officials were charged with the regulation of the marketplace. There were official wood and coal measurers, and officials to supervise the packing of beef and pork. There were fence wardens and chimney wardens and church wardens, who levied taxes on land, chattels, servants, slaves, and money-at-interest, and who inspected, ordered, regulated, controlled, and punished for what most believed was the common good. The colonial legislatures of the tobacco-growing colonies established inspection procedures and inspectors to ensure the shipment of good-quality tobacco. Early in the eighteenth century, magistrates in Philadelphia appointed inspectors for the meat, bread, flour, and grains which had become the principal exports of that growing town. Such regulation was based on the assumption that the good of the community was best served—and the interests of the wealthiest, most powerful men as well—by community control of markets and trade. Since almost all assumed that only those who owned property and controlled wealth were the community (they were the only people who counted), in colonial circumstances where many owned land, and many controlled at least their own labor, the regulation of the local markets was in the hands of the people most engaged in those markets. No trader, merchant, seller, or entrepreneur, however small or large, is without the desire to control the marketplace: law, custom, the new ideals of commonwealth, the widespread ownership of land, and near-universal engagement in trade all combined, in eighteenth-century America, to reinforce the tradition of community market regulation and control.

The development by the English government of the practices Adam Smith later labeled "mercantilist"—practices begun in the late seventeenth century and continued to the American Revolution—was an extension and abstraction of the tradition of market regulation, based on the newer notions of the Commonwealth. The mercantilist laws and regulations governed the movement of goods, and trade, to and from England and all her colonies within England's empire (in effect, an attempt to create a single imperial "market"), and they regulated the trade of England's colonies with other European nations. The regulations required that goods be carried in ships owned and manned by subjects of the king; they encouraged the production of some goods and discouraged or prohibited others; they required the colonists to ship most of their goods to England (or to the English colonies), thereby assuring English merchants of colonial profits while producing revenue through duties and taxes to the English government. The same regulations assured colonists of exclusive entry for their goods into English markets. While the laws were made by English magistrates and merchants to assure their own control of the markets, trade, and profits of the colonies, for nearly a century after the first of the Navigation Acts was passed, colonial merchants, freemen, and magistrates prospered under such regulation.

Increased colonial wealth, population, and trade by mid-eighteenth century combined with growing perceptions of the value and power of local commonwealths and local control of available markets to bring disillusion among colonials with the mercantilist system. The crisis preceding independence, from 1763 to 1776, which was brought on by the deliberate attempt of the English government to enforce and impose more stringent mercantilist policies and market control, gave Adam Smith's attack on mercantilism in *The*

Wealth of Nations a ready audience in Revolutionary America. Americans still believed that markets ought to be controlled and regulated—but not by distant, imperial governments.

Virtuous and Useful Business

Benjamin Franklin's long life (1706–90) spanned most of the eighteenth century and encompassed a variety of activities. He was, among other things, a printer, writer, publisher, and successful tradesman; a politician, something of a courtier, and a bureaucrat; a scientist, experimenter, inventor, and gadgeteer; a leading philosopher of the Enlightenment; a revolutionary leader in his seventies; a Founding Father, diplomat, and darling of Parisian salons. He was a colonial American, born in Boston, who ran away from his apprenticeship to his brother, and built fortune and position for himself in Philadelphia by working shrewdly at his trade, by marriage, by speculation, and by becoming more involved in local government as he became more successful. As his wealth and position became established, Franklin turned more and more to public affairs and to the leisure activities of a gentleman. He did not enjoy being reminded, when he was older, that he had once been in trade, or that entrepreneurial success had made him a gentleman. He was a child of the eighteenth century, and he believed—with most other Americans—in an ordered hierarchy of social classes, perhaps somewhat changed by the Revolution, but nevertheless dominated by natural gentlemen and aristocrats.

Yet Franklin was a revolutionary—particularly in his advocacy of a conscious American business ethic (the word "business" would very soon after Franklin's day be commonly used to mean commerce, trade, and marketplace activity). "The way to wealth," he wrote in 1748 in *Advice to a Young Tradesman,*

> if you desire it, is as plain as the way to market. It depends chiefly on two words, *industry* and *frugality;* that is, waste neither *time* nor *money,* but make the best use of both. Without industry and frugality, nothing will do, and with them every thing. He that gets all he honestly can, and saves all he gets (necessary expenses excepted), will certainly become *rich,* if that Being who governs the world, to whom all should look for a blessing on their honest endeavors, doth not, in his wise providence, otherwise determine.

Franklin anticipated Adam Smith (another Enlightenment moral philosopher) in associating honesty, industry, and frugality exclusively with wealth and "the way to market." And he flew in the face of ordinary reverence by portraying "that Being who governs the world" as unreasonable if He did *not* reward industry and frugality with wealth and success "(necessary expenses excepted)."

It was twenty years or more after his death in 1790 that Franklin was taken up by nineteenth-century Americans as the homely philosopher of business, of the Protestant work ethic, and of the virtues of commercial and industrial discipline. In his lifetime, Franklin was not peceived as a fatherly, folksy writer of truisms (that they became truisms is a measure of his ultimate success as a revolutionary). He was a radical advocate, a clever propagandist of the Enlightenment's "practical" vision of the human universe. In *Poor Richard's Almanack* (whose widespread sales made him wealthy), Franklin subtly combined folklore, accepted religious truths, moral ideals, the search for profit, and the widespread American concern with markets and trade. For nearly half a century, *Poor Richard* provided advice to Americans (almanacs were widely used by all—farmers, tradesmen, merchants), concentrating on "hints for those that would be rich."

"God helps them that help themselves," Poor Richard said repeatedly, making God a participant in trade. "He that hath a Trade hath an Estate, and He that hath a Calling hath an

Office of Profit and Honour; but then the Trade must be worked at, and the Calling well followed," Richard advised. "If we are industrious we shall never starve; for . . . at the working man's House Hunger looks in, but dares not enter." Furthermore, "God gives all things to Industry." "If you would have a faithful Servant," Poor Richard said, "and one that you like, serve yourself." "If you would be wealthy . . . think of saving as well as Getting." "Fools make Feasts, and wise Men eat them." And Poor Richard warned: "Think what you do when you run in Debt: you give to another power over your Liberty. . . . Then since the Borrower is a Slave to the Lender, and the Debtor to the Creditor, disdain the Chain, preserve your Freedom; and maintain your Independency: Be industrious and free; be frugal and free."

Franklin challenged accepted truth by accepting the moral propriety of selfishness, and advocating profit-seeking, social leveling, and individual independence. He asserted that men could earn estates, and high offices of profit and honor, which belonged to the upper classes, through trade and work. Only very slowly, after years of dissent, argument, and strong resistance, did Franklin's ideas begin to seem reasonable rather than "far out," funny, cranky, or dangerous, to many Americans. It took the American Revolution, the ideals and ideology of which Franklin helped to shape, to establish any widespread sense among Americans that independence, industry, frugality, liberty, and individual self-serving were logically connected; that work, wealth, and morality were not incompatible; and that all society was served by democracy, equality, and commerce.

In 1782, as the War for Independence was coming to an end (but *long* before a majority of Americans accepted the ideals of the Revolution), Franklin continued his advocacy in his *Information to Those Who Would Remove to America.* There are in America, he wrote,

> . . . few People so miserable as the Poor of Europe, there are also very few that in Europe would be called rich; it is rather

a general happy Mediocrity that prevails. There are few great Proprietors of the Soil, and few Tenants; most People cultivate their own lands, or follow some Handicraft or Merchandise. . . .

Much less is it adviseable for a Person to go thither, who has no other Quality to recommend him but his Birth. In Europe it has indeed its Value; but it is a Commodity that cannot be carried to a worse Market than that of America, where people do not inquire concerning a Stranger, *What is he?* but, *What can he do?* . . . The Husbandman is in honor there, and even the Mechanic, because their Employments are useful. The People have a saying, that God Almighty is himself a Mechanic, the greatest in the Universe; and he is respected and admired more for the Variety, Ingenuity, and Utility of his Handyworks, than for the Antiquity of his Family. . . .

If they are poor, they begin first as Servants or Journeymen; and if they are sober, industrious, and frugal, they soon become Masters, establish themselves in Business, marry, raise Families, and become respectable Citizens. . . .

The almost general mediocrity of Fortune that prevails in America, obliging its People to follow some Business for subsistence, those Vices, that arise usually from Idleness, are in a great measure prevented. Industry and constant Employment are great preservatives of the Morals and Virtue of a Nation.

An American society based upon that "general happy Mediocrity" did not exist when Franklin wrote. For many years after Franklin died, successful American businessmen sought to be considered gentlemen, among the "idle rich," rather than industrious tradesmen. But Franklin's long lifetime of radical advocacy, despite his own ambivalent behavior, began the process of weaving a tight fabric of specifically American business beliefs out of the loose threads of American colonial ideals and circumstances. The result would not be clear until Americans born in Revolution and undisturbed by the necessities and beliefs of Englishmen in a colonial world began to take control of American society.

The Fabric of a Business Civilization 1776-1850

By 1850, the peculiar combination of idealism and market behavior which the rest of the world sees as characteristic of American business civilization had developed. By 1850, the majority of free white Americans who worked in public (and many who worked in the home) were entrepreneurs, directly engaged in marketing their goods, their labor, and investing their capital for profit. More than at any other time in our history, most Americans in the years between Independence and the mid-nineteenth century were in business for themselves.

The men who pledged their lives, their fortunes, and their sacred honor by signing the Declaration of Independence in 1776 understood that achieving political independence from one of the most powerful nations on earth would not be easy. They were, when they signed the Declaration, already engaged in the world's first colonial war of liberation. That war did not end until a treaty was signed in 1783 in which Great Britain recognized the independent existence of the United States of America.

The Declaration, however, went far beyond the matter of political independence. It started a revolution. The Declaration became the ideological basis of a continuing revolution in America, postulated on logical and necessary connections between independence, equality, democratic government, individual liberty, the republican welfare of an orderly commonwealth, the individual pursuit of happiness, and the common good of all society.

The very idea of independence as a stated, primary, consciously sought goal for a nation and its people was revolutionary in the eighteenth century. Indeed, it had long been the ideal of the English landowner to acquire an *independency:* to own his own land, not to pay deference to others in order to use it, and to have sufficient income from it to provide for his own, his household's, and his family's needs without having to depend on anyone else. But this was an ideal admitted to be unrealizable in most cases, possible only for the few. The Revolution made this vision of independence the goal of every individual American and family: it was the ideal for a whole nation.

From the Revolution until well after the middle of the nineteenth century, Americans devoted much of their collective time and effort to the creation of governments, the writing of constitutions, the passage of laws, and the constant movement of people into and out of political office and power. Revolutions and rebellions became part of the pattern of political and electoral life. The first federal government and thirteen state governments were created in the course of the Revolution itself. A new federal government was created in 1787 by a convention in Philadelphia, in part because of a rebellion led by Daniel Shays against the Massachusetts government (in 1786). The Whiskey Rebellion against the constitutional government in 1794 took President George Washington into the field with a force of militia to put it down. Political parties began to form late in the 1790's, modeled on revolutionary organizations and devoted to the overthrow of people in power and to their replacement by others. The "revolution of 1800" put Thomas Jefferson in the Presidency and elected a majority of his new party of "republicans" to Congress. Once in power, Jefferson and the republicans permanently tied the growth and expansion of the nation to the ideals of independence and democracy. And in 1812 the United States went to war against Great Britain for a second time, in order to confirm its independence. The British invaded, the new capital at Washington was captured and put to the torch; the war ended in 1815 even before the significant victory by Andrew Jackson at New Orleans.

In 1823, President Monroe enunciated a doctrine of idealism and independence which extended national influence to the whole of the Western Hemisphere. In that decade, too, the party of republicans split, and the popular leader of the "democratic" wing, Andrew Jackson, overthrew the "national" republicans under John Quincy Adams and brought yet another revolutionary movement—of Westerners, mechanics, and common men—into control of the federal government. Democrats and Jacksonians were overthrown by a new party, with a new more "democratic" campaigning style, in 1840, when the Whigs, with their "log cabin and hard cider," their national conventions, and "Tippecanoe and Tyler too," won the Presidency and control of the federal government.

By 1850, thirty-one state governments and a half-dozen territorial governments were organized. Dozens of political parties had been established, elected, changed, and overthrown. Revolutionary governing procedures had been put into effect time after time as Americans moved westward, assimilated immigrants, and expanded. Hundreds of local governments had been constituted, changed, overthrown, and reestablished between 1776 and 1850 as well. Americans thus gradually built the patterns of their revolution into their expectations of all institutions and the way they should run.

In the years between 1776 and 1850, individual mobility became a portent and symbol of the independence and the happiness Americans were free to pursue. As soon as the War for Independence started, Americans began to cross the mountains to settle "the West." Tribes of Indians were driven off their lands over "trails of tears" to make room for the new settlers. People left their villages and moved off their farms, to go West, to go down to the sea in ships, to try life in the mills, to find opportunity in cities. They opened a trail to Santa Fe in the 1820's, looking for trade (and hoping for cities of gold). They sent trappers and traders out for furs, and settlers followed. Americans began moving into Texas in the 1820's, declared their independence of Mexico in 1836, and for nine years maintained the Republic of Texas before joining the United States. In the 1830's, Americans opened a trail to Oregon and California; by the early 1840's, thousands were making the two-thousand-mile trek from the Missouri to the coast each year. And in the 1830's and 1840's, tens of thousands of migrants—from Ireland, the states of Germany, Scotland, England, Wales, Scandinavia, and the Low Countries—poured into the United States, drawn by the dream of land, independence, and plenty, but pushed, too, by starvation, famine, and the brutal suppression of revolution in Europe. They moved to cities as well as to farms, worked on canals and railroads, took jobs in the new mills and factories, and built new communities in the West.

War with Mexico, from 1846 to 1848, confirmed the annexation of Texas and expanded the national territory from Santa Fe to the Pacific. By 1850, there were more than a hundred thousand Americans in California (most in the goldfields, and more on the way), the fertile Oregon country was settled, and the American population extended from coast to coast (although there were large areas in between still "open" and occupied by Indians).

The achievement of independence and an expanded American nation was not merely a matter of governments, politics, and war. It was the concern of every individual. The Declaration had postulated the logical connection between political and national independence and individual liberty and the individual pursuit of happiness. Independence, by that logic, could be found in the marketplace by every individual. Americans were accustomed from their colonial experience to working to produce goods and market them for profit. In their new nation, they were surrounded by assumptions of the social superiority, the independence, and the happiness of successful merchants and farmers. They grew rapidly accustomed to the forms of governing communities, groups of people, voluntary organizations, and business companies. After the Revolution, Benjamin Franklin's argument that individual material success not only brought happiness and social and political clout but was also good for the whole society became widely popular. So did Adam Smith's ideas that human beings were naturally commercial, and that independence could be found if every individual were free to enter the marketplace. His argument that social good would inevitably be produced by the activities of individuals seeking profits in markets was only slowly accepted, but it won adherents because it fit the logic of American independence.

Individual and national independence had to be paid for. It was the process of achieving, funding, and expanding independence—for the United States, for its people, and for individuals—that created the social fabric of business civilization between 1776 and 1850.

Paying for Independence

Much business in the years after the beginning of the Revolution was devoted to devising ways to pay for independence. Americans opened up new lands, built transport networks, developed manufacturing, and tried to find new markets—all in order to pay for independence. They had to find ways to collect, pool, invest, and manage what capital they had in order to make it possible to survive outside the old imperial mercantilist system.

The Revolutionary War disrupted markets, the flow and value of currency, and the everyday patterns of production and exchange of goods. As the crisis which led to independence had developed, between 1763 and 1776, normal human inertia kept most Americans hoping to do "business as usual." But open warfare after April 1775, and independence after July 1776, meant that the patterns of finance, communication, and transportation which had sustained the markets in the colonies, in the West Indies, and in Great Britain, in which Americans had done most of their business, were hopelessly disrupted.

An army was recruited and trained and led into battle by George Washington and his officers, and by the officers of the militias of the newly created states. But there were no available government establishments to feed, clothe, supply, and arm the army and navy. The only possible suppliers—the only available people with experience in markets and in the accumulation of goods—were merchants and businessmen. There was no national treasury with connections to the owners of wealth, to bankers, and to financiers which could finance a great war. The congressional government and the state governments were distracted by the problems of directing a political revolution. They turned to American businessmen to supply and finance the war.

Robert Morris's career as one of the leading suppliers of the American armies and one of the leading financiers of the American Revolution suggests how business provided military necessities while trying to grapple with the longer-term problems of paying for independence. In 1775, Morris became chairman of Congress's Secret Committee for the procurement of supplies for the rebellion. He was already a successful Philadelphia merchant, partner to the wealthy, established Thomas Willing, another member of the Secret Committee. Like most successful merchants in American regional market centers, Morris participated in a network of merchants, shippers, financiers, and political leaders throughout the colonies and overseas, which enabled him to trade, finance his operations, ship goods, and invest in markets from New England to Georgia, the West Indies, Britain, and Europe.

But with an armed rebellion to finance and supply, the traditional, established avenues of trade as well as the principal sources of capital and manufactured goods—cloth, blankets, gunpowder, guns, and knives, for example—were closed to Morris and to other American merchants. They were forced to find new sources of funds, new avenues of trade, new supplies of manufactured goods, and at the same time protect themselves from Britain's army and navy.

When independence was declared, in 1776, Americans had to choose either to continue to be British, loyal subjects of their king, part of the protected and comfortable connection to a mother country, or to give up the familiar patterns and expectations and loyalties. Many remained loyal to king and country. Merchants and businessmen had the additional complications of knowing that commercial connections, markets, and protections with which they were familiar (and in which the successful had succeeded) were going to be altered by the Revolution—if it was successful—in unpredictable ways. There were, as a result, merchants and businessmen among the Tories and Loyalists, as there were among the Patriots, who supported the Revolution.

Robert Morris supported independence; he even saw it as a business opportunity. Morris seemed to enjoy the frenetic activity involved in the formation and dissolution of companies and partnerships to supply provisions for the war. Businessmen from almost all the thirteen revolutionary colonies, as well as men from St. Eustatius, Martinique, Paris, Amsterdam, and London, participated in Morris's companies, partnerships, and deals. He and his syndicates bought and sold prize ships, traded with the French and the Dutch and the Spanish in the West Indies and in Europe, bought and sold American lands, invested in manufacturing in America and abroad, invested in clothes and cloth, grain and flour, gunpowder and guns, and borrowed, lent, paid, collected, and transferred money and credit throughout the Western world. Furthermore, as the Revolution went on, Morris and many of his business colleagues became convinced that trade controlled by individual businessmen for the realization of their own profit could bring socially desirable results. Adam Smith's arguments for trade freedom seemed to many, like Morris, similar to American arguments for independence from Britain and individual liberty.

As chairman of the Secret Committee from 1775 to 1779, Morris saw to it that the firm of Willing & Morris was given contracts to provide supplies for the army (at a 2½ percent to 5 percent commission). Morris partnerships with merchants in Connecticut, Boston, and Philadelphia were also given supply contracts. The Philadelphia merchant William Bingham was sent to Martinique as an agent of Congress to arrange trade with the markets of the French empire (which would perhaps substitute for lost British markets). Bingham in partnership with Morris bought French goods which were sold to the Secret Committee. Silas Deane, a Connecticut merchant in Paris as Congress's agent to arrange loans and subsidies from the French government, also acted as a partner of Morris. Morris's ventures were generally successful—both those on his own account and his great venture of financing and supplying the American war effort. When he was appointed Superintendent of Finance under the Articles of Confederation government in 1781, he was one of the wealthiest men in America.

Morris remained Superintendent until 1785. During that time, he helped found the Bank of North America, one of the first chartered corporations of the new United States and part of what Morris hoped would be a strong financial structure for the United States. The bank opened its doors in Philadelphia on January 7, 1782. Morris was one of its stockholders, and Thomas Willing its first president. The bank was established to issue notes, redeemable in specie, and to provide loans to the government of the United States. Since not many bought the bank's stock, Morris (as Superintendent of Finance) invested Congress's money and made the U.S. government the majority stockholder of the bank. The Bank of

North America—operating in cooperation with Morris—was able to provide a relatively stable currency and fiscal structure for the new nation until the end of the war in 1783. However, Morris's hope that the bank would become a major, permanent institution for capital collection and government contribution in the long-term financing of independence was not realized.

Morris tried to provide a permanent fiscal structure by proposing programs for payment of the interest on the war debts through taxes and for the establishment of a standardized currency. But powerful distrust of centralized economic power—a result of the long years of crisis and war with the mercantilist British government—defeated his program in Congress and in the states. Not until a decade later were enough Americans convinced—by the debates over the Constitution, the Bill of Rights, and the proper form of the new federal government, and by the conviction that some national economic standardization was desirable—to permit the measures first proposed by Morris to be enacted.

Throughout his public career, Morris advocated the creation of a strong, economically active central government, which could, he believed, create and maintain a stable financial and fiscal structure within which trade could move freely and markets operate to increase national wealth. Such a government would act to generate capital and economic opportunity on a grand scale, which in turn, Morris believed, would insure the continued independence and prosperity of the new nation.

Alexander Hamilton, first Secretary of the Treasury (from 1789 to 1795), advocated a program similar to Morris's. It included funding the war debts of the federal as well as the state governments, the establishment of a Bank of the United States funded by the U.S. government, a tax and customs program to provide government revenue, and government investment in manufacturing and economic development. Hamilton, like Morris, was committed to financing American independence. Morris, Hamilton, and their many adherents among successful merchants and gentlemen believed that American society and all government should be controlled by "people of the better sort" and operated to their advantage. They believed that upper-class status could be achieved by business success and its attendant wealth; once wealth was achieved, they believed that all the traditional perquisites of position, power, and deference should belong to the wealthy, and that they should govern. At the same time, Robert Morris (like Benjamin Franklin, and many other of his contemporaries) was eager to hide his business success because it was success in trade, and to pretend that he was an aristocratic gentleman of leisure who governed by right, who lived lavishly and publicly, and who never soiled his hands in trade.

The issues raised by Morris and the Hamiltonians—concerning the power of the national government to intervene in and regulate the economy, the right of the wealthy and successful to govern and to reap the rewards of government—have been sources of tension in American life since the Revolution. Morris, Hamilton, and other wealthy and ambitious men based their advocacy on the success of British mercantilism as they had perceived it, and on their belief in the superiority of gentlemen. They argued, in essence, that independent America should be an improved version of Great Britain (as understood by a colonial). Opposed to them were men who were equally devoted to independence and equally committed to the virtue and social utility of business success. Led by Thomas Jefferson after 1790, when he became the first Secretary of State, these opponents of Hamiltonianism generally distrusted a powerful, economically active central government. Jefferson in particular emphasized the pivotal—and egalitarian—place of American farmers in the establishment of independence. He gave expression to the mythology which has controlled the American perception of agriculture since the beginning of the nineteenth century. Jeffersonians believed in the democratic possibilities of great numbers of successful farmers controlling independent local communities and governments for the greater social good. They rejected the idealization of the traditional governing class, in favor of the egalitarian independent yeoman. And they rejected centralized government and economic intervention in favor of local, popular economic regulation, control, and encouragement.

Both Hamiltonians and Jeffersonians believed—and this made them peculiarly American—that successful business activity was, and ought to be, the path to independence. Social and political power—"equality," in this new democracy—should follow from business success. Both Jeffersonians and Hamiltonians believed that individuals as well as communities, social groups, and nations ought to seek independence and liberty, and that independence could be found in the marketplace.

When Robert Morris left the government in 1785, he renounced activity as a merchant in order to appear to be a gentleman of leisure. He continued, however, to act as a financier and as a businessman but in "respectable" pursuits which were connected to government (and were therefore, in eighteenth-century English terms, more "gentlemanly"). He bought and sold the confiscated property of Loyalists, bought into new manufacturing establishments, acquired a contract from the farmers of the French tobacco monopoly to supply American tobacco to the French market, speculated in millions of acres of lands, and invested in a manorial-industrial community development scheme in Morristown, New Jersey. Late in the 1790's, his complicated financial and land speculations collapsed in a declining market and resulted in hundreds of lawsuits and foreclosures. At the time he was declared bankrupt, Morris and one of his partners, John Nicholson, had over $12 million worth of promissory notes outstanding (in which there was a considerable speculative market). Morris spent three years in debtors' prison in Philadelphia. He was released in 1801. Until he died in 1806, he and his wife lived with his old friend Gouverneur Morris (no relation). He was visited in debtors' prison by George Washington, among others, and helped publicize the movement (successful after his death) to abolish debtors' prisons in America. It was Robert Morris's final contribution to business independence.

Business on the land

From the beginning of the Revolution to the middle of the nineteenth century (and beyond), the great majority of Americans were farmers. In 1850, nearly five million of the free Americans ten years old or older who "earned money . . . or . . . assisted in the production of marketable goods" worked on farms (two-thirds of the free work force). Well over half of them owned the farms they worked. Nearly twenty million of the 23.3 million Americans (slave and free) lived and worked in rural areas.

Farming provided the nation with its food, with the fibers from which almost all clothing was made, with the leather essential to all land transportation (except railroads), and with the marketable commodities which earned profit and capital from the rest of the world. Farming provided full employment for a rapidly expanding population, and it accounted for most of the value-added and savings generated in America before 1850. It was the sine qua non for American economic development. Indeed, arable land continues to be America's greatest resource.

Farming was hard work, and done almost entirely by hand—with some help from animals. More efficient plows were introduced and widely used by 1850 (although Southern planters continued to supply their slaves only with hoes), but reaping machines, threshers, and other mechanical aids to the cultivation and harvesting of crops were not widely available or used until the second half of the nineteenth century. Farm production was not, by later standards, efficient, and many farm families were barely able to produce enough to feed themselves. Yet the desire to produce "cash crops" and to sell what was produced for profit in a market seems to have motivated the vast majority of American farmers, who sought farmsteads with access to transportation—waterways, roads, canals, railroads—which could take produce to markets.

While the ideal of self-sufficiency and independence might seem to have encouraged subsistence farming, only a small minority of farmers chose to remain at what many came to think of, pejoratively, as "subsistence level." The yeoman ideal, which influenced farm owners, their families, farm workers, and tenant farmers alike, was to achieve freedom from subservience to and dependence upon wealthier, more successful farmers, merchants, and bankers of the community. American farmers after the Revolution believed they could live better and become more independent if they worked hard to produce more, carried their goods to market, and sold in the marketplace for a profit. They could then afford the goods they wanted, improve their lives, own their farms and homes, and be "beholden" to no one. The dream of the farmer was to acquire independence through successful business.

Farmers were producers, and the staples of their commerce were foodstuffs and fibers. On the frontiers, corn and animals were the preferred crops—corn because it was easily grown and provided large yields in relation to the labor required, and animals because they could forage in areas only partially cleared for plowing and because they could be driven to local markets. The list of produce is long, a reflection of farmers' ingenuity in the search for marketable goods. Tobacco, sugarcane, rice, and cotton were the commercial staples of the South. Flax and hemp were essential sources for cordage for ships, as well as for yarns and bagging and canvas. Hay and peas and beans, oats and wheat and other grains were staples of farm commerce everywhere. Work animals as well as people required food, and in urban areas demand for their food was great. Potatoes began to become important commercial crops after the beginning of the nineteenth century. Apples and apple products—cider, applejack, and vinegar—were long-established staples. Farmers and country dwellers shot wild birds for sale—the raising of poultry did not become commercially important until late in the nineteenth century. Vineyards were not popular, because they were expensive, slow to produce, and labor-intensive. Fruit and vegetable farming became major businesses in the growing urban areas as the century progressed. Maple sugar, produced primarily in New England, provided between ten and twenty percent of American sugar. And ice, cut from Northern lakes and ponds by farmers in the winter, stored in sawdust provided by Northern timber businesses, was shipped all over the world to provide refrigeration during long, hot summers.

The demand for grain in the European nations easily accessible from the Atlantic from the 1790's to about 1812 or 1813 made the overseas marketing of those crops which were most easily produced exceptionally profitable. Combined with the rapid expansion of farming across the Appalachians and into the Ohio and Mississippi Valleys from the 1780's onward, and with the expansion of cotton production in the South after the 1790's, the commercial production of grains and fibers joined established commercial tobacco production as permanent parts of American farming.

In 1803, President Jefferson bought New Orleans from the French in order to secure access to markets for the Western farmers, who could get to markets only down the Mississippi River system. Jefferson, who distrusted the use of central power, nevertheless used the power of the federal government to buy not merely New Orleans but all of the Louisiana Territory (the land north of Texas between the Mississippi River and the Rocky Mountains)—and thereby confirmed the important connection between business, farming, independence, democracy, and expansion. "While the property and sovereignty of the Mississippi and its waters," Jefferson said to Congress,

> secure an independent outlet for the produce of the western States, and an uncontrolled navigation through their whole course, free from collision with other powers and the dangers to our peace from that source, the fertility of the country, its climate and extent, promise in due season important aids to our treasury, an ample provision for our posterity, and a widespread field for the blessings of freedom and equal laws.

Jefferson himself did not believe that Adam Smith's "invisible hand" in the marketplace would regulate commercial activity for social good, but he did believe that commercial farming, tied to the expansion of American territory, would make farmers who were prosperous, independent, and democratic. Jefferson's belief that "men are disposed to live honestly, if the means of doing so are open to them," became the basis on which American farmers argued for the acquisition of more territory, and for the liberal distribution of lands to people who were going to farm them. In 1785 and 1787, the Congress (under the Articles of Confederation) established the fundamental policies for dividing up, distributing, and colonizing the "western" lands. The land ordinance of 1785 (which Jefferson helped write) established standards and patterns for surveying the public lands, an essential preliminary to dividing the land into plots which could be individually owned. A system was also devised to provide an income for the federal government from the distribution by sale of millions of acres of land. Once surveyed, the public lands were sold at auction to the highest bidder. A majority in the Congress in 1785 felt that the lands should go to the wealthier, "better" men who were already speculating in Western lands, so the minimum price and acreage set required any buyer to have several hundred dollars cash.

By the first census in 1790, a hundred thousand Americans

had moved West—two and a half percent of the population. By 1850, forty-two percent of the population (nearly ten million people) lived west of the Appalachians. Every family that went West tried to acquire land. Nearly everyone in frontier settlements bought land, sold it, cleared and farmed it, and moved the produce to market.

The sale of public lands not only encouraged westward migration and the expansion of agriculture, it also encouraged the almost universal practice of speculation in land. "Until the era of big business, large capitalization, and million-share companies," Paul W. Gates has written in *The Farmer's Age,* "the favorite medium of speculation was land." Between 1790 and the 1860's, the difference between speculation and investment in land was often nonexistent: people and companies with capital bought and sold land without seeing it, divided it into house lots, and planned cities. Others improved the land by clearing it, plowing it, planting crops, fencing, putting up houses and buildings, and then tried to sell it at a profit. For those who had capital, there were many ways to profit. Land could be bought cheaply at auction. It could then be sold at a considerable profit to migrants who wanted to farm or to squatters already on the land. Since few squatters had cash—like the Iowa squatter mentioned by Gates who had no way to get his produce to market in 1841, had "five yoke of oxen, two or three cows, a good horse, 3,000 pounds of pork, and 400 to 500 bushels of corn," but no money—the speculator with capital could lend at a high rate of interest. Then either the speculator collected his interest—it was never under ten percent and often ranged to thirty percent or more per year (it went over one hundred percent in the speculative boom of the 1850's)—or, if the squatter or farmer defaulted and the land was repossessed, the speculator had improved land to sell again.

Land companies, funded with capital from investors in the East—particularly from Boston, New York, and Philadelphia—bought land, established banks, lent money, supervised investments for speculators and absentee landlords, collected on mortgages, sold land, and even operated land investments themselves. Smaller speculators often bought, on credit, more land than they could possibly clear and work themselves, hoping always to be able to sell some at a profit in order to pay for the rest.

Growing Western populations, increasingly powerful political demands for more egalitarian policies, and periodic financial depressions all brought successive changes in the land laws between 1800 and 1862 to permit increasingly wider distribution of the public lands to individuals likely to farm. The passage of the Homestead Act in 1862 changed official policy from sale of the public lands (to provide support for the government) to government grants of public land (in order to provide support for important public policies). The Homestead Act also established in law the principle that land should be available to anyone willing to work it or "improve" it. The land market in America had, by that time, become a major center of business activity and continued to be so after the U.S. government ceased to be a major participant. In 1860, there were seventy-eight U.S. Treasury branch Land Offices, and "doing a land-office business" had become synonymous with high-volume business—a minimum of one million acres every year between 1829 and 1862 were auctioned off at those offices.

While most farmers were poor struggling people who were not speculators, the temptation to buy and sell land was always present. It was there because American farmers were—unlike most of their European counterparts—frankly and consciously in business. They believed their independence, their freedom, and their prosperity lay in their ability to market their produce, and their land, for profit.

Merchants and New Routes to Profits

Merchants engaged in international trade had been, throughout the colonial period, the wealthiest men in America. It was they who collected the produce of agriculture, provided the ships, crews, agents, insurance, capital, and marketing networks necessary to sell that produce in markets, and to buy goods abroad to sell here. Capital had accumulated in their hands.

The Revolutionary War, the battles on land, the British blockade of many American ports, and the hazards presented by British warships disrupted the patterns of American trade. Some established merchants, and many younger ones, took up "letters of marque" or commissions as privateers—which legally empowered them to arm their merchant ships and capture and keep the ships and cargoes of the enemy. Nearly 1,700 commissions for privateers were registered with the United States government during the Revolution, many more with individual states. Operating principally out of Massachusetts and Pennsylvania (New York was held by the British, and the Chesapeake was effectively blockaded), more than ten thousand men were employed on privateers. As the war went on, the ships became bigger, better armed, their captains more skillful, and the profits they acquired—both in trade and in preying on British shipping—grew. The British lost £18 million worth of goods, two thousand ships, and twelve thousand sailors during the Revolution, the great majority to American privateers.

Privateering was not without risks. Of the two hundred privateers that went out of the port of Salem, Massachusetts, one-third were captured or destroyed by the British. But the surviving ships, large, well manned, fast, and officered by men experienced in trade and warfare, were essential to the establishment of a strong peaceful trade after the war.

When the war was over, American merchants were gradually able to reestablish contacts with British merchants and gain access to some British markets. The British market for American cotton expanded steadily throughout the nineteenth century, but never after the Revolution did Britain dominate American trade. American merchants carefully cultivated markets in France, Holland, Spain, and some of their colonies. The West Indian trade revived. Still, merchants sought new places for trade and new and more profitable goods to carry and exchange. Merchants from Salem and Beverly, Massachusetts—the Cabots and E. H. Derby, for instance—sent one of their ex-privateers into St. Petersburg in 1783, and by 1790 more than twenty-four ships from Salem and Beverly had entered the Baltic trade. They carried tar and turpentine, rice, sugar, and tobacco from Southern and West Indian ports to the Baltic, and brought back iron bars, hemp, cordage, cables, canvas, and bagging, which was either used in Salem or resold in other American ports. Salem ships brought a cargo of pepper out of Sumatra in 1795—without consulting the Dutch, who were trying to monopolize the pepper trade. Hundreds of thousands of pounds of pepper were, ultimately, shipped into Salem and transshipped, to the profit of Salem merchants, to other American ports and to Europe. American ships also moved into the Mediterranean, trading in Spanish, Italian, Adriatic, Turkish, Levantine, and North African ports. Opium from Turkey entered American merchant calculations, and so did the "Barbary pirates."

In November 1784, Elias H. Derby of Salem sent his big ex-privateer *Grand Turk*, Jonathan Ingersoll, Master, to the Cape of Good Hope loaded with cheese, salt, sugar, butter, and ginseng (which grew wild in New York State, and which was much in demand in China and "the Indies"). In Table Bay (Capetown), *Grand Turk* met the *Empress of China*, a New York ship owned by a syndicate which included Robert Morris, which was returning from Canton—the first American ship to have traded into China. In Table Bay, *Grand Turk* traded her cargo to an East Indiaman in return for teas and silks and nankeens from China. In December 1785, *Grand Turk* again left Salem, bound for Capetown, but this time she sailed on to Canton and docked alongside the *Empress of China* (on her second voyage). *Grand Turk* loaded a cargo of

75 cases of chinaware, 140 cases of cassia, 415 chests of bohea tea, and enough chests of hyson, singlo, and Congo teas to make a full cargo. She returned to Salem in May 1787: the China trade had become a lucrative and important part of American international trade. The syndicate which had sent *Empress of China* on her first voyage in 1784 had realized a twenty-five percent profit on its investment in ship and cargo combined.

John Jacob Astor of New York became, in the decade before the War of 1812 and in the period immediately following that war, one of the most successful of the many American merchants in the China trade. An immigrant from Germany, Astor became a fur trader and actively entered the China trade in 1800 when he bought part ownership in his first ship. By 1807, Astor owned three ships outright and was sufficiently important in the China trade to finagle permission—on a specious pretense—from President Jefferson to send a ship to China during the import/export embargo (imposed by Congress in response to the Napoleonic Wars).

In 1808, Astor formed the American Fur Company to help establish the American claim to the Oregon country and its rich furs as well as to attempt to control the American fur trade. In 1811, the company established a trading-post fort, Astoria, at the mouth of the Columbia. Although Astoria was lost to the rival Canadian North West Company in 1813, the American Fur Company did ultimately succeed in controlling most of the trade in American furs along the Great Lakes and up the Missouri from St. Louis to the Rocky Mountains. Astor tied the fur trade to the trade to China after the war with Britain ended in 1815, and for ten years or so—the fattest years of the China trade—he monopolized it.

Astor's trade with China was a complex pattern of moving and turning over cargoes which produced profit at each step: his ships left New York loaded with American goods, mostly agricultural, for trade; they called at western South American ports, in Chile particularly, where they traded for copper and wines and brandy; they called at California ports (which were Spanish colonies until 1821 and part of Mexico until 1848) to trade for furs and hides and foodstuffs; they traded foods, arms, ammunition, and other provisions into fur-trading posts in the northwestern parts of North America (run principally by Astor's own American Fur Company and by British-Canadians and Russians) for fine furs; they called in Hawaii to acquire sandalwood in exchange for food, cloth, brandy; and they traded fine furs, sandalwood, copper, specie, and some brandy and wine in China for teas, silks, furniture, and chinaware. In the China trade, as in much international trade, the Americans were handicapped by a lack of gold, silver, and an established banking system. The Americans' great rivals, British merchants of the East India Company, had all three—and a near-monopoly on the opium that proved most negotiable in China.

In the 1820's and 1830's, the China trade gave birth to a new and elegant variety of ship—the clipper—designed (by American shipbuilders) to move lightweight, not very bulky cargoes at the highest possible speeds over great distances. Carrying vast areas of canvas, worked of necessity by large crews, these graceful, beautiful ships raced with their cargoes of tea, silks, and porcelain to American (and later European) ports, making sailing records which are still unbroken. Elegant as they were, the China clippers did not long sustain the China trade. By mid-century, British merchants and American lack of cash had brought an end to the American luxury trade to China.

In 1834, John Jacob Astor dissolved the American Fur Company at what seemed the height of its domination of the New York and London fur markets. Astor had already sold his ships in the China trade. Other merchants, too, sold their ships, dissolved their trading companies and partnerships in the 1830's, and moved their capital out of international trade as quickly as they could "realize" it (turn it into cash). Since there was still profit to be made in the "carrying" trade, and in the selling of American agricultural produce overseas, some remained in those businesses. But many of the merchants of great wealth, and their sons and heirs, deserted the old avenues of trade and invested their capital in a new market.

American merchants began seeking profits within the growing United States. The expansion of the nation and its population to the Pacific was followed by merchants seeking and creating markets. International trade was left to the British and others, whose manufacture and commerce expanded into international markets. American merchants saw opportunities closer to home, more easily and directly supervised and much more accessible to them than to foreign merchants. The inward turning of merchant activity helped to create America's economic independence. It also removed a significant American presence from international markets—with the result that Europeans were far less aware of the massive American industrial, transport, and financial development in the middle years of the nineteenth century.

Trade in Salem—a major American market and merchant center—reached its peak in the years just before the embargo of 1807 closed it down. Salem merchant activity in international markets recovered after the War of 1812 but never reached the heights it had attained between 1791 and 1807. Salem merchants—like other successful American merchants—had made investments in local roads and turnpikes, bridges, banks, insurance companies, and canals, and many had invested in or speculated in land, as ways to "balance" their risks in ships and cargoes. They were accustomed to moving their investments—they often sold the ships as well as the cargoes—and dividing their risks. After the War of 1812, the shrewder and luckier among them, slowly, almost imperceptibly, began to shift their investments to the American market—to land, merchandising, transportation, and manufacturing operations in the hinterlands. Some of them moved—to Boston, New York, Springfield, Albany; some even farther west, to Buffalo and Cleveland. Salem declined as a center of trade and wealth as its businessmen moved both their investments and themselves away from international markets.

John Hare Powel is an example of a very successful Philadelphia merchant who moved his investments in the 1820's and 1830's from overseas trade and involvement in European markets to the development of improved dairy farming and marketing in America. Powel gave up being a merchant to become a "gentleman farmer," scorned by "dirt" farmers as incapable of successful farming. He invested his fortune in the purchase and import of improved dairy stock from England, and transferred his successful techniques of management, accounting, marketing, and operation to the production of better dairy cattle (and dairy products) for what he saw as a steadily growing American market. He consistently made a profit at his new business—and contributed greatly to the improvement of the dairy business in America. There were many other merchants like Powel who transferred their capital and their operations to the business of agriculture and to the development of domestic markets.

John Jacob Astor moved much of his capital into land (as merchants traditionally had done). But his land was in New York City, and ultimately all of his (and his son's) time, work, and capital were profitably engaged in the management of urban investments. After the Erie Canal opened a highway from the West to New York in 1825, it was not coincidence that investments in New York City looked better to a shrewd merchant like Astor than ships in the China trade or fur traders scattered across a continent. The attraction lay in the possibilities of direct control and direct management of one's own business, right here in America. Such control—it seemed to many American merchants—was the way to independence.

The Useful Corporation

Capital, cash for investment, and the skills necessary to create profit were in short supply in America after the Revolution. A continuing problem for those who wanted to create large enterprises for socially useful, and profitable, purposes was to find enough capital. Banks and governments were both used as sources of large-scale investment. But merchants and other men of wealth who were eager to accomplish community-wide projects and make a profit at it sought large pools of capital and direct control of it. Between 1776 and 1850, many turned from proprietorships, partnerships, and loose companies of partners to the corporation as the preferred device for pooling capital and controlling its management. The corporation had the added advantage that it brought with it profitable government benefits.

The corporation has become so characteristic of American business that it is difficult to conceive of business without it. An American economist (E. S. Mason, in 1960) has written that "something very like the modern corporation is the inevitable product of an industrializing society." Yet only in America—not in Great Britain, France, Germany, Japan, or any other major industrial nation before the middle of the twentieth century—has the corporate form been an important instrument of business organization. The development of the corporation into a widely used business institution is peculiarly American, a product of the Revolution and the growth of American business between 1776 and 1850.

Only seven business corporations had been created in the American colonies before the Revolution. Several of the colonies themselves were corporations—and one British corporation, the British East India Company, did business in America, which contributed directly to the crisis of the American Revolution. It was not until 1781, when Congress chartered the Bank of North America, that a business corporation was created in the United States. In the next ten years, thirty-three corporations were created by the states and one more by Congress, the Bank of the United States. By 1800, there were 295 business corporations, and thereafter hundreds and then thousands more. Why? Why did Americans after the Revolution seek to use a device that they had so rarely used before?

When the corporation started to be used extensively in America, it was, as Oscar and Mary Handlin pointed out in their article "Origins of the American Business Corporation" (*Journal of Economic History*, 1945),

> conceived as an agency of government, endowed with public attributes, exclusive privileges, and political power, and designed to serve a social function for the state. . . . The community, not the enterprising capitalists, marked out its sphere of activity.

Corporations had originated in English law. A charter of incorporation was granted to a body of people, who were made a single *corpus* by the grant, by the king as sovereign, in order to carry out tasks useful or desirable to the government of the kingdom. In effect, the king made the incorporated body his agent, and granted the body the right of government and the right to exist for the duration of the charter (corporations could be immortal in law, if their charter did not specify a time of termination). Charters of incorporation ordinarily specified the rights granted to the corporation, the duties and responsibilities it was expected to carry out, and the ways—cooption, residence, election, purchase—by which its membership was to be established and renewed. Typically, charters of incorporation were granted to cities, towns, and municipalities—which were their charters of "liberties" and self-government. Charters were granted to colleges, to guilds of artisans and merchants (the companies of goldsmiths, of drapers, of vintners, etc.), and to companies of merchant-adventurers for the development of trade and colonies (like the Massachusetts Bay Company, the Muscovy Company, or the East India Company). Ordinarily the liberties and privileges granted to a corporation would not be granted to another in the same business, craft, geographical area, or trade. They were monopolies.

Because they were agents of government, corporations were under the active supervision of the sovereign. Charters were granted for government purposes, and they could be taken away—as the Massachusetts Bay Company found out when its charter was revoked, and Massachusetts became a royal (not a chartered) colony.

After the Revolution, Americans took a new course in regard to corporations. The sovereign was now the people; governments were agents of the sovereign responsible for the common weal, the commonwealth. State legislatures, which were representatives of the people, began to use corporations to build or develop useful projects for the common welfare. They also created banking corporations, to help establish sound credit and currencies, as well as to pool capital for other desirable enterprises.

The "enterprising capitalists" (mentioned by the Handlins) petitioned state legislatures for charters of incorporation, accompanied by privileges and monopolies—the right to collect tolls, to condemn property, to operate a bank in a particular place, to receive government funds—with the clear expectation of profit. Once they gained incorporation, they used every means at their command—lawyers, money, political support, the courts, bribes, threats—to keep their charters and their corporations independent of government supervision or control. Businessmen saw in corporate charters a means to create permanent, self-governing, autonomous communities of interest (all revolutionary ideals) specifically dedicated to operating in a market for profit and also directly associated with the public good and public welfare. By the 1820's, businessmen were battling in legislatures and the courts to attain incorporation and corporate privileges. They argued that the corporation was a model of democratic, community organization—the epitome of the voluntary association of independent individuals devoting their capital, their labor, and their skills to the public good. It was, many felt, the right of democratic, revolutionary Americans to be able to incorporate.

At the same time, the creation of corporations was opposed in the United States after the beginning of the Revolution, and often bitterly opposed. It was argued by many—workmen and mechanics, revolutionary politicians, convinced democrats from varied backgrounds—that all corporations were anti-democratic, aristocratic, subversive of revolutionary principles of equality and democracy, destructive of individual independence. Mechanics in New York City in 1785 objected that

> all incorporations imply a privilege given to one order of citizens which others do not enjoy, and are so far destructive of that principle of equal liberty which should subsist in every community . . . nothing but the most evident public utility can justify a further extension of them.

If everyone were to be granted incorporation, these New Yorkers argued,

> . . . the State, instead of being a community of free citizens pursuing the public interest, may become a community of corporations influenced by partial views, and perhaps in a little time (under the direction of artful men) composing an aristocracy destructive to the Constitution and independence of the State.

Corporations had a "natural tendency" to "promote the spirit of monopolizing," according to objections made by Pennsylvania legislators to the recharter of the Bank of North

America in the 1790's. For half a century, from the 1790's to the 1840's, urban mechanics and workers, farmers, and other independent businessmen fought corporations because they gave away "common rights" and the "privileges or powers of the state" to "little aristocracies" who gained thereby "profit, influence, or power." After the panic of 1819, caused in part by the restrictive currency policies of the Bank of the United States, many Western farmers and businessmen joined with Eastern workers and tradesmen in a political struggle for increased democracy and increased equality of opportunity to use the economic privileges (such as public lands, public works, and corporate protections) which they believed belonged to the commonwealth of independent Americans. Andrew Jackson became the political leader of a democratic movement which used the "monster" Bank of the United States (the largest American corporation) as its symbol of the evils of aristocratic, monopolistic, corporate privilege. Indeed, the continuing tradition which associates corporations with hateful upper classes, anti-democratic privilege, and monopolistic "monsters" is based in the Jacksonian belief that corporations are subversive of equality, individual freedom, and independence.

In the course of the decades-long debates over the nature and uses of corporations, legislatures began to create general incorporation laws in order to try to meet some of the objections. Starting with the Massachusetts law of 1799 for the creation of library corporations, these laws made it possible for any petitioners to be granted corporate charters for the purposes established by statute, without special acts of the legislature. By the 1830's, all states had enacted general incorporation laws covering business corporations, banks, and nonprofit organizations, which provided for the grant of corporate charters to any group of people who filed applications, paid the required fees, and registered with the state government. The corporate device was thus made available to anyone who wished to use it.

General incorporation laws did help remove some of the stigma of privilege from corporations. Andrew Jackson's decision to remove U.S. government funds from the Bank of the United States and place them in many banks in several states, despite the provisions of the Bank's charter, destroyed the Bank. It was also a public, national, and symbolic blow against corporate privilege. In 1837, Jackson's Chief Justice, Roger Taney, announced the Supreme Court decision in the Charles River Bridge case which made corporate monopolies unconstitutional. (In 1819, in the Dartmouth College case, the Court had decided that corporate charters could not be withdrawn by the legislatures that had granted them.) By late in the 1830's, the corporation had ceased to be a privileged monopoly.

As models for voluntary association in what was becoming a "nation of joiners" eager to form communities to work for the common good, corporations emphasized the voluntary and independent nature of their members. Qualification for membership depended on wealth, since membership in business corporations was bought through shares, but that membership was available voluntarily, freely, to anyone who cared to invest. By the 1830's, states had limited the liabilities of individual corporate shareholders, so people of limited means could consider investing in corporate ventures. Even earlier, in the 1820's, it had become possible to buy corporate shares in open markets. Those shares provided equal and democratic participation in the corporation's government, the liability of each shareholder was limited to the price of the share, and the liability of the corporation itself was limited to its assets. Corporate privilege (as it had been understood fifty years earlier) had, by the 1840's, gone the way of corporate monopoly.

By the 1840's, businessmen had developed the belief that the corporation was a device for the democratic organization and management of the pooled resources of a group of independent individuals. It was a device increasingly favored for the organization of business and community affairs. It was available to all—and thus arguably appropriate to the ideals of democracy and equality. Its primary privilege was that of governing its own affairs and operating freely in the marketplace. Corporate directors and stockholders also argued that corporations should be independent of regulation or intervention by any government, that they were entitled to individual freedom and independence. However, many Americans, including many in business, continued to disagree. They saw the corporation, not as a device for the service of the commonwealth and the enrichment of individuals, but rather as a monster of privilege, a monopoly that threatened the freedoms of independent people and required control by democratic government.

Roads to Independence

There were not many miles of roads in the colonies before the Revolution. Those that existed were short, generally straight (whatever the obstacles), poorly maintained, and frequently impassable. Roads were very expensive, the colonies had been relatively poor, and most colonial settlements had been sited on or near navigable waterways (and so had few roads).

After the Revolution, Americans began to create the basic "infrastructure" of a national economy. Of course they did not call it that, and most of them did not think in such abstract, specifically economic terms. Singly and collectively, they were seeking independence. They wanted their country to expand, and they wanted to get themselves and their goods to markets. They were, collectively, no richer than they had been before the Revolution, but they began to pool their resources and build roads, bridges, turnpikes, then canals, and later railroads so they could get there—wherever "there" turned out to be.

The roads they built were hardly comfortable. An 1804 law

in Ohio prohibited stumps over one foot high in the public roads. It was usually easier to travel in the winter, when roads were frozen, or to carry goods on sledges or "boats" when they were muddy. Nevertheless, state and local governments attempted to provide for the common welfare by encouraging the construction of roads and bridges and ferries. Petitions from businessmen who wanted to build bridges, establish and operate ferries, and construct and maintain roads for profit were granted by legislatures. Slowly at first, and then with increasing rapidity by the beginning of the nineteenth century, state governments created corporations to provide transportation and communication services and charge the public for those services. These early corporations were very similar to modern "Authorities," which are created by government to provide transportation services (turnpikes, airports, piers), which require privileges exclusive to governments like eminent domain, are governed by businessmen, and are funded by private investment (bonds today, stock in earlier corporations).

The first transportation corporation in the United States was the Proprietors of the Charles-River Bridge, chartered in Massachusetts in 1785. The stock was quickly sold, and on Bunker Hill Day, 1786, the bridge was opened with a celebration planned by the stockholders to show "a most pleasing proof of how certainly objects of magnitude may be attained by spirited exertions" and to demonstrate "the greatest effect of private enterprise in the United States." A parade of the bridge builders and their tools, of the stockholders, of state and city government officials, of "officers of the late Continental Army," of "the President and Directors of the Massachusetts Bank," and many other dignitaries was watched by twenty thousand spectators, while cannons were fired from Copp's and Bunker's hills and the Christ Church bells rang. Eight hundred guests sat down to a meal on Bunker Hill and drank toasts, accompanied by cannon fire, to "the bold and successful effort of ingenuity and enterprise." The bridge proved a financial success, it paid its stockholders at least ten percent per year on their investment, and it increased land values around the bridge. In 1837, the Charles River Bridge corporation was party to the Supreme Court case in which it was decided that corporate monopolies were unconstitutional. Throughout the course of American expansion, the need for bridges generally brought government action, renewed fierce debate about the common benefits to be gained by private investment in public utilities and about the evil or beneficence of corporations, and produced a scramble to use the powers of governments for profitable investment by promoters, speculators, salesmen, builders, engineers, financiers, retailers, merchants, and transporters of goods.

The first of the great American turnpikes to be incorporated (in 1792) and built (in two years) was the President, Managers, and Company of the Philadelphia and Lancaster Turnpike Road. When the books of the Lancaster Turnpike were opened to sell stock, Philadelphia investors put thirty-dollar deposits on over two thousand shares in a few hours—although only half of the total of 1,208 shares had been allocated for sale in Philadelphia (the other half was reserved for Lancaster). The company finally conducted a lottery for the shares—each depositor receiving a lottery ticket. The market in the tickets rose to a hundred dollars, and when the lottery was held, each winner received a share of stock, and losers had their deposit refunded. It cost nearly $500,000 to build the Lancaster Pike's sixty-two miles of stone overlaid with gravel. It was "a masterpiece of its kind," according to an English traveler in 1797, and it was one of the most successful of the hundreds of turnpikes which were eventually built in America. It paid dividends in most years, averaging about three percent on the initial investment.

There was strong opposition to the Lancaster Pike, from democratic legislators who argued that the state's power of eminent domain should not be used to acquire right-of-way for private profit. The argument was overridden by legislative majorities who believed that the common welfare was better served by having the roads—and by not taxing the people in order to get them. Local farmers living near the road were granted concessions by the legislature, after considerable complaint, so that they did not have to pay tolls to move themselves, their livestock and goods across the road or very locally on it.

Turnpike building developed gradually, and then boomed after the War of 1812. In the Eastern states, as well as in Kentucky, Tennessee, Ohio, and Indiana, tens of thousands of miles of pikes were built and millions of dollars spent on them. Some state governments, most notably Pennsylvania and Kentucky, invested heavily in turnpike corporations which were managed by stockholder-elected directors in order to assure construction of adequate roads. There was a short-lived boom in plank roads in the 1840's, because they were cheaper to build and were effective high-speed roads while they lasted—which turned out not to be very long. Turnpike construction declined in the 1850's and ceased by the time of the Civil War—not to start again until the 1930's.

Turnpikes were built for long hauls with heavy goods. But they proved to be very expensive for long-haul freight, principally because the animals used were expensive to feed, and with tolls added, the costs were prohibitive. By the mid-1830's, for example, when turnpikes had become plentiful, it cost $3.50 per hundred pounds to ship goods by wagon over turnpikes from Philadelphia to Pittsburgh—about four hundred miles. It cost $1.50 per hundred pounds to ship the same weight from Philadelphia to Pittsburgh by ship and steamboat via New Orleans and the Mississippi and Ohio Rivers—about four thousand miles. As a result, turnpikes were not used for long-haul freight, and so most of them proved to be very unprofitable ventures. Nevertheless, businessmen for decades believed they could be profitable—it seemed logical, since there were so many people eager to move goods to and from markets—and invested heavily in them.

As more and more pikes were built and interconnected, they made the movement of people, goods, and mail much easier and swifter. Short-distance, local freight movements and longer-distance movements of people were well served. So their unintended contribution to the spread of population, the development of regional market centers, and the ease of communication was enormous—but not profitable to investors.

Getting the Goods to Market

The Erie Canal was a great success. It was celebrated in song and story—"Low bridge, everybody down, low bridge, for we're comin' into town"—and promoted by bankers, brokers, engineers, legislators, small-town and big-city boomers, landowners, farmers, and even by immigrant Irish laborers. Americans like to tell success stories. We particularly enjoy stories about movement, mobility, and getting there. We tell and tell again the story of the big success in a particular business or venture—and tend to forget the many failures.

When the New York State legislature decided, in 1817, after long and violent debate, to build a 350-mile canal between Albany on the Hudson River and Lake Erie, there were fewer than one hundred miles of canal in the entire United States, and the longest was the Middlesex Canal, which ran twenty-seven miles between the Merrimack River and Boston. New York actually proposed to build two canals, one linking Lake Champlain and the other Lake Erie to the Hudson near Albany, at a cost estimated at $6 million—or four dollars for every man, woman, and child in the state—at a time when a hardworking man could hope to earn a dollar a day in wages. Furthermore, there were no trained engineers (other than surveyors) in the United States. The men who built the Erie—some of them were elected to do it—learned by doing. One young surveyor, sent to England by New

York's governor DeWitt Clinton, walked two thousand miles along English canals to study their construction. He returned to become the Erie's chief engineer. Despite what seemed to be insuperable obstacles, the Erie was built, and rather well built. It also proved immensely profitable (when tolls were abolished in 1882, the canal had made a net profit after "cost of construction, improvement, superintendence, and repairs" of nearly $42,600,000).

In 1825, the entire length of the Erie Canal, four feet deep and forty wide, from Albany to Buffalo and from Lake Champlain to the Hudson, was opened to traffic. The occasion was celebrated by a flotilla that moved from Buffalo to New York City carrying dignitaries and casks of Lake Erie water. The celebration ended at Sandy Hook, where Governor Clinton dumped waters from Lake Erie into the Atlantic: "vials containing water from the Mississippi, Columbia, Thames, Seine, Rhine, Danube, Amazon, La Plata, Orinoco, Ganges, Indus, Gambia and Nile Rivers" were also emptied into the ocean. The exuberance of the celebration seemed appropriate to the achievement.

The Erie started a canal-building boom. In all, over 4,400 miles of canals were built. Construction continued until well after the Civil War, and at least $125 million were spent on initial construction, and tens of millions more on improvement and maintenance. Because canal construction was so difficult and expensive, it had to be financed with government funds. Only by taxing, selling state bonds and state public lands could such massive amounts of capital be raised. Eager canal boosters tried, and failed, to get the federal government to fund canals. But state governments created canal corporations and sought individual business investors and managers; governments bought canal-company shares, lent construction money, used their powers to acquire land and rights-of-way, and subsidized canal operations. Some states granted public lands to canal corporations to be sold to finance the canals.

The wealth produced by goods moved on canals was staggering. The prices of agricultural products of all kinds increased permanently along the routes of completed canals and along the roads and streams that fanned out into the countryside from canals. Farm populations and urban centers clustered near canals. Business boomed as the markets for farmers' goods expanded wherever canals reached. There were 3,600 new dwellings built in New York City the year the Erie Canal opened (and that city with its auction markets, banks, and growing exchanges became the commercial center of the United States). The populations of Ohio, Indiana, Illinois, and Michigan increased rapidly in the years immediately after the Erie was completed. "Then there's the State of New York where some are rich," went an 1830's Michigan ballad:

Themselves and a few others have dug a mighty ditch,
To render it more easy for us to find the way,
And sail upon the waters to Michigamia,
Yes, yea, yea, to Mich-i-gam-i-ay.

Independence—achieved by growing markets and increasing numbers of people moving themselves and their goods to those markets—was the goal of the legislatures, the governments, the people, and the businessmen who fought, argued, invested, and worked to build canals and better ways to move across America. However, independence—of government ditches in their back yards, of interfering, pushy businessmen who thought they were better than the next man and who used power they shouldn't have in a democratic society—was the goal of the people who tried to prevent the canals and who fought against state governments investing so much in them. And freedom and independence were the goals of the thousands of workers who moved the earth with picks, shovels, and wheelbarrows, and built the locks, and got soaked, chilled, starved, or died of malaria and pneumonia by hundreds, in order to earn enough to live.

In 1815, two years before construction on the Erie Canal started, John Stevens obtained a New Jersey charter to run a railroad between the Delaware and Raritan Rivers. Ten years later, he had not built the road, but he had designed and built and run the first American steam locomotive. Eight years after that, in 1833, Stevens's sons obtained a charter, raised one million dollars capital, and started scheduled rail service between New York and Philadelphia—using an English-built locomotive. In the same year, 1833, the South Carolina Canal and Railroad Company completed its 136-mile railroad from Charleston to Hamburg (across the river from Augusta, Georgia) and operated scheduled service on the longest line in the world. By 1836, the Baltimore and Ohio had built a line from Baltimore to Harpers Ferry, had a thirty-seven-mile branch line to Washington, D.C., was operating seven locomotives, 1,078 freight cars, forty-four passenger cars, and had an annual revenue of $260,000.

Americans actually started building railroads in 1830. By 1840, $75 million had been invested in the construction of three thousand miles of railroad (only 1,800 miles of railroad had been built in Europe, including Great Britain, by that time, at far greater cost). By 1840, too, Americans had designed the T-rail and used it on all their roads. The standard American locomotive had been designed and built (by James Brooks and Henry R. Campbell)—the eight-wheeler, four on the bogie truck and four drivers. The cowcatcher, the steam whistle, and the great kerosene headlamp had all become standard equipment. The corridor-type passenger car was in use, as was the double-bogie, which allowed cars to be longer, carry more, and corner better. And, by 1840, William Harnden and Alvin Adams had established "railway express" businesses, carrying packaged goods in rented baggage space on scheduled passenger trains.

Americans gambled heavily that these new engines, machines, and cars would carry more goods, farther, faster, and create more markets, more freedom, and more profit than before. By 1850, they had invested $310 million in nine thousand miles of railroads (more than double their investment in canals). Railroads became, as we shall see, the biggest businesses in America by the 1850's. The investment had come from state and local governments, supplemented by individual investors. State lending programs alone had provided nearly one-third of the railroad capital invested by 1850. And in 1850 the federal government initiated a program of granting federal public lands to states, to help the states finance railroad construction.

Government subsidies, as they would be called today, were essential to the growth of all the large-scale businesses in America before the middle of the nineteenth century (as they would continue to be thereafter). Invariably, the governments were state and local. Those were the governments which most Americans considered important and effective before the Civil War. The federal government was distant and (most people hoped) limited in its powers. State governments had, all agreed, wide powers particularly to regulate and encourage the markets and economic opportunities available to their citizens. The arguments in state and local governments before the Civil War were almost entirely arguments over who should benefit from government economic participation, not (as they would be later) whether such governments had any power to control economic activity or markets.

Virtually every railroad was a corporation, chartered by a state legislature to provide transport for the commonwealth. Dozens were chartered in every state. Some were granted monopolies. Many were given financial advantages—tax exemptions, the right to raise capital by lotteries, banking privileges, outright subsidies, loans raised by state bonding. All were given the right to use eminent domain in order to acquire rights-of-way (a privilege British railroads were never granted), which made land acquisition relatively inexpensive. All railroad corporations were governed by boards and officers elected by the stockholders—only in very rare circumstances were they appointed by governments, or were there government representatives on their boards.

The businessmen who invested in railroads were usually merchants eager to see their local markets extended by better transportation. Longer, larger railroads were often financed by wealthy merchants who shifted their investments from international trade in the 1830's and 1840's. Accustomed to supervising investments over great distances, and eager to invest in new businesses they could hope to dominate, they formed railroad companies, merged small companies into larger ones with longer lines, poured capital into them, and also bought land, banks, mines, mills, and other businesses along the railroad lines.

The enthusiastic response to turnpikes and plank roads, canals, and railroads was more than the simple desire of businessmen to make a profit. Being on the move has always been part of the Great American Success Story. And since the Revolution, Americans have invested their work and money (and insisted that their governments also invest) in roads, turnpikes, highways, canals, railroads, airlines, subways, streetcars, buses, elevateds, monorails, and helicopters so that everyone can move.

The Richest Men in America

On December 26, 1831, Stephen Girard died in Philadelphia in the midst of a flu epidemic. He was in his eighty-second year, and he was believed to be the richest man in America. The same was said of his friend, John Jacob Astor, when Astor died seventeen years later at the age of eighty-four. The public response to the deaths and testaments of these two wealthy men (as Sigmund Diamond has shown in *The Reputation of the American Businessman*) provides a vivid demonstration of the changing attitudes toward business and the accumulation of wealth in the years after the Revolution.

Girard was born in Bordeaux, France, in 1750, the son of a French sea captain and merchant. He went to sea at fourteen and set up on his own as a merchant in Port-au-Prince in 1774. In 1776 a sloop he commanded, trading out of New Orleans, was driven by storm and a British frigate into Philadelphia. Girard's sloop was confiscated by the rebel Americans, and he set up shop as a merchant on Water Street. In 1778, he became a citizen of Pennsylvania, and Philadelphia remained his home until he died more than fifty years later.

Girard became a successful merchant during the Revolution. In the years that followed, his ships and cargoes moved in all the directions of American trade—to Europe, to England, to the West Indies, to the Mediterranean, and to the Far East. He invested in American land, in the stocks of American banks, and in the securities of state governments and the new federal government. He invested and speculated in financial markets in America, in London (where his correspondents were Baring Brothers), and in Amsterdam, where Hope & Company were his bankers. In 1812 he bought the building that had been used by the first Bank of the United States (whose charter expired in 1811) and went into the private banking business.

Girard's Bank was instrumental in financing the first American government loan in the War of 1812. Girard formed a syndicate with John Jacob Astor and David Parish which took $10 million of a $16 million loan. According to Donald R. Adams in *Finance and Enterprise,* it was the first American investment syndicate, which "set the tone for subsequent syndicate operations by introducing a system of pooled purchases of government bonds on the one hand and subcontracted sales on the other." Girard was instrumental in the founding of the second Bank of the United States in 1816, was involved in its government until 1820, and continued to hold a large block of its stock until his death.

Girard's own bank operated primarily in the commercial paper market, making secured short-term loans to merchants, manufacturers, and other businesses. The bank issued notes, and accepted the notes of other banks for deposit. Only in the last few years of his life did Girard's Bank begin to invest in long-term capital ventures. In 1812, when he founded his bank, Girard moved his capital out of foreign trade and into the American market. The several hundred thousand dollars he had on account with Barings in London and Hope in Amsterdam were transferred to America, and while Barings kept an open credit line of at least £50,000 (about $250,000) for him, Girard's European investments rarely approached that figure after 1816.

Girard was, as one biographer, Harry Emerson Wildes, called his book, a *Lonely Midas.* Not a pleasant man, he was rigid, chilly, unsympathetic. He tyrannized his associates and used employees like "machines or instruments." His relationships with family (he had no children) in France and America were bitter, acrimonious, and unloving. His relatives insisted his will be read over his corpse before he was buried. His funeral was a public occasion—the largest funeral Philadelphia had seen—because of rumors that he had left large amounts to the city. The Catholic bishop of Philadelphia permitted interment in the Catholic church grounds because Girard had been baptized, but Masons in full regalia conducted the service.

Girard's estate amounted to over $6 million. He left about $350,000 in legacies to his family and bequests to various charities. The Commonwealth of Pennsylvania was granted $300,000 for the improvement of canals, and the city of Philadelphia was given $500,000 for the development of Water Street and Delaware Avenue. Nearly 280,000 acres of "rich plantation land and its slaves" were given to the cities of New Orleans and Philadelphia for beautification. The rest was left to found a college in Philadelphia for "poor white male orphan children," with the proviso that no minister of any religion was to set foot in it.

This "poor, outcast, ignorant, and wandering boy," as one

paper described Girard, had by "sobriety, prudence, economy, industry," his great intelligence, remarkable knowledge of world markets, creativity, a "passion for production," and his belief in the duty of hard work become "the architect of his own fortunes." "His immense wealth," according to the Philadelphia *Inquirer*,

> was accumulated solely through his own industry, exertions, and enterprise. His character through life was distinguished for sobriety, honesty, and consistency throughout, and his whole career presents a beautiful example of the success of industry and economy, when added to good sense, perseverance and the moral virtues.

Girard was the epitome of the independent individual who had found freedom and success in the marketplace. His business was his work. The moral virtues—industry, honesty, sobriety—and common sense, were seen, by 1831, to be business virtues that crowned his life with success and wealth. The relationship between work, morality, business, and success which Benjamin Franklin had portrayed in *Poor Richard* nearly eighty years earlier had been made real by businessmen like Girard.

This successful immigrant was an outstanding example of American independence, too, according to *The Saturday Evening Post*, because he "considered himself merely as an agent, or steward" of his wealth. "Mr. Girard looked upon the wealth and prosperity of individuals," the *Post* said, "as blessings that are given in trust, to be used and disposed for the common good of society." There was no hint here that it might be possible to believe that individual wealth was in itself beneficial to society. On the contrary, wealth was given to an individual in trust, to be used and disposed of for social benefit and public utility. Girard's meanness could be overlooked and his tyrannies ignored, because he devoted the rewards of his greed to the benefit of his society.

Seventeen years later, attitudes had changed. When John Jacob Astor died in 1848, he left only about $500,000 of his estate for public charities, principally for a public library in New York. The rest of his estate—about $20 million—was left to his family. There was considerable furor that Astor did not leave his fortune to the public. Horace Mann described Astor as "the most notorious, the most wealthy, and considering his vast means, the most miserly of his class in this country." Mann thought that "nothing but absolute insanity can be pleaded in palliation of the conduct of a man who was worth nearly or quite twenty millions of dollars, but gave only some half million . . . of it for any public object." James Gordon Bennett, the publisher and editor of the *New York Herald,* straightforwardly asserted that Astor's fortune was created not by the man but by the society he lived in:

> . . . *one-half of his immense property—ten millions at least—belonged to the people of the City of New York*. . . . The farms and lots . . . which he bought . . . have all increased in value entirely by the industry of the citizens of New York. Of course, it is plain as that two and two make four, that the half of his immense estate, in its actual value, has accrued to him by the industry of the community.

Bennett concluded that this "modern Croesus," the "self-invented money making machine," owed his fortune to the community and should have returned a great portion of it to the community. Bennett's and Mann's attitudes, shared by many, were based on the assumption made by most Americans since the Revolution that individual freedom, independence, and success had ultimately to serve the whole society. Only then could greed or meanness be condoned. Their shock (which most Americans today would find surprising) came from the widespread belief that a democratic society demanded service in return for freedom from individuals.

"We are not enemies of the rich," a Baltimore paper editorialized on the publication of Astor's will, "but this does not prevent us from despising as the meanest of men, the miser who accumulates and aggrandizes a family, and leaves nothing for the people at his death, except a library." The aggrandizement of a family smacked, for most Americans of the day, too much of aristocracy, of European decadence.

On the other hand, many Americans defended Astor's will and argued that a man had a perfect right to leave his fortune to his family. Wealth, they argued, was the proper reward for individual work. If wealth was acquired by an honest, industrious, enterprising individual who had entered the marketplace and achieved success—as Astor had done in the fur trade, in the China trade, and in large ventures in New York real estate—then wealth itself was a social good. The moral and economic ideas of Adam Smith were combined with Benjamin Franklin's espousal of the social utility of work and wealth to defend John Jacob Astor. Individual success itself was equated with social good, in these arguments, just as business activity was equated with morality. American democracy was protected, and society served, according to these increasingly popular arguments, by the very efforts of the individual to acquire wealth and the independence long associated with wealth. Once the individual had succeeded, the wealth acquired made the whole society larger, richer, and better.

By 1850, many Americans associated work, industry, frugality—virtues they agreed were moral and good—with business (which they generally agreed was the seeking of independence in the marketplace). However, they did not all agree that business success and wealth served a democratic, egalitarian American society.

The Business of Working Machines

The expansion of agriculture, the development of transportation, and the growth of manufacturing all required the labor of human beings, supplemented by the labor of animals, the use of tools, and the energy of wind and water. The search for independence generated by the Revolution made many Americans increasingly receptive to new, practical ways of getting work done. To be independent of the work of one's own hands—to be a person of leisure—had long been taken as a sign of the upper classes (or of laziness!). One of the ways of gaining such independence and getting more work done at the same time was with machinery. Machinery was "labor-saving" almost by definition. It could do work faster than human beings, it could do work human beings were incapable of, and it could as a result make its owners or operators persons of comparative leisure. Americans took to machinery with increasing enthusiasm.

Machines gradually became part of American life—as they did of the life of Western Europe—in the eighteenth century, along with Newtonian physics, the Enlightenment, modern rationalism, and scientific thought. Skilled craftsmen in that century, in Europe and America, had begun to try to build skills into tools they called "machines." The surprising machines of ingenious tinkerers—like Jacques de Vaucanson in France, Thomas Newcomen and James Watt in England, Benjamin Franklin in America, to name only a very few—were based on the careful observation of human and animal movement. Using the knowledge thus acquired, inventors broke down movement into discrete parts, and reintegrated those parts with mechanical devices—wheels, gears, levers, pulleys, and screws—so that skills were built into the machines. Energy to drive the machines and mechanical ways to transmit energy were also based on the new laws of physics—Newcomen's steam engine (1712) used the new awareness that the atmosphere had weight for its operation, and James Rumsey's first steamboat (1786) used Bernoulli's theorem of the dynamics of flow for its water-jet propulsion. Americans particularly delighted in saving labor, improving life's comforts, and providing social utility through machines and gadgets of all kinds: some had borrowed stationary threshing machines from England (patented there in 1732) by the time of the Revolution, Benjamin Franklin founded a society for the Promotion of Useful Knowledge in 1743, and a group of Philadelphia businessmen in 1790 built the first completely mechanized flour mill, in which gears, pulleys, and levers powered by a waterwheel carried grain to the gristmill, ground the grain, collected and bagged the flour, and moved the bags to storage.

While steam engines and machines have become associated in our minds with industrialization, and industrialization seems inevitably to be connected with business, they were not connected in the minds of Europeans or Americans in 1776. Only gradually, between the late eighteenth and the mid-nineteenth century, on both sides of the Atlantic, were steam engines, and machines, and manufacturing coordinated, and the products marketed.

In 1793, a Connecticut tinkerer with a late-Enlightenment education, who was working as a tutor on a Southern plantation, designed and built a machine which made mechanized cotton-textile manufacturing possible. Eli Whitney's engine ('gin) could efficiently and on a large scale remove the short fibers of upland cotton from its tenacious seeds. It made the Southern United States a commercially successful cotton-producing region: five million pounds of cotton grew there in 1793 and two and one quarter billion pounds were produced in 1860. The gin also contributed to the enormous expansion of slavery since it made possible the expansion of cotton production.

Whitney had a central place in the folklore of American business, because he also introduced and sold to the federal government the idea of interchangeable parts for guns manufactured by machines and put into production in his own armories. Interchangeable parts, the design of special machines to make those parts, and the organization of the assembly of such parts all, as we shall see, very slowly became the basis for a peculiarly American system of manufacturing. But in his own day Whitney was one among many Americans and Europeans who played with machinery and attempted to build businesses based on machine manufacturing.

The mechanized manufacture of cotton textiles—the first modern industry—was started by English inventors and businessmen and spread to America. With it came the complex processes of designing and manufacturing industrial machinery and the creation of the machine-tool industry, which in turn made it possible to create machines for all kinds of manufacture. Between 1764 and 1799, Hargreaves, Arkwright, and Crompton had perfected machinery in England for spinning quantities of fine, strong cotton threads. Spinning mills and later weaving mills developed, and with them the demand for cotton which Eli Whitney's gin made it possible to meet.

In 1787, George Cabot set up a mill in Beverly, Massachusetts, with horse-driven machinery for cotton spinning. It ran for nearly five years before it was abandoned. In 1789, an Arkwright employee named Samuel Slater emigrated from England (despite laws prohibiting skilled cotton-textile workers from leaving). Financed by the Providence merchant firm of Almy and Brown, Slater designed and built machinery for a seventy-two-spindle mill using power from the Pawtucket River in Rhode Island, which opened in 1791. Within three years, three other spinning mills were opened in Connecticut, and one in New Jersey. Increasingly, Americans invested in spinning mills, the design and manufacture of machines for textile making and machines for machine making, and the development of techniques for "putting out" machine-spun thread for handweaving into cloth. By the beginning of the War of 1812, at least one hundred spinning mills were in operation in New England, and by the time the war ended (in 1815) there were between 140 and 165 mills in operation within thirty miles of Providence alone.

American cotton-textile manufacturing in its early years did not, as the British did, use steam to drive its machinery.

Waterpower was plentiful in New England, where there were businessmen with large sums of available capital to buy machines and build mills. The extensive use of stationary steam engines in America for manufacturing power awaited the development of coal mines and of railroads to move the coal to the engines—which would begin in the 1830's and expand rapidly by 1850.

Americans made their earliest, and very important, contributions to the development of steam machinery by using steam to *move.* The Marquis de Jouffroy d'Abbans in France (1783) built the first successful steam vessel. It was, however, the Americans James Rumsey (1743–93), John Fitch (1743–98), John Stevens (1749–1838), and Robert Fulton (1765–1815) who designed and built effective, operating steamboats. Robert Livingston, a New York businessman and brother-in-law of John Fitch, acquired a monopoly of steamboat operation in New York State in 1802 and then hired Robert Fulton (an American jeweler-artist-designer-inventor living in France) to build him a steamboat. The Fulton–Livingston ship, *Clermont,* made a round trip between New York and Albany in August 1807 and demonstrated the business potential of steam navigation. By 1815, steamboats were operating on many of America's numerous rivers (well supplied with available wood on their banks)—making them two-way highways for the movement of goods between farms and markets. Americans and their goods were even more mobile after steam railroads began to be built in the 1830's. Machines very rapidly became symbols for Americans—of work and its most efficient organization and production, and of swift mobility as well. In 1841, Theodore Parker wrote:

> The head saves the hands. It invents machines, which doing the work of many hands, will at last set free a large portion of leisure time. . . . At the voice of Genius, the river consents to turn his wheel, and weave and spin. . . . Fire and Water embrace at his bidding, and a new servant is born, which will

> fetch and carry at his command; will face down all the storms of the Atlantic; will forge anchors, and spin gossamer threads, and run errands up and down the continent with men and women on his back. This last child of Science . . . is already a stout giant.

In 1813, Francis Cabot Lowell organized a group of Massachusetts merchants into the Boston Manufacturing Company and constructed a new kind of mill in Waltham, Massachusetts. Lowell had seen power looms (weaving machines) in England, and he was taken with the idea of designing and building a mill in which the entire process of making cloth from raw cotton could be done by machinery and in one "plant." Lowell brought Nathan Appleton and his own brother-in-law, Patrick Tracy Jackson—both successful merchants—into the management of his newfangled mill. He hired Paul Moody, an "able mechanic," to design and build machinery based on his memory of the English weaving machines. In 1814, the specially designed mill in Waltham in which the entire process of manufacturing cotton textiles was accomplished by machinery under one roof went into production: the first modern industrial factory. The Waltham plant also had its own machine shop for the design, manufacture, and repair of its machines, a bleaching and dye works, and, later, a print shop—all in close proximity to the factory and all integrated into the factory process.

The invention of the industrial factory by Lowell and his associates was the first major American contribution to industrialization. (British industrialists did not adopt the idea until much later in the century.) The factory was itself a complex machine which required the integration of energy, capital, numbers of human beings, and many complicated engines into a self-contained process which produced a volume product. The factory-machine was based on the ideal of self-sufficient independence: everything necessary for the process was contained within the unit, integrated into a community of effort which resulted in a product salable in the marketplace. Of course the raw cotton, and the waterpower, came from "outside"—self-sufficient individual independence was also not ultimately perfectible—but it was the vision of such independence, and the effort to achieve it, which underlay the attraction of the factory for Americans.

The idea spread very slowly before 1850. It required the concentration of a great deal of capital, the courage to manage a great many different enterprises at the same time, a willingness to use what seemed to most contemporaries to be an exceptionally revolutionary concept, and to do all that with a method new to world commerce. Even enthusiastic Americans, consciously revolutionary and eager for business opportunities, were initially cautious about factories.

While steamboats, mills, railroads, factories, and machinery were, before 1850, evidence of an American fascination with machines and the possibilities of independence and success they offered, yet hand labor and older techniques of production and manufacture prevailed until well after mid-century. It was not, for example, until 1880 that the horsepower produced by steam in manufacturing exceeded the power produced by water; it was not until 1893 that ship tonnage powered by steam exceeded that under sail. Machines driven by new sources of power were—most Americans agreed by 1850—wonderful ways to get work done and work saved. But it was more important, and probably more profitable, to control, order, and organize the ways people worked than it was to put more machines to work.

The Spirit of Manufacturing

The mechanized manufacturing we call industry—as well as the "industrial revolution" we tend (mistakenly) to think of as the immediate result of the creation of Watt's and Arkwright's and Whitney's and Fulton's machines—spread very slowly. It took all of the nineteenth century for industrialization to reach everywhere in American manufacturing and business. But well before industrialization was complete, there had been a revolution in the organization of work.

In 1791, in his *Report on Manufactures,* Alexander Hamilton had proposed that the federal government embark on a program to invest in and encourage the development of manufacturing. Hamilton did not use the word "manufacturing" as modern Americans do—to mean the mechanized production of goods—but he also did not mean simply "making by hand." He wanted the federal government to encourage the large-scale organization, discipline, and control of the productive work of numbers of skilled people—in order to make Americans independent of European manufactures, and in order to counteract the effects of British mercantilism, which had discouraged manufacturing in America before independence. Hamilton's program was rejected by a Congress which believed that it was mercantilist and not within the province of the new federal government.

Rejection meant that Americans did not want the power of the federal government to be extended so far—not that they rejected the idea of encouraging manufactures, or of state-government investment in manufactures. Individually, and through their state and local governments, they began to develop manufacturing on an ever-increasing scale. But, as an Englishman observed at the time:

> . . . It is not enough that a few, or even a greater number of people, understand manufactures; the spirit of manufacturing must become the general spirit of the nation, and be incorporated, as it were, into their very essence. Knowledge may be soon acquired; but it requires a long time before the personal, and still longer time before national habits are formed.

English manufacturing, particularly the weaving of cotton and woolen textiles by hand, was already highly organized, capitalized, and quite productive at the end of the eighteenth century. It was based on skilled human labor and a system of "putting out" the yarn and thread to weavers, and then collecting, transporting, and selling the finished textiles; and the English sold their manufactured goods all over the world, and not least in their former colonies. Many Americans were eager to catch up with and surpass the manufacturing of the mother country.

Daily life, in America as elsewhere, was traditionally organized on a solar schedule: people slept when the sun was down; they rose and worked when the sun was up. In winter—particularly in northern latitudes—they slept more; in summer they worked more. There was little difference in life rhythms between those who were agriculturalists and those who manufactured goods—they were often the same people at different seasons or times of day. There was little difference between those who lived in the countryside and those who lived in cities. There were differences between social classes, however. Those who could command wealth could afford artificial heat and light. Those who could command the work of other human beings did not themselves have to work, and they could induce or force others to modify their habits and do more or different work. Useful work was arranged by specializing tasks, assigning tasks on the basis of ritualized training, sex, and social and communal status, and dividing the tasks among all the available people. Productivity was measured by the tasks performed and the goods produced, without regard to the numbers of people required. The more people who could be put to work, the more goods were produced and tasks performed.

As machines were introduced to parts of the manufacturing process, useful work began to be measured by the machines. Weavers were expected to weave increasing numbers of spindles of yarn because the machines were able to spin them. As people began to move the site of their work from home or shop to mill or factory, the clock—already in the early eighteenth century a precision-made machine (the first)—replaced the sun as the measure of days, work, and the rhythms of life. Clocks associated with signals—bells, whistles, semaphores—marked the significant events of daily industrial life: waking, eating, working, resting, coming and going. People were trained by the use of clocks to be more machine-like, to coordinate their activities with machines. The making of clocks became an early and important part of American industry—their distribution and sale a vital part of American business.

The early machine-run mills and the more complex mechanized factories impressed on their "hands" or "operatives" that time, measured by clocks and bells, and by the running of machines, was at the core of industrial life. In 1850, in the new, carefully designed manufacturing city of Holyoke, Massachusetts, the following was the (typical) mill timetable:

Morning bells: 4:40 a.m. and 5:00 a.m.

Mill gates open from first bell until ten minutes past last bell. Work commences ten minutes past last bell. Anyone "caught out" when work commences is not permitted to work until after dinner.

Breakfast bell: 7:00 a.m. (October 1 to March 31), 6:30 a.m. (April 1 to September 30). Work bell: 30 minutes after breakfast bell.

Dinner bell: 12:30 p.m. Work bell: 1:00 p.m.

Evening bell (work ends): 6:30 p.m. except on Saturdays when the sun sets before 6:30, in which case the evening bell is at sunset.

In this mill, "the first stroke of the bell" marked the time.

Machines changed the organization of time and the rhythms of daily life and work. They also brought fundamental changes in the social organization of work. Productive work in Europe and America before industrialization was organized in households. A father was the head of the household and the master of its manufacturing or trade, responsible for production, quality control, work supervision, and training. The mother/mistress of the household was usually responsible for the feeding, cleaning, clothing, nurturing of all members of the household—and was usually a skilled worker as well. There were servants in the household who were skilled workers, and children and apprentices who were workers-in-training. Both farming and manufacturing households used day laborers (journeymen, hired hands, employees), who often boarded in the household and were part of the working organization of the household even when they lived elsewhere. Everyone in the household—including servants, women, and children—did productive work. This "paternalistic" household system of work was the only model available for organizing industrial work. It remained a powerful influence on the ideas of the proper organization of work—whether of mill owners, farmers, factory managers, industrial engineers, or workers—throughout the long process of industrializing the whole society.

The population—predominantly rural and agricultural—grew very rapidly after the Revolution (as the population of England had expanded earlier in the eighteenth century). Many of the young men as they approached adulthood left home and went West, or tried their luck at road building or canal building, or sought jobs in the new mills. But children and young women were caught in what seemed to be a double bind: their economic value declined in farm households with increasing numbers of males available, and because of their age and sex, they could not go West on their own or seek jobs requiring strength and living in common with men.

Samuel Slater hired children to tend the spinning machines in his first mill in Pawtucket. Children were quick, small, able to spot and retie broken threads on the fast-moving machines. Slater was master of the mill, and children fit easily and logically into the household model of labor organization. Under the care and guidance, the discipline, of a master, children could become properly trained "machinists" or "operatives"—new words to describe the skills of running machines, not the old hand skills of artisans.

As Slater and others built more spinning mills in the 1820's and 1830's, they built them in rural villages in Rhode Island, Connecticut, Massachusetts, and New Hampshire where there was waterpower available and where there were young people to attract to work. The thread produced in the mills, by the machines and their young operatives, was "put out" to weavers and their families working in their own homes or shops in nearby village communities. Very often the mill hands were children and young women from weaving households. The weavers brought the finished bolts of cloth back to Slater's mill, where the quality was checked and they were paid, after the cost of the thread was deducted, in scrip or credit at the Slater-owned store in the mill village.

Francis Cabot Lowell and his associates in the Boston Company in 1813 sought out young women, as well as children, to be operatives in their Waltham factory. And in the 1820's the Boston Company built the first planned industrial city in America—Lowell, Massachusetts—and hired young women from the surrounding countryside. Boardinghouses were built by the company, provided with house "mothers," strict rules of behavior, and cultural activities appropriate for young women, and the operatives were required to live in the houses. This Lowell "experiment" did not last long: other populations (immigrants and permanent city dwellers) became available as mill operatives, and the household model of work organization and labor discipline proved inadequate in mills and factories with dozens of great machines and hundreds of people attending them. It was possible, by the 1840's, for a mill supervisor to say, "I regard my work people just as I regard my machinery"—not a comment possible for the master of a household of skilled workers. "So long as they can do my work for what I choose to pay them," the supervisor went on, "I keep them, getting out of them all I can." The head of a family of servants (the use of indentured servants had ceased by the 1830's), journeymen, apprentices, and young people in training had not perceived his household as a set of machines, or his relationship to them as a matter of "pay" for "work."

The advantages to the mill master of using young and female workers seemed obvious: they could be trained to work with machines regardless of their lack of traditional skills. Further, before 1850, men were paid twice as much as women and ten times more than children (a pattern which continued into the twentieth century). Machines provided the important skills in factories that men provided in traditional craft work. Women and children were believed to be socially inferior to men and therefore could be subjected to harsher discipline and forced to adjust to machines more quickly. A work force of women and children could be sent back "home" when they were not needed—when mills stopped running because of low or frozen water, high inventories, or poor markets. They would be cared for at home and be available when needed in the mills. Like the machines, mill workers could be "turned off" when they became inconvenient or expensive. Paternal responsibility often disappeared in the relationship between master and mill hand, but masters retained control. Masters and hands alike slowly and often reluctantly came to the conclusion that their relationship was more like the one of haggling and confrontation which Adam Smith had idealized of the marketplace than it was of the paternal household. Masters and workers sought their own profit and advantage with less and less thought of social responsibility to the other.

Such views, however, did not spread far by 1850. Masters and mill hands were a tiny part of the working population. Most Americans, young and old, saw themselves as entrepreneurs, in business for themselves, marketing their labor when they had no goods to market, in order to earn profit and independence.

Mills and working machines were *not* accepted eagerly or

easily by most Americans. Many fought bitterly against machinery and all it implied of loss of human skills and dignity. From the beginning of the nineteenth century, distrust of science and the machines that many believed were its result engendered an extensive popular literature based on the horrors of human beings becoming machine-like monsters or of machines becoming increasingly human and dominating human beings. The visions of humanity being controlled and dehumanized by science and machines have continued in American society to the present—computers which run amok and cute little robots rescuing damsels in distress are direct descendants of Frankenstein's monster and of giant saws moving nearer and nearer to Vera.

On the other hand, employment attending machines in the new mills offered freedom, independence, mobility, active engagement in the marketplace, and productive work to young, eager Americans and to new immigrants. It offered women the possibility of breaking away from dependence on parents, family, household. Lowell's boardinghouses and those of many other mills offered a way out of the family, and economic profit and independence. The disillusionment of many who went to the mills to work, the terrible weariness that came from long hours attending moving machinery, the sense of exploitation that sooner or later came to mill and factory hands, did not destroy the sense that involvement with machines and mills was a revolutionary act. Measured against what they had known before, independence, freedom, and profitable work awaited those who went down to the mills.

Manufacturing did increase in the United States, steadily and impressively, between 1776 and 1850. Although the majority of the population remained agricultural, the spirit of manufacturing—the ideal of producing "made" goods, and marketing them—spread rapidly, even among farmers. But the great majority of Americans who manufactured goods by 1850 still did so by hand at home or in small shops as part of fiercely independent manufacturing organizations in autonomous, self-governing communities. David Montgomery in his article "The Shuttle and the Cross" (*Journal of Social History*, 1972) described the manufacturing town of Kensington, Pennsylvania, in 1840, a suburb of Philadelphia in which eighty-nine percent of the three thousand adult workers were in manufacturing and trades. The richest residents of the town were master weavers, shoemakers, victualers, gunsmiths, shipbuilders, lumber merchants, ship carpenters, and furniture makers. Almost all were manufacturers, but none of them in mills and none (except the gunsmiths) was involved in significant work with machines. There were glassworks and iron mills in the town, so there were a few machinists and some mill hands. But the ships, textiles, shoes, furniture, and clothes produced in large quantities were not produced by machines. Production was organized on what amounted to a communal or guild basis. The business companies were rather like extensive households of workers and managers, part of whose production was done by "putting-out." There were unions in Kensington as well, voluntary community organizations of the working people (who viewed themselves as mechanics and artisans) devoted to protecting wages and prices, providing quality control, and maintaining work levels. They were based on the use of the master-day laborer-apprenticeship system modeled on the traditional household. In the 1840's, when there was a great strike in Kensington, it was—unsuccessfully—waged by the unions of these entrepreneurs against the introduction of machinery into their crafts, and against the increasing numbers of immigrant Irish Catholic workers, who were excluded from the unions because of their religion and their recent migration to the community, and who were feared because their poverty and dire necessity made them willing to work with machines and have their work organized in new, machine-like ways. The new spirit of manufacturing, with its mills and machines, based its organization of human work on the old vision of the poor: that those who worked at machines were young, unskilled, lazy, and had to be regimented and tightly controlled if they were to be made industrious and productive. The union members of Kensington, who knew themselves to be virtuous, productive, skilled, hardworking, and successful (they included the wealthiest members of the community)—like many other established workers in America by 1850—wanted no part of the new industrial order.

The community ideal—that independent Americans should freely gather together and build autonomous, democratic communities which were self-sufficient—was powerful and very influential not only among those in new settlements in the West, and those fighting to preserve their freedoms in places like Kensington. It was also strong among those who were building mills, creating factories, inventing new machines, and trying to industrialize America. Slater and Lowell and their associates clearly tried to create communities modeled on the household tradition. But industrialists and businessmen who followed them tried to imbue their new communities with the "modern" spirit of manufacturing. Mill companies (themselves corporations—voluntary, democratic communities working for their common welfare and profit) often created whole new physical towns—as in Holyoke, Massachusetts, or in Manchester, New Hampshire, in the 1840's and 1850's. Those communities were carefully structured to focus on the mills, and the patterns of integration of mills, machine shops, canals and water systems for power, boardinghouses for single workers, family homes for operatives, for overseers, and for managers, stores for food and other necessaries, fire services, and even churches, doctors, lawyers, and other professionals, reflected the vision of the complex machine (as factories themselves did). Such communities were designed to run by machines. Few of those industrial towns were actually completed as machine-like as they were designed, but where they still remain they give a haunting physical reality to the early-nineteenth-century ideal of the spirit of manufacturing.

Managing Slavery

The planters of the South, those who aspired to be planters, and the many more who simply wanted to be successful, independent farmers devoted themselves in the years between the Revolution and the Civil War to the profitable and productive organization of work. Agriculture expanded across the southern part of the United States as it did elsewhere. Millions of acres of new lands were put into production, and Southerners produced for market as eagerly and in as great a proportion as other American farmers. But with the expansion of Southern agriculture came the expansion of the South's peculiar institution, slavery—the business of buying, selling, and exploiting the lives, bodies, and work of black Americans.

In 1860, before the Civil War began, just over one-third of the American population lived in the South—about eleven million people. Nearly four million were slaves. Of the seven million whites in the South, 385,000 were slaveowners. The majority of those slaveowners owned five or fewer slaves. But the great majority of the slaves lived on plantations with twenty or more slaves.

There were about 46,000 whites in the South who owned twenty or more slaves in 1860. (There were 312 who owned two hundred or more slaves; fourteen who owned over five hundred; and one South Carolinian who owned more than one thousand slaves.) Those 46,000 whites, with their families, were the "planters"—the active, successful business people who dominated the economy as well as the politics and social order of the South.

The most important crop produced in the South before the Civil War was corn. It was used to feed the plantation population, and it was extensively shipped and marketed, as grain, as pork, and some of it as whiskey. Annually, in the 1850's, there were eighteen million acres of corn grown in the South, compared to five million acres of cotton (and 400,000 acres each of sugar and tobacco, and 70,000 acres of rice). The value of the corn crop was $209 million, compared to $136 million for cotton (and $63 million for wheat, $35 million for sugar, and less than half that for tobacco and rice). While cotton was the most visible Southern crop outside the South, and undoubtedly king of Southern crops in the world's markets, where it earned cash for Southern businessmen, planters and slaves alike devoted much of their time and energy to the growing of corn.

The planters were conscious of their active participation in business and markets; they were aware that they—like other American businessmen—were engaged in a search for increased production, better markets, and higher profits. For the most part, they saw themselves as thoroughly modern nineteenth-century businessmen seeking to impose order and rationality, predictability, and control, by whatever means available on their businesses, their property, their markets, and their society. "Let there be order," a Georgia planter wrote in 1851,

> start by time, work by time, rest and sleep by time, and if the overseer has sense and energy . . . there will soon be but little use for cowhides or track dogs under such an administration, and at the end of the year, the wear and tear will be much less, and the bags of cotton and barrels of corn quite as many.

The Southern planter differed from businessmen in the rest of America in his use of slaves to do his productive work. During the period after the Revolution, racism became the explicit justification for slavery. Racist attitudes had been implicit in colonial perceptions of Indians and Negroes, but bondage, coercion, and enslavement had not then required a racial justification so long as the general English and colonial attitudes about the poor, the uncivilized, and the un-Christian prevailed. Indeed, the eighteenth-century attitudes about those "lower orders" continued in the beliefs of many to justify harsh discipline and training, as well as confinement or restriction of movement. However, American enthusiasm for independence, liberty, and equality after the Revolution forced a search for a new logic of justification for slavery. Inferiority of social class or social order—indeed, the idea of a class society—had been explicitly rejected by American ideology. Difference of race, however (race was, to eyes eagerly seeking inferiority, "physically" and "naturally" visible, imposed by the Creator, or by Nature), could and did logically exempt some people from the civil and human rights Americans came to assume were the birthright of whites. With a terrible irony, the ideals of the Revolution—liberty, equality, and the protection of civil and human rights—were applied only to whites by those who wished to maintain slavery.

If black Americans could be viewed—as they were—as less than civilized, as a different, inferior race of beings, then it became possible for whites to justify to themselves the continual lifelong enslavement and coercion of all black men, women, and children. As that view became current in the early nineteenth century, white slaveowners began to view slaves as machines (tools with skills built in), or as parts of machines or factories, as gears, wheels, drivers, as sources of energy and productive work—like waterwheels, steam engines, or spinning machines. They were property—and the increasing use of that word (always carrying the meaning of "slaves," whatever else it may have meant as well) in Southern rhetoric and politics through the Civil War is one example of the strength and ubiquity of racism and slavery in Southern society.

Property was, for early-nineteenth-century business people particularly, directly connected to work and its organization. Buildings and machines were the property of mill owners, bonds and contracts the property of merchants and bankers, lands and slaves the property of planters, servants' bonds and workers' contracts the property of employers. Property was to be used, exploited, invested, and managed for the profit of its owner: "There are planters," a citizen of Mississippi wrote in *De Bow's Review* (a New Orleans agricultural journal) in 1847,

> who regard their sole interest to consist in large crops, leaving out of view altogether the value of negro property and its possible deterioration by unskilled usage like any other property. To say nothing about morality, this is a great pecuniary evil. . . .

Independence and liberty could be goals only for masters and whites in a slave regime, but the "pursuit of happiness" at least should be, many slaveowners argued, the one important American ideal that could be applied to the management of slaves. "Plantation government should be eminently patriarchal, simple, and efficient," a Georgia doctor wrote in 1860. "Wherever this is the case, peace, happiness, contentment, cheerfulness and good order reign supreme." "Happiness" of the slaves as a goal of plantation management is a recurring theme in the literature of Southern slaveowners (a collection of which can be found in James O. Breedon's *Advice among Masters*). "System," "uniformity," "management," "discipline," and "pecuniary benefit" were, however, the predominant concerns of slaveowners, as they were of mill owners, railroadmen, and other large-scale businessmen trying to organize large work forces and machine production. "The time has been," said an article in *Southern Cultivator* in 1849,

> that the farmer could kill up and wear out one Negro to buy another; but it is not so now. Negroes are too high in proportion to the price of cotton, and it behooves those who own them to make them last as long as possible.

"The most important part of management of slaves is always to keep them under proper subjection," a *Farmers' Register* article said in 1837.

> They must obey at all times, and under all circumstances, cheerfully and with alacrity. It greatly impairs the happiness of a negro to be allowed to cultivate an insubordinate temper. Unconditional submission is the only footing upon which slavery should be placed. It is precisely similar to the attitude of a minor to his parent, or of a soldier to his general.

Overseers, who were essential to the management of any plantation of moderate size, were too often "as trifling and contemptible as the negroes," one writer warned in 1838, since they were mere "hirelings," not committed, by ownership of property and hope of profit from it, to the proper management of work or a business.

Slavery created wealth for the owners of slaves, as machines did for their owners. As James Oakes has shown in *The Ruling Race*, poverty in America was widespread by 1850, and as much "a phenomenon of cities and immigrants as of rural destitution." Slaveowning did not cause undue poverty among nonslaveowning whites in the South, but it did expand the "highest stratum" of white society. The twelve wealthiest counties in the United States, in 1860, were in the South. "As slavery became the most popular means of acquiring wealth and status," Oakes wrote, the "restraining force" of the traditional paternal obligations of the household model virtually disappeared. A distinctive feature of planter society in the nineteenth century, for instance, "was the systematic effort to dehumanize slaves by treating them as property," by forcing slave women to "breed," by bartering slaves for money, debts, goods, food.

It was not only slaveowners who became wealthy through the exploitation of blacks. By 1859, as Philip Foner has shown, New York City merchants did $200 million worth of business with just five cotton-producing Southern states. Many merchants, bankers, brokers, investors, and other businessmen outside the South jointly owned and operated plantations and their slaves with Southerners. And, of course, the entire cotton-textile industry, which was the basis for the mechanization and industrialization of all of American business—the basis of the "industrial revolution"—got its cotton from the bondage, coercion, dehumanization, torture, affliction, and slavery of millions of innocent Americans who were black.

Samuel Colt and the American System

In 1851, a Great Exhibition of industrial machinery and machine-made products was opened by the British government in the Crystal Palace in London. Confident of their industrial superiority, the British invited exhibits from all industrial nations. Americans exhibited sewing machines, rubber goods, woodworking and machine tools, hand tools, cutlery, precision instruments, clocks, firearms, carriages, pianos, agricultural machinery, and paper bags. The American goods were not beautiful by European standards: they seemed crude, they lacked finish and polish. They were lightweight and looked hurriedly made. Americans used wood whenever possible, even for gears and machinery. But American machines worked—and went on working. When they broke, it was cheap and easy to replace a part or two, as the parts of many of them were standardized, interchangeable, and manufactured by ingenious machines specifically designed for a specific task. Cyrus McCormick's reaper surprised Europeans by its sustained performance and its rugged design. Samuel Colt's revolver was equally impressive for its remarkable performance and its standardized manufacture. Admiration for what Europeans began to call "the American system of manufacture" grew (grudgingly) among businessmen, government officials, engineers, and others who attended the Great Exhibition. In that same year, 1851, Samuel Colt opened a factory in England for the manufacture of his patented revolver—and became thereby the first exporter of American know-how and American arms.

Samuel Colt was born in Hartford, Connecticut, in 1814,

nearly forty years after the beginning of the Revolution. He was always going somewhere (sometimes simply getting out of town), moving, seeking his own independence from family, institutions, other investors, marketing his ideas, his work, his skills, his goods for a profit, delighted with useful, practical things and ideas, fascinated by science and machines, and determined to build his own freedom, and his own community. Rejecting apprenticeship to a farmer when he was eleven, Colt went to school, worked in his father's mill in Ware, Massachusetts, and played with "galvanometry" (batteries and electricity). On July 4, 1829, in a spectacular explosion, he blew up a raft in Ware Pond by igniting gunpowder on it with an electric spark from a battery on shore transmitted under the water through wires he had coated with rubber. He was sent to Amherst Academy to keep him out of trouble, and a year later was apprenticed to Captain Spaulding, of the brig *Corlo,* on a voyage from Boston to Calcutta. The ship carried missionaries, ice from New England, and miscellaneous cargo. While on the voyage, Colt carved a wooden model of a pistol with a revolving chamber worked and held by a clutch connected to the trigger—similar to the clutch on a ship's capstan. He returned from sea in 1831 and talked his father into paying for two pistols made from the model (two working models were necessary for a patent).

Colt went back to the Ware mill, became something of a chemist in the dye works, and learned about nitrous oxide ("laughing gas"). The pistols were made in 1832, but they did not work. Colt's father refused to pay for more, so Colt found a gunsmith in Baltimore willing to start work on new models, and he left Ware and went "on the road" as "Dr. Coult of New York, London, and Calcutta," lecturer and demonstrator of laughing gas, in order to pay for the pistols. For three years, he toured the United States and Canada (including trips up and down the Ohio and Mississippi Rivers with his brother John, a riverboat gambler). Beautiful models of the pistol were ready in 1835, and they worked. Colt went to

London, obtained British and European patents, came back and obtained an American patent, and in 1836 incorporated the Patent Arms Manufacturing Company in New Jersey. He never fully paid the gunsmith for the models.

The profitable manufacture of arms in quantity depended from the beginning on the federal government. Eli Whitney, early in the nineteenth century, sold the federal government the idea of making guns using interchangeable parts. Each part for a gun, in Whitney's view, was made by a special machine or machines, designed specifically to make that part; then the whole gun was "assembled" by a single workman supplied with all the parts. Whitney had not successfully made all the necessary machines, but the idea had been adopted at the government's arsenals—at Springfield, Massachusetts, and at Harpers Ferry, Virginia—and private arms makers had taken it up. The expense of designing and making the special machines was great. From Whitney's day to Colt's (continuing to today), anyone who wanted to produce arms in quantity sought government contracts large enough to pay for the machinery (provide the capital) to go into production.

As soon as he had his patent, Colt began lobbying congressmen, administration officials, military officers, and militiamen in an effort to get government contracts for his revolver and for revolving rifles and carbines which he also believed he could make. He gave away samples, and tried to get soldiers and militiamen in the Seminole Wars and in Texas (which was engaged in sporadic warfare since its independence in 1836) to use the revolver. Many soldiers (including President Andrew Jackson) liked the "Colt" and its firepower. Colt's fame grew as he spent company money and pawned guns to pay his often lavish travel and entertainment expenses. The company produced 2,700 revolvers and 2,500 rifles, carbines, and shotguns, but production was stopped in 1840 because the stockholders and managers felt that Colt was spending far too much of their money (he even lost a $6,000 check) and getting no contracts. He did sell a few hundred revolvers and some rifles to the army and the Texas Rangers in 1841, but production was never resumed. The stockholders dissolved the company in 1845.

But the Patent Arms Company was only one of Colt's businesses. In the late 1830's he had designed a waterproof cartridge and what he hoped was an effective underwater mine—both based on his early tinkering with rubber-coated wires and galvanometry. In 1841, he became friends with the Boston painter, inventor, and entrepreneur Samuel F. B. Morse, who was also lobbying in Washington. Colt's waterproof cable was vital to Morse's telegraph—the problem was to transmit an electric impulse over wires and not lose the impulse because of damp or wetness. In 1841, Colt formed the Submarine Battery Company, on the strength of a $20,000 federal-government contract for the development of his mine. In 1842, he successfully blew up a ship in New York Harbor (the mine was stationary on the bottom, and only effective if it was set off from shore as a ship passed directly over it). Between 1842 and 1844, he made several more successful tests, but the government did not buy any of his mines. Undaunted, he formed a cable company in 1844, and sold cable for Morse's telegraph. In 1845, under license from Morse, he established a company (the New York and Offing Magnetic Telegraph Association) which telegraphed news of incoming ships from Coney Island to the Battery and sold the news to subscribing merchants. He opened a similar company in Boston. Once all these companies were in operation, Colt left them in other hands, took shares or sold out his interest, and went on to other investments, other adventures.

In 1846, the beginning of the Mexican War brought orders to Colt for revolvers (Colonel Walker of the Texas Rangers had helped Colt—who was now a lieutenant colonel in the Putnam Phalanx of the Connecticut Militia—to redesign and advertise the revolver). He subcontracted to Eli Whitney, Jr., to Remington, and to other arms makers in Connecticut, and delivered a thousand revolvers in 1847. In 1848, Colt opened a plant of his own in Hartford, using machinery he bought from Whitneyville. In 1849, he renewed his patent and his armory was in full production supplying revolvers to emigrants to the California goldfields. He hired Elisha Root, whom he had known in Ware in his youth, to help design machinery, and he and Root developed the machines and the techniques for mass production of the revolver and other guns. In 1849, Colt went to Europe, where he found a ready market for the revolver as a result of the revolutions of 1848. He supplied Kossuth's army in Hungary and the Sultan's guard in Istanbul, and his advertising, entertaining, and lobbying began to spread the word in Europe that there was an American system of manufacture which could make more of anything, faster, and more uniformly than humanity had ever dreamed possible.

Back home in 1850, Colt moved his factory to larger quarters in Hartford, and began construction of a huge, new factory community by the Connecticut River. The next year, he went to the Crystal Palace Exhibition in London, demonstrated his revolver personally (as McCormick did his reaper), and stayed to build a Colt plant in England. He licensed manufacture in several European countries, sold thousands of revolvers to the British army and navy, and by the time of the Crimean War (1854–56), all the armies in the war were using Colt revolvers.

As the Crimean War began, the British government proposed to build a new factory for the production of small arms at Enfield. A Committee of the Ordnance Board—two senior artillery officers and an inspector of machinery (an engineer)—was sent to the United States with urgent orders to investigate the American system of manufacturing and buy machinery which was most representative of that system for the new factory. The committee made a several-months-long tour of the principal manufacturing towns and cities in the United States, bought machinery, and reported its findings to the Ordnance Board and to Parliament.

"The Americans display an amount of ingenuity combined with undaunted energy, which as a nation we would do well to imitate," the committee wrote, "if we mean to hold our present position in the great market of the world." The manufacture of interchangeable parts and mass production were the core of the American system, the committee reported, and they recommended its establishment in England not only in the arms business but in dozens of others. "The tools and machinery used for making wooden tubs and pails," they reported, "enables a few hands to turn out 1,000 per day"; a similar system applied to furniture meant one factory made four hundred chairs per day; and "a very clever machine is employed for making wooden matches at the rate of 15,000 per minute."

The committee tested interchangeability at the Springfield Arsenal by selecting ten muskets, each made in a different year, taking them apart, and handing the parts at random to a workman, who "assembled" them "with the use of a turnscrew only." The committee was impressed that the workman did not make or "fit" the musket parts but only assembled them with a screwdriver: "with regard to the fitting of these muskets when thus interchanged, the Committee are of opinion that all the parts were as close, and the muskets as efficient, as they were before the interchange took place."

It was the factory system, the committee reported, "got up by Corporations," using an "extreme subdivision of labor," and "with machinery applied to almost every process," each machine doing a single operation, in which the entire product is "made on the premises from the raw material" (and even the machines themselves are made on the premises), which made American mass production possible.

The machines themselves, the committee believed, which were "employed by engineers and machine makers" were "upon the whole behind those of England." But inferior machine-tools did not deter Americans; while "the work" such machines produced "may not in every case come up to our notions of finish," the committee reported, "it is produced cheaply and quickly." Materials and workers were both high-priced in America, and "the extreme heat of the weather during summer" reduced American productivity. Therefore, "the only reason" Americans could produce arms "cheaper than in England," the committee wrote, "is altogether owing to the productive capabilities of the machinery and tools that are employed."

American workers impressed the committee, despite their being "absent from their employment to an extent which could not be tolerated with us." Nevertheless, the committee reported, "every workman seems to be continually devising some new thing to assist him in his work," which very often resulted in new, labor-saving machines. Workers and owners alike "avidly laid hold of any new idea and improved upon it." American workers generally were clean and sober, drinking only "immense quantities of water" (often iced). A "distinguishing feature" of American factories was "the ample provision of workshop room," according to the committee, which gave space for expansion but most importantly allowed "order and systematic arrangement" of the process of making and assembling products.

System was what the committee found "striking" and "admirable" in American manufacturing. "This applies . . . to the selection and adaptation of tools and machinery," the committee concluded, "to the progress of the material through the manufactory," and also "to the discipline" of the workers. The Americans made special machines for everything "in order to obtain the article at the smallest possible cost." They "sunk" their capital "to a great extent" into specialized factories where they had departments "set apart for the express purpose of making the special tools and contrivances required." For Americans, factories themselves were giant, integrated machines. The British were surprised, and impressed—in their view, industrial machines were simply tools (not systems), to be well made and used with skill, in order to help human beings produce highly finished products.

The committee concluded its report by expressing regret that the first time it visited Colonel Colt's factory in Hartford it had eight feet of water in it from the flooding "connected river" (presumably the Connecticut), and on the second visit they saw only Colt's "new establishment, now in the course of erection, the magnitude of which quite astonished them. When completed, this will be the largest and finest armory in the world."

In the spring of 1856, Colt's new Hartford Armory (part of which still stands) went into full production. Two hundred fifty finished revolvers were produced each day. Special machines were used for every step of the process, machines designed by Colt or one of his many machinists and built in the factory. Colt's workers were supplied with housing near the plant, and Charter Oak Hall, seating a thousand persons, was part of the factory community and used for cultural and community events. Dikes were built to keep the Connecticut's floodwaters out of the factory and the community, and willow trees planted to keep the dikes in place. Then a community of German wicker-workers (who were provided housing and a beer garden) were imported to make wicker products out of the willows. Colt built a great mansion to overlook his factory community, and in June 1856, the forty-two-year-old bachelor married.

Six years later, Samuel Colt died of gout and rheumatic fever in the midst of the Civil War. The Colt Armory produced 387,017 pistols, 113,980 muskets, and 7,000 rifles for the United States government during that war—as well as tens of thousands of pistols for private buyers (among whom were agents of the Confederacy). Colt's great factory was representative, early in the 1850's when the British Committee saw it under construction, of the future of American manufacturing, of the massive organization and mass production which would make possible the Civil War's destructiveness, as well as the vast growth of late-nineteenth-century American wealth, industry, and manufacturing.

Colt had built his armory, and his business, on a pattern of attitudes which he and his workers and most Americans shared: curiosity and mobility; independence of decision; the search for "useful," "practical" knowledge and ideas; fascination with machines; the desire to apply knowledge, machines, and systems to the production of marketable goods or services; the desire to be liked; the measurement of popularity and approval by investment, sales, monetary support (and votes); the desire to make a buck and be somebody. He found his capital and made his money from lyceum and theater audiences who wanted entertainment, from the "scientific" curiosity of Americans, from family and relatives, from the federal government, from state and local governments, from investors willing to gamble, from new inventions applied to old desires or necessities, from marketing a mass-produced "consumer" item, from lobbying and advertising, and from intense, worldwide marketing and selling. Gradually, during Samuel Colt's lifetime, all those attitudes and characteristics had been woven together by Americans to form the fabric of a civilization in which almost all Americans were, like Colt, in business—for themselves, their families, and the common welfare.

Big Business and the National Market 1850-1925

Between the middle of the nineteenth century and the third decade of the twentieth, wars, moving and increasing populations, and an enormous increase in wealth changed the American world. The Civil War, from 1861 to 1865, was the most destructive war Americans have ever fought. We engaged as well in a "splendid little war" (in the words of the Secretary of State at the time) in 1898, which brought us the remnants of Spain's colonial empire. We participated massively but briefly in the Great War of 1914–18 (World War I), which destroyed European Victorian civilization. And we fought less extensive but very important wars against Indians and Filipinos.

In the same years, the American population increased four hundred percent. Land in agricultural production more than doubled. The American people were distributed across the continent, millions of immigrants swelled the population, slavery was abolished, and the United States became the world's leading industrial nation.

Between 1850 and the 1920's, big businesses were created and came to dominate the American economy. These giant, corporate, complex, interdependent organizations of capital, machines and factories, extensive labor forces, transportation, purchasing, processing, and marketing systems were created by men who set out to revolutionize business—and succeeded. Big businesses brought machines, factories, and large-scale operations to every significant kind of manufacture and production. They brought the majority of working Americans into their employ. They transformed America from a society in which the majority of working people were entrepreneurs—business people—operating in markets for their own interest and profit, into a society in which the majority were employees in a labor "market" from which they could hardly withdraw.

Big businesses transformed the laws, the Constitution, and legal traditions. They forced the redefinition of property, contracts, and individual liberty in the courts—and in the public mind. They changed the powers of state and federal governments and the relationships between them. Big businesses invaded and destroyed most local and regional markets, along with the many businesses and jobs which had operated in those markets. In their place, big businesses created a national market which they dominated. By the 1920's, big business had become a much admired, widely imitated model for the government (the management or administration of the affairs) of all organizations, corporate bodies, municipalities, communities, and societies in America.

The successful were the immensely wealthy, peculiarly visible symbols of the Americanness of big business. In no other industrial nation, at the beginning of the twentieth century, were there so many or such large individual fortunes created by industry. In Britain, France, Germany, and Japan, the great fortunes of the early twentieth century belonged to landowners, bankers, merchants, and other members of long-established wealth-controlling upper classes. In America they belonged to the successful creators of big business corporations engaged in industrialization. The successful individual was redefined by big business.

Big business, the national market, and industrialization were the result—according to arguments increasingly popular by the 1920's—of a great historical process called "the industrial revolution" or "progress," which could not be prevented or denied. Furthermore, it was argued, big businesses produced so many jobs, so much wealth, such an unbelievable quantity of goods, that they were obviously in the interest of the entire nation.

The idea that rational, calculated self-interest drives all economic behavior (and that economic motives are fundamental to all human behavior) is the common premise of modern economic thinkers, from Adam Smith and the classical economists, Karl Marx and his diverse followers, to Maynard Keynes and Milton Friedman and every other contemporary economist. This premise has become one of the major myths of the twentieth century—almost universally assumed to be self-evident reality. It was taken up by the defenders of big business late in the nineteenth century and made the basis of understanding "rational interest," "business principles," "free enterprise," as well as "common sense" and "reason."

Along with the premise of rational self-interest, the notion that human behavior in the aggregate always proceeds progressively was taken up as well by those who defended the growth of big business and its national market. Since the Revolution, Americans had made much of the idea that America was the refuge of liberty, the last best hope of the world, that American life was constantly improving, that America was the embodiment of human progress. With additions from Darwinian evolutionary ideas, it was an easy step for Americans to the belief that societies, institutions, and all of human life progress, that everything evolves, develops step by step, stage by stage, from the lesser to the greater, from the "backward" to the "advanced," from the worse to the better, from the "undeveloped" to the "developed," from the simple to the complex, from the small to the large, from the primitive to the civilized. Even those who rejected Darwinian ideas came to accept "more is better" and "growth is good" as imperatives.

On the basis of such logic, many Americans by the 1920's had come to believe that an inevitable "industrial revolution" had taken place and that, inevitably, giant business corporations ruled by shrewdly capable, immensely wealthy businessmen were symbol and reality of American wealth, power, and success. While there were many who fought against big business—farmers, workers, unions, Grangers, Populists, small businesses, local and state governments, even the federal government—and there were many whose rational interests were opposed to those of big businesses (including blacks, Indians, most immigrants, most employees), nevertheless most of these people and interests were seen (and often saw themselves) as trying to block progress and prevent the inevitable.

Yet there is little in the creation of big business which is necessarily inevitable or progressive. The big corporations of the late nineteenth century were the result of individual businessmen pooling their resources and seizing opportunities to control transportation, manufacturing, resources, markets, workers, and to influence governments—opportunities which just began to exist at mid-century. They used the available assets, opportunities, inventions, popular ideals and tolerances to achieve their goals. Their aim was to achieve conditions and markets they could control, and they built giant market-busting, regimenting, bureaucratic organizations capable of overriding local concerns, businesses, and governments, as well as community ideals, community welfare, individual needs or desires, and the power of democratic governments in order to do what they set out to do. They created vast bureaucracies long before governments did, and in the process they gradually redefined government.

The big-business revolutionaries had grown up with the values of a civilization based on democratic ideology and individual entrepreneurship. While they did want to create businesses on a scale greater than had been seen before, they did not intend entirely to destroy the business civilization they inherited, and they did not intend to change the nature of their own beliefs in independence, freedom, equality, democracy, and success. But as the many who fought them felt, those changes in scale—of transportation, of mechanization, of organization of work, of communities—all created changes in the nature of the society and of the beliefs that supported it. Between 1850 and the 1920's, the big-business revolution tore, and forever altered, the fabric of America's civilization.

Working on the Railroad

Railroads were the first big businesses. The techniques of big-business management and control were first developed in consolidated and extended railroad companies after the 1840's. The construction of transcontinental railroads and the national integration of rail lines after the Civil War made a national market possible for the first time. The transcontinentals were the first businesses to be subsidized on a massive scale by the federal government. National railroads were the first big businesses to be regulated by the federal government. Railroads were models for the business revolution.

The first big railroad companies were put together during the 1850's when the total railroad mileage in America increased five hundred percent to a total of 30,000 miles. They were the New York and Erie, the Pennsylvania, the Baltimore and Ohio, and the New York Central. Each required greater capital than the largest textile mills, the largest slave plantations, and the largest canal systems. Railroad operating costs were much higher than those of the great textile mills (which were, in the 1850's, the largest industries): Pepperell Mills's (the largest single factory complex in America) annual operating costs were just over $300,000 during the 1850's, while the Erie Railroad's costs were nearly $3 million and, by 1860, the Pennsylvania's were approaching $5 million. By 1855, the Pennsylvania Railroad employed four thousand people (Pepperell Mills employed eight hundred), and by the late 1880's, when no manufacturer in America had more than two thousand employees, the Pennsylvania alone employed nearly fifty thousand. Finally, the number of daily financial transactions on the big railroads—tickets sold, freight charges collected, rents and taxes paid, coal, water, wood, metals, paper, and other materials purchased, employees paid—exceeded by hundreds the daily transactions of any other businesses.

On roads dozens and ultimately hundreds of miles long, it was obviously no longer possible to have men running in front of the trains to warn of their approach or to arrange for passengers and freight. But "size was only one dimension of the unique challenges facing managers of the new, large railroads in the 1850's" according to Alfred D. Chandler, Jr., in his article "The Railroads: Pioneers in Modern Corporate Management." Daily railroad operations required "far many more and far more complex decisions than did the working of a mill, canal, or a steamship line." Railroads operated "shops, terminals, stations, warehouses, office buildings, bridges, telegraph lines" as well as tracks and trains. It was not possible for a single owner, director, or manager to make all the decisions, operational and planning, required to run a great railroad. "Not only were administrative decisions of coordination and appraisal more complex" for the large railroads, but, according to Chandler, "so were the still longer range ones" which involved purchase, construction, and expansion of the roads and their operations, and the financing both of operations and of expansion.

The Erie, Pennsylvania, and B & O in the 1850's, and the New York Central after the Civil War, invented the principles and major techniques of business management—for the government of big business. American railroads were already larger and far more extensive than railroads anywhere else in the world, so there were no models to follow for their management. Engineers, owners, and directors who wanted to build longer, more complicated roads, control them, and make them profitable tried to think out and apply rules, organizational schemes, systematic behavior, and allocations of responsibility that could help. Louis McLane and Benjamin Latrobe of the B & O created the "first functionally departmentalized, administrative structures for an American business," according to Chandler. Their system was elaborated by Daniel McCallum on the Erie and applied by J. E. Thomson to the Pennsy. The system divided the railroad into operational divisions, headed by superintendents and charged with the complicated day-to-day running of the trains and traffic. There were also functional divisions, headed by agents and engineers, responsible for planning, policies, and general supervision of the various kinds of work the company did: divisions for passengers, freight, wood (later coal), telegraph, road repair and maintenance, locomotive repair and maintenance. All the operational divisions reported to a general superintendent. He, in turn, along with the heads of the functional divisions, reported to the president, who was ultimately responsible for the entire company. There was also a Financial Department responsible for collecting, assessing, and presenting to the president and the Board of Directors financial information on all operations, and responsible for supervising the company's finances.

Reports, both immediate and accumulated, a carefully arranged hierarchy of authority and responsibility, and a system of rapid communication were the essentials of big railroad management. McCallum on the Erie insisted on hourly telegraphic reports (on train movement and delays), as well as daily, weekly, and monthly reports from those responsible for departments and divisions. Modern accounting was developed to determine costs and profitability, and to arrive at standardized management decisions.

Thus, modern corporate bureaucracies were invented. Some of the railroads used decentralized operational control combined with centralized reporting, accounting, and policy-making departments. Others, like the Vanderbilts on the

New York Central system, used management departments which were entirely separate from each other, and operations which were also controlled from central headquarters. However the bureaucracies operated in detail, they were all designed to make complex, sprawling, diverse operations controllable and manageable from one headquarters.

The scale of financing required by big railroads was, like their management, of an unprecedented order. Like the turnpike and canal companies before them, railroads had sought capital from state and local governments to supplement (and to help generate) investment from private sources. Railroad officials quickly became experienced lobbyists. By the 1840's, they sought help from the federal government as their roads were built across state lines and companies began to consolidate roads in more than one state. In 1850, the Congress granted public lands to the state of Illinois to be used to subsidize railway construction—which the state government then granted to the Illinois Central railroad. And in 1862, during the Civil War, the Congress initiated a program for the direct granting of federal lands to build transcontinental railroads. Federal subsidies ultimately were worth hundreds of millions of dollars to the railroads.

Investment in railroad companies and construction of railroads boomed after the Civil War. Land grants provided 170 million acres to the railroads by 1871, while federal loans secured by the expectation of land grants provided millions of dollars for construction. Businessmen scrambled to form railroad companies, woo congressmen and government officials, and spend money on rapid construction in order to get the loans and grants. By 1900, there was nearly a quarter of a million miles of railroad in the United States, and track was still being laid.

While the big railroads devised management structures which were models for later businesses, it does not follow that big railroads were well managed. Nearly all transcontinentals were haphazardly built; on some, miles of track had to be rebuilt before trains could run over the whole line. Only one of the great early transcontinentals, James J. Hill's Great Northern, did not go bankrupt by the time it was completed, and did not require extensive rebuilding before trains could run across the continent on it. Great scandals grew around the railroads and their construction—the Union Pacific Company's major stockholders formed a railroad-construction company, Crédit Mobilier, which used up all of Union Pacific's capital and ran it into bankruptcy to build the UP track. The construction company made huge profits, paid its stockholders handsome dividends and its government officials handsome bribes.

In 1873, a financial panic originating in the building and financing of the Northern Pacific Railroad closed the doors of the banking house of Jay Cooke. Cooke was a Philadelphia banker, investor, and speculator who had put a minimum of $100 million into the railroad, received tens of thousands of acres of public land grants, and built barely five hundred miles of track from Minneapolis to Bismarck. A depression followed the panic, and there was widespread unemployment and violence among railroad workers. Railroad scandals, slumping construction, and sporadic labor violence characterized the second Presidential term (1873–77) of Ulysses S. Grant. For some years after the panic of 1873, it was difficult to revive the large-scale investment in railroads, from Europe as well as from America, which had been available in the years before.

Thousands were employed on the construction of the railroads and many thousands in their operations. The first mass migration of Chinese to America came because the Central Pacific contracted for thousands of poorly paid, poorly fed "coolie" laborers (many were virtually kidnapped and brought to America). The railroads made possible the opening and occupation of millions of acres of land (which, of course, raised the value of the acres granted the railroads). They made it possible for farmers and ranchers to exploit the seemingly boundless lands of the Far West, and send what they produced to market. In 1868, when the railroad first arrived in Abilene, Kansas, for example, 75,000 head of Texas cattle driven there over the successor to the Chisholm Trail were sold for shipment East. In 1871, 700,000 head were sold in Abilene, and millions more in other "cow towns." The railroads not only meant markets for the new Western farmers and ranchers, they meant food and sustenance for growing urban centers all over the United States. By the beginning of the twentieth century, railroads had created the possibility of a national market. A producer of goods, agricultural or manufactured, could reach customers anywhere in the United States—a revolutionary change.

By the twentieth century, the railroads were national big businesses. Two-thirds of the nation's rail mileage was in the hands of seven groups of investors identified with or controlled by E. H. Harriman, the Vanderbilts, James J. Hill, the Pennsylvania Railroad (in which Andrew Carnegie had interests), J. P. Morgan, George J. Gould (the son of Jay Gould), and W. H. Moore (of the billion-and-a-half-dollar Rock Island system). There were many who had come to believe that a railroad system was like a giant octopus (the title of a late-nineteenth-century Frank Norris novel about a railroad) squeezing farmers, local businesses, their own employees, and the poor of the great cities with extortionate charges, monopolistic practices, and vast profits for their Wall Street speculator-owners. From the 1870's to the twentieth century, some of the most bitter strikes were against railroads—many brought on by wage cuts. Among the earliest national labor unions were the Railroad Brotherhoods. And in 1892, the National People's Party (the Populists) platform called for the federal government to take over and operate the railroads.

Federal regulation began late in the nineteenth century as the railroads (and other big businesses) successfully destroyed the power of local and state governments to control them. Until that time, the traditional distrust of the federal government combined with the strong common-law and Revolutionary tradition of local control had kept state and local governments actively creating and enforcing price and service laws and regulations for railroads as for other public corporations. Late in the 1860's, the Illinois legislature, pressed by farmers and the Grange, enacted legislation which set not only railroad rates but the warehouse storage rates charged by railroads. The railroads went to court. In 1877, in the case of *Munn v. Illinois,* they lost. Chief Justice Morrison Waite of the U.S. Supreme Court, in the majority opinion, upheld the "living tradition" of the power of the community to regulate business activity and "to fix a maximum charge to be made for services rendered, accommodations furnished, and articles to be sold" by businesses operating in the public interest. "To this day," Justice Waite wrote,

> statutes are to be found in many of the States upon some or all of these subjects; and we think it had never yet been successfully contended that such legislation came within the constitutional prohibitions against interference with private property.

The large railroads, and big business generally, continued the fight to destroy the power of any government to regulate their businesses. In 1886, in the case of *Wabash, St. Louis and Pacific Railway Co. v. Illinois,* corporate lawyers using new constitutional arguments before a new generation of judges convinced a majority of the U.S. Supreme Court that railroads were in interstate commerce and could only be regulated by Congress. The result was not cessation of regulation, as the railroads had hoped, but passage in 1887 of the Act to Regulate Commerce by which Congress created the Interstate Commerce Commission and gave it power to regulate railroad rates. The practice of regulating business gradually shifted to the federal government.

Twentieth-century business people, economists, and some

historians have convinced themselves that the efforts to regulate the railroads with the Granger legislation of the 1860's and the federal government's Interstate Commerce Commission were *new*, changes from what have been assumed to be the laissez-faire attitudes of the mythical golden age of nonregulation of business. No such age existed. What was new in the regulation of business in the second half of the nineteenth century was big business, big railroads, and the federal government. Federal regulation was a result of business success in reducing the power of local and state governments—power big businessmen believed stood in the way of the creation of a national market. But as the national market grew, American tradition called for democratic regulation of it in order to protect the rights of all and provide for the common welfare. It was the big businesses, not the defenders of regulation, who were the revolutionaries; they fought, not unsuccessfully, to prevent federal regulation in the national market from becoming as extensive and as controlling as government regulation had been in state and local markets.

Civil War Business

The Civil War (1861–65) was the most destructive war Americans have yet directly experienced. As a result of that war, slavery was destroyed and nearly four million Americans were freed from bondage. The power of Southern planters, and the society based on those planters, was destroyed. There were many at the time, and there have been many since, who believed the Civil War was a revolution which brought fundamental changes to social, political, and economic life.

The war itself did not bring significant changes to the patterns or the processes of business. The transcontinental railroads, other big business, and millions of acres of new farms appeared immediately following the Civil War, but the war does not seem to have caused those developments, nor did they first appear during the war. In his book *The Economic Impact of the Civil War,* historian Ralph Andreano wrote that during any war "the operation of market forces usually produces a drastic reordering of economic life," and "wartime conditions and responses can restructure an entire economy in a relatively short time period."

Such views have been widely accepted in America since World War II, because Americans have been eager to believe that that war did restructure the economy and make it successful after the depression of the 1930's. Certainly it did revive the economy. But it is not clear that the Civil War either fundamentally restructured or revived the economy. It had an impact on business. The social experience of the war made a strong contribution to the acceptance of industrialization and big business. But, generally, there were no sharp changes in economic structure immediately before, during, or immediately after the war.

The war did destroy the business of slavery. The capital represented by slaves ceased to exist. The power of slave-owners and slave-merchants was broken. However, the cotton-plantation business was only locally and temporarily affected. As soon as the war was over, plantations (often with different owners) continued to grow larger, and profits from cotton production increased until near the end of the nineteenth century. Cotton-textile manufacturing, North and South, showed the same wartime dip, followed by decades of growth, expanded production, and continuing profit.

The Confederacy was defeated and the effort to create an independent nation out of a region of the United States was aborted. And the Southern states, with their rich agriculture and large populations, remained (as they had been before the war) part of the system of markets, employment, production, and business which was growing, expanding, and developing all over the United States. The affirmation of the political and legal unity of the U.S.A., which was the result of the Confederate defeat, contributed powerfully to the nationalism of the postwar decades—and to the growth of big businesses and the national market.

Public lands were released and distributed on a vast scale after the war was over, under the railroad land-grant program and the Homestead Act. Both were passed by Congress in 1862, because Southern opponents were no longer in Congress. Railway construction after the war and the swift opening of the Far West was made possible under these acts. But the war did not change the process of land distribution, nor did it change the eagerness with which Americans sought to acquire and farm land.

Tariffs were imposed by the Union government during the war to provide additional income. The effect of their continuation after the war was to close the national market to a great variety of foreign manufactures. Industry was effectively protected from overseas competition. As historian Howard K. Beale pointed out in 1930, the radical Republicans in Congress after 1866 "insured the permanence of a protective system, which since the election of 1866 has been seriously threatened only twice and never overthrown." Tariffs during the war had no noticeable effect on business. Only after the war was over, and the tariffs continued, did protection materially aid the growth of some businesses.

The scale of financing necessary during the war—on both sides—gave a generation of bankers and financiers experience raising and investing very large sums of money. The techniques used for floating loans, financing large-scale spending, and investing quickly and effectively in many kinds of goods and services were adapted by banks, governments, financiers, and investors to the development of big business after the war. But the change was a change in scale, not a restructuring or a change in the nature of financial practices.

For most businesses, the Civil War did not mark any great watershed. There was little change in railroads, iron and steel, and coal—the basic industries of the day. Iron and steel manufacturing capacity in the North did not expand. The capacity proved adequate to fill all war needs, normal civilian requirements, and the requirements for continued westward expansion. Iron and steel production in the South suffered but recovered quickly afterward. The war destroyed Southern railroad mileage but brought its restoration as well. The Union developed techniques of rapid construction which were used to build transcontinentals after the war. Some men were trained in railroading during the war, but many wartime railroaders were already experienced and there were no significant wartime developments in railroad management techniques. Daniel McCallum, the Erie's innovative management genius, was in charge of the Union's railroads during the war. General Grenville Dodge, who became the Union Pacific's chief of construction after the war, acquired rank and combat experience in the war, but he was a civil engineer and railroad builder when the war started.

The war brought changes in scale to several businesses, as well as experience in the collection and distribution of much larger quantities of goods. The armies of the Civil War were much larger than any previous American armies, and immense systems had to be quickly devised to supply millions with food, clothing, weapons, medical care, and shelter. The Union quartermaster's department, for example, designed a "pup-tent" (a two-man shelter, half of which could be carried by each man) that was mass-produced. The quartermaster standardized the sizes of men's shoes and boots and devised a sizing system for ready-made men's clothing in order to provide millions with boots and clothes that fit. Ready-made men's clothing had been available before the war, as had machine-made boots and shoes. War contracts and standardization increased the use of machinery and brought greatly increased production. After the war, the men's clothing and shoe businesses immediately turned to the growing urban markets and sought—generally successfully—to sell the goods their great capacities made possible. Widespread sales of ready-made clothing and footwear for women developed much more slowly.

The design, quality, and manufacturing processes for guns and armaments changed very little during the Civil War. The scale of production, distribution, and use did increase enormously. Technical changes in arms did not seem to be speeded up. The changeover to steam-powered, propeller-driven iron or steel ships (and armored warships) continued throughout the war, but not at greater pace. The pistols, muskets, carbines, and rifles used had all been developed and manufactured before the war. Colt's revolver, used very widely in the war, had been in production for at least fifteen years. The Pratt & Whitney Company of Connecticut sold machinery and technical advice to Krupp in Germany after the Civil War, but American business had been exporting arms and machines to make arms for at least a decade before the war started. Many more guns were made, and many more Americans than in any previous generation knew how to use them, and used them. But the business of arms manufacture and sale was not restructured by the war.

The experience of large-scale national organization was the Civil War's contribution to the big-business revolution. The experiences businessmen had in financing the war, in producing goods for it, in collecting, transporting, and distributing goods were used, applied, and transformed in creating big businesses after the war was over. But more important was the experience of millions—more than ten percent of the population—in the mass armies of the Civil War. In those armies, for the first time young Americans had the experience of being regimented to work, move, fight, eat, and sleep in company with and in coordination with thousands of others. Six hundred thousand young men died—more than have died in all the other wars America has fought. And millions carried their experiences home with them—the experiences of regimentation, mass life, and mass work. They came home believing that the large-scale effort of masses of people—if the masses were large enough, and if they were systematically organized and well-supplied—could change the world.

The businessmen who wanted to change the economic

world after the Civil War relied on the wartime experiences of nationalism and regimentation. They set out to create national, large-scale, centrally controlled, systematically organized corporate businesses. The logic of the Civil War experience implied a rejection of the old paternal-household model (taken to its logical—and horrible—extreme in slavery) and of the old belief in the coercion of the poor as the bases for the organization of work. The war's logic offered instead the regimentation and hierarchical organization of masses of voluntary wage workers, who were trained to act in machine-like ways and the value of whose product was to be measured by standardization and uniformity. The war helped to mechanize, industrialize, and regiment the tradition of the "work ethic."

Big-Business Revolutionaries

John D. Rockefeller incorporated the Standard Oil Company in Ohio in 1870, five years after the Civil War ended. The company had capital of one million dollars, and it was the largest single refiner of petroleum in the United States. Rockefeller, who was just thirty years old, had already earned a reputation as a shrewd and successful businessman who had built a fortune in a wholesale merchant firm during the Civil War and increased it in the oil business after the war. Rockefeller was joined in his new company by Stephen V. Harkness, who had made his fortune in whiskey and distilling in Ohio; by Henry M. Flagler (Harkness's nephew by marriage), who had already been Rockefeller's partner in the oil business; by Samuel Andrews, a refining expert; and by William Rockefeller, John's brother and an outstanding salesman. These men, with a few who joined the firm after it was formed, came to be known as "the Rockefeller associates" or "the Standard Oil crowd." They built Standard Oil into a nationwide trust by 1882, worth at least $70 million, that controlled ninety percent of all American petroleum products. By the beginning of the twentieth century, Standard Oil was a great corporation (broken up by an anti-trust suit in 1911) controlling billions of dollars in assets, which monopolized American petroleum and distributed and sold its products all over the world. With a single company, in a single generation, these men made vast personal fortunes, created an enormous business (the parent of the present Exxon Corporation, Mobil Corporation, Standard Oil of California, Standard Oil of Indiana, Standard Oil of Ohio, Atlantic-Richfield, and Continental Oil), and led the big business revolution.

Rockefeller was the leader of the Standard Oil group. He devised company strategies and seemed to possess the clearest vision of what was to be done and how to do it. His vision centered on control, predictability, and large scale. He long maintained the principle that it was foolish, risky, unpredictable, and very expensive to drill or own oil wells. He wanted to acquire and control all petroleum production from the American oil fields (which were, when he started, simply the Pennsylvania fields near Cleveland, his headquarters), and to refine petroleum on the largest possible scale in the most efficient, well-organized refineries possible; he wanted to control the distribution of petroleum products through the United States (and later the world) and their sale on the greatest possible scale to the largest possible number of people. He wanted to produce and market his goods in an orderly, predictable manner, with maximum control of the process and minimum risk. He carefully specialized and departmentalized the work in his company, regimented his workers, and systematically structured company activities, authority, and responsibility. He intended to profit from the business, and he did.

The primary petroleum product, from the time the Pennsylvania oil fields were opened in 1859 until the advent of mass-produced automobiles in about 1910, was kerosene—a not-very-volatile petroleum derivative which burned with a bright light and provided the world's first inexpensive source of artificial light. It was a product which could be sold to masses of people. Rockefeller worked all his life to develop more efficient refineries and more uses for petroleum in order to make his products less expensive, and in order to sell more of them. He welcomed the automobile because it made another "by-product"—gasoline—widely salable and profitable.

Rockefeller's awareness of the possibilities presented by the growing network for control of distribution (which he shared with other business revolutionaries) seemed uncanny to people who lived in a world in which a national railroad network was only just becoming a reality. When the Standard Oil Company was formed, it joined with the Pennsylvania, Erie, and New York Central Railroads to form the South Improvement Company, through which Standard Oil's shipments of petroleum were distributed only to the three railroads in agreed proportions, in return for which the railroads gave rebates to Standard Oil on its own and its competitors' oil shipments, and also provided Standard with information on the rail shipments of its competitors. South Improvement Company lasted only two years. The Pennsylvania legislature (acting to regulate a corporation in the public interest for the public welfare) withdrew its charter in 1872 as a result of public outcry and pressure from other railroads and from oil-refining competitors. But Standard Oil had used the information and rebates in the two years to buy or force several competitors out of business. Other rebate arrangements were quietly made with all the railroads Standard used until the 1890's, when ICC regulation began. Rockefeller and his associates did not hesitate to buy into recalcitrant railroads, bring financial pressure to bear on them through banks, or refuse to ship on the railroads that did not grant satisfactory rebates. The rebate system enabled Standard Oil to ship its products all over the United States at prices which gave it an advantage over competitors and helped guarantee large and predictable profits.

Standard acquired companies which built and operated pipelines out of the oil fields, and so controlled crude-oil production. Well owners and independent refiners in the 1870's and 1880's tried to break Standard's control by building their own pipelines out of the Pennsylvania fields toward the big Eastern cities where there was great demand for oil. Standard fought them in the courts, in legislatures, and used its power with banks and in financial circles to stop their financing. In 1883, the independents settled for eleven and a half percent of the crude in their pipelines; the rest went to Standard.

Standard acquired the patents for railroad tank cars and, through a separate company, controlled American tank-car production. The company leased its cars to users, and provided Standard information on who was shipping how much, where, and to whom. The leases provided Standard income from every oil shipment in the country.

Rockefeller insisted upon receiving information in minute detail from all parts of his company and from every possible source. An elaborate committee structure was developed to collate, assess, and report all this intelligence data to Rockefeller and his associates (as Board of Directors, Board of Trustees, or Executive Committee at various times in the history of Standard Oil). The data was used to plan all company strategy and to make operational decisions for the company's many departments.

The company was organized on lines very similar to the management system devised by the big railroads. Various operations—refining, shipping, sales—were divided into departments. Strong central accounting and finance departments collected the daily, weekly, and monthly telegraphic and written reports, analyzed, and reported on them. A specialized bureaucracy, each division bent on becoming more expert, informed, and efficient, provided policies, supervision, research, and engineering for the multitude of businesses the company was engaged in.

Standard had its own marketing and sales organization.

Standard people sold only Standard products; their livelihoods and careers depended entirely on the company (Rockefeller had started his own career as a commission merchant and knew that independent wholesalers and retailers could not be controlled as employees could). The organization was divided into regions, with headquarters controlling district organizations—much as the larger railroads used geographical operating divisions. Sales at the local level were made through a variety of company organizations. Independent companies and distributors with local names and reputations were kept in existence after purchase or acquisition by Standard, so that Standard could benefit from their good reputations. Advertising and selling campaigns, even price wars, were used to develop local sales and convince the public that Standard was fiercely competitive, democratic, and beneficial to all.

Rockefeller and his company were not alone. Others after the Civil War used the rail and telegraph networks, pooled large assets, and created businesses on a national scale. Their cumulative effect was to create a national market (and many, like Standard Oil, moved into foreign markets as well). The Swift brothers, as well as Armour, and Morris & Cudahy, made meat-packing and the sale of meat and animal products a national big business. James B. Duke manufactured cigarettes by the billion, and created a national marketing and advertising organization to sell them; R. J. Reynolds and P. Lorillard followed suit. James S. Bell, who founded General Mills, and his nearest competitors, the Pillsburys, transformed flour milling from a local affair in which thousands of millers participated into centrally controlled, mass-producing corporations marketing standardized flour across the nation. Andrew J. Preston began importing tropical fruit, and integrated its production, transportation, and national sales in the United Fruit Company. Cyrus McCormick built his agricultural-machinery empire into a national corporation after the Civil War, as did several of his major competitors.

William Clarke bought into Singer Sewing Machines (whose first patent dated from 1846) and made it a national, and international, selling organization. United States Rubber, National Biscuit, Distillers Securities, and many other corporations followed a similar pattern.

The new big businesses sought markets in the growing cities, as well as in towns and countryside. In the process of creating business bureaucracies and regimenting their workers and managers, they bought up, consolidated with, or simply put out of business thousands of entrepreneurs and their employees. Their purpose was to create a national market they could control, and their revolution ultimately succeeded. But their success destroyed local and regional markets, and entailed the destruction and failure of uncounted thousands of small businesses. The resentment against these big-business revolutionaries and their octopus-like corporations among Americans accustomed to individual entrepreneurship and expecting to find their success and independence by being in business for themselves was fierce and lasting (and only very gradually balanced by the consumer pleasures attainable from national mass production and mass marketing).

Agribusiness

Throughout the nineteenth century, the principal activity of the federal government was the organization, distribution, and exploitation of the public lands of the United States. In the thirty years following the Civil War, 430 million acres of new agricultural land were put into production, more than doubling farm acreage. Agriculture continued to be the most important American business until the end of the nineteenth century, but industrialization, growing cities, and big business gradually changed even the nature of farming (as they changed every other aspect of American life and business).

The number of Americans who farmed, and the number of farm families, increased in every decade the Census was taken from 1800 to 1930. But after the Civil War the proportion of the total population which was rural declined steadily, and after 1920 an increasing majority of all Americans lived in cities. The number of tenant farmers (who did not own the land they farmed) increased steadily after the Civil War: by the 1920's, nearly forty percent of all farmers were tenants. Mechanization, increasing capitalization, and corporate organization became characteristic of American farming—and so did productivity.

The produce of American farms had been sold in international markets since the seventeenth century. As agricultural production increased in the nineteenth century, so did exports. In the 1860's, about thirty-five million bushels of wheat were sold abroad annually; by the beginning of the twentieth century, two hundred million bushels a year were exported. Pork and beef exports quadrupled between 1865 and 1900. Nearly a billion pounds of cotton were exported each year in the late 1860's, and an average of three and a half billion pounds a year were sold overseas in the first decade of the twentieth century. The increasing, rich produce of American agriculture (the United States today possesses more arable land than any other nation on earth with the possible exception of China) created much of the savings and capital and enticed an increasingly large flow of foreign investment to the United States, upon which the big-business revolution and industrialization was based.

From the beginning of the Civil War, the business of farming was actively supported and encouraged by the federal government. The Homestead Act of 1862, and the other land-grant acts which followed, distributed millions of acres of public lands to farmers, ranchers, and lumbermen directly, as well as indirectly through grants to railroads, colleges, and Indian tribes (which put the lands into cultivation themselves or sold to others who did). The government established a Department of Agriculture to serve farmers and farm business, and it established programs for agricultural education and for agricultural research and experimentation.

In the first half of the nineteenth century, most Americans had grown up on farms and acquired farming skills. Farming technology had only required the investment of labor and those skills (along with land, some tools, and seed) in order to farm and enter the marketplace. However, as cities, industries, and the nation grew, the capital required to start a farm and to keep it productive increased steadily.

In the years immediately following the Civil War, a homesteader's farm in the West was calculated to require an investment of at least one thousand dollars—in animals, buildings, tools, fences, machinery, and seed—the equivalent of nearly three years' total annual wages of an industrial worker. If the farmer or rancher had to buy land, as many found it necessary to do, then the costs were much greater. Since farm laborers were scarce, machinery to farm the 160-acre homestead was a necessity—at the very least steel plows and harrows, seed drills, and harvesting machinery. Farmers quickly learned that the machinery needed to farm a 160-acre homestead could farm a 640-acre section, or more. It was inefficient and hazardous, in a competitive-market world, to invest so much in the smaller plot. But large-scale farming obviously required still more capital. As farming expanded, so did the investment that poured into it—from railroad companies, from banks and investors in land companies, mortgage companies, ranching and farming companies, from insurance companies, and from English, Scots, French, Dutch, German, and even Russian investors who wanted to operate in and profit from the amazing and increasing production of American farms and ranches. Corporate farming and ranching had become central to agricultural production by the twentieth century. Family farms did continue to operate, and continued to be the agricultural ideal, but corporate farming was more efficient and more profitable.

Farming became inextricably involved with and dependent upon big businesses. Only the transcontinental railroads were able to carry the goods needed to open the plains and mountain areas to farming and ranching—lumber for shelter, timber and wire for fencing, tools and machines for working the land. Only railroads made it possible for the produce of the farms and ranches to move to markets in quantity. The manufacturers of the machinery so essential to increased agricultural production grew rapidly into big-businesses marketing nationwide. The manufacturers of newly invented barbed wire, whose product was essential for fencing, became a corporate monopoly as well as a national big business.

While farmers formed part of the expanding national market for goods and services, they also produced for the national market, and new big businesses grew based on the collection, processing, and distribution of farm and ranch produce into the national market—and beyond. Starting in 1878, with their first shipment of butchered meat in refrigerated railroad cars from Chicago to the East, Swift & Company built meat-packing plants, stockyards, feeding stations, and cattle-and-hog-buying operations along a railroad-based network all over the Middle West. It also developed a national distribution and sales system based on regional wholesale houses. In the 1880's and 1890's, Swift systematized its buying operations, developed uses and sales of by-products, introduced new lines of meats and animal products, and moved into international markets. By the beginning of the twentieth century, meat packing and sales was a national, organized, centrally controlled, departmentally specialized, highly profitable corporate operation.

When the Civil War began, flour milling had been the most valuable manufacturing industry in the United States (the annual output of American flour mills was worth $207 million, while that of textile mills was worth only $115 million), but flour mills were small (an average of two workers per mill), they served only local markets, and there were more than 13,000 of them. By the 1890's, the small mills had disappeared, and flour milling was big business dominated by three companies based in Minneapolis and controlled by four families—the Washburns, the Bells, the Pillsburys, and the Crosbys.

Minneapolis had distinct market advantages for big business—available waterpower in St. Anthony's Falls on the Mississippi, access to the new wheat lands of the Great Plains by rail, and water and rail highways to growing urban markets. The big millers developed machines to make fine white flour from the hard-kernel, high-gluten wheat of the northern plains.

One of the largest corporations in the United States today started in the sale and transportation of grain in 1865, when Will Cargill bought a wooden grain elevator in Conover, Iowa, at the end of the railroad line. Cargill and his brother bought and built other elevators—financed in part by Milwaukee banks eager to attract grain trade to Milwaukee. The Cargills arranged rebates from railroads as their grain traffic grew, and sold coal and other necessities to farmers, so that their rail traffic and sales became two-way. Competition for the ownership of elevators developed with Frank Peavey (who became the Grain Elevator King of the World by 1901), but the Cargills survived and prospered by controlling grain supplies and transportation as well as storage facilities. Ultimately (by 1980), the Cargill Corporation became one of America's largest multinationals, involved in the worldwide buying, selling, and transportation of grain; it was also involved in land, petroleum, scientific research, agriculture, seed production, edible oils, and the transportation business. It remains a closely held, family-run business.

By the 1920's, the business of independent yeoman farmers had become big, industrial, corporate, and national.

Robber Barons

On January 4, 1877, Cornelius Vanderbilt, nearly eighty-three years old, died in his house in New York. He left more than $100 million, most of it to his son, William H. Vanderbilt (who died in 1885, leaving $200 million to his heirs). The two Vanderbilts had put the New York Central railroad system together—based on money Cornelius ("the Commodore") had made before the Civil War in steamboats, ferries, coastal shipping, Central American railroads, and transatlantic shipping. In 1869, E. L. Godkin wrote sarcastically (in *The Nation*) about Vanderbilt's "railroads and river boats" as "witnesses to an energy and a luminous sagacity" which had "bought whole legislatures, debauched courts" and "crushed out rivals, richer or poorer." He compared Vanderbilt to "the unmoral, unsentimental forces of nature" that "grind down whatever opposes their blind force." Finally, he said, Vanderbilt was a "robber baron" (a figure of romantic evil in popular Victorian literature), who

> was not humanitarian; and not finished in his morals; and not, for his manners, the delight of the refined society of his neighborhood; nor yet beloved by his dependents; but who knew how to take advantage of lines of travel; who had a keen eye for roads, and had the heart and hand to levy contributions on all who passed his way.

Vanderbilt was quite probably the richest man in America when he died, and he was widely eulogized and widely attacked in the popular press as a result (as Sigmund Diamond has shown in *The Reputation of the American Businessman*). Although America's centennial year had just ended and the violence that marked 1877 had not yet begun, and despite his being a "robber baron" of giant railroads and big business, Vanderbilt was most frequently judged by the same standards that had been applied to men of great wealth (like Stephen Girard and John Jacob Astor) years before in the Jackson era of individualistic entrepreneurs and popular involvement in markets and business. Vanderbilt, like those earlier successful businessmen, was praised in the obituary literature for his exceptional character, for his virtuous pursuit of profit, and for his hard work, frugality, industry, and devotion to business.

And like them, he was castigated as a miser who lived off the poor working people whose labor created his fortune, and, like Astor, as an aristocratic ingrate who did not leave any of his fortune for the benefit of the community. The attitudes characteristic of that earlier fabric of business civilization (in which Vanderbilt grew up) were very much alive in 1877.

But there were new arguments in the public response to Vanderbilt's death which indicate a change in the way Americans after the Civil War viewed successful big businessmen. Many newspapers portrayed Vanderbilt as a "man of the people," a person whose character in no way differed from the ordinary. They pointed out that he was not very well educated, his language was not polished, he respected and honored his mother, he was not religious, he wanted to be rich, and he lived unostentatiously—he did not set himself above the common people. He was, in short, an exemplar (although they did not make the implicit logic of their arguments explicit) of a democratic, egalitarian society—he was a product (as it might be put today) of the American system.

The change in attitude indicated in this new explanation of Vanderbilt's success (which was by no means the only explanation widespread at the time) is important because it is so different from the earlier general assumption that it was the exceptional character and virtue of a Girard or an Astor which enabled them to succeed and become rich. Vanderbilt became rich, according to the new arguments, because he wasn't exceptional. As the New York *Graphic* put it:

> His vast power and property were the legitimate results of the old democratic notion that everybody should be allowed to do anything short of direct robbery or murder without let or hindrance from the Government. . . . It was the individual on the make. . . . He belongs to the system.

Every American could become a robber baron by such logic. Vanderbilt's wealth and his big business were the products of democracy, the outcome of egalitarianism, the triumph of individualism. At a time when opposition to big business was increasing, and opinion makers like Godkin were suggesting medieval barons as models of big businessmen, explanations that big businesses were the logical result of democracy and the American system were certainly welcome to the advocates of big business.

The second new perception appearing in the obituary comments about Vanderbilt was the argument that the very business organizations which Vanderbilt had created and grown rich from were great and lasting contributions to the good of the society. The ideal that every independent American must also serve the commonwealth was combined with Adam Smith's assertion that the social good was best served by the individual pursuit of profit in the marketplace, to defend Vanderbilt's immense wealth. By building and running the New York Central and his other railroad systems, according to this new argument, Vanderbilt had given work to thousands of people, he had provided millions who lived along his railroads with food, clothes, and goods of all kinds. If Vanderbilt decided, *The Public* in New York wrote,

> that $60 million would be better employed in building up, maintaining and defending against all competition, the great railway which now forms the main artery of the commerce of this city, it is at least possible that he thereby established a more useful benevolent institution than any other which his money could have founded. It is better . . . to permanently promote the industry, commerce and prosperity of a great state and city, thereby giving millions of workers a better chance to earn a living, than to found any number of hospitals.

According to this view, the wealthy, successful big businessman did not have to give his fortune back to the society, because through his business he had contributed greatly to the social good. "He worked for himself," the New York *Sun* wrote about Vanderbilt, "but in so doing he served the public as well as himself—as every powerful individuality must always do." The logic of the argument was explicit: big business automatically served the public good (a logic which many twentieth-century Americans accept as the obvious conclusion of rational economic self-interest).

In 1882, when asked if he ran his railroads in the public interest, William H. Vanderbilt, the Commodore's son, replied: "The public be damned." He explained that the "public" wanted all it could get from the railroads, and "of course we like to do everything possible for the benefit of humanity in general, but when we do, we first see that we are benefitting ourselves," he said. He concluded that railroads were "not run on sentiment, but on business principles, and to pay." Business principles, his statement implied, are rational and unexceptionable. Many agreed, but there were those who, like the New York *Irish World* when his father died, thought that "sharp practice—in plain words, swindling," along with "bribery and corruption" were the essence of those business principles. A large tax on "towering riches" would, according to such arguments, bring "a more equal division of wealth, a higher tone of morals in business circles, and a happier state of society generally." Not all Americans were willing to agree that the "principles" of big business were unexceptionable, or of benefit to the commonwealth.

Counterrevolution

Organized efforts to counter the big-business revolution came initially from rural populations and small farmers—not surprisingly, since the majority of Americans were rural, and the majority of business people were farmers. Big businesses, so it seemed to many rural Americans in the late nineteenth century, brought the destruction of family and community by seducing the young and uncommitted to the city and the factories with promises of work and wealth. And they choked off the profits of farmers and other rural business people by their control of transportation, credit, land, and manufactured goods. Big businesses put thousands—ultimately millions—of Americans out of business, and destroyed their sense of independence and community in the process.

In 1867, the Patrons of Husbandry—a fraternal organization for farm families based on local lodges called Granges—was founded to improve the quality of rural life. The Grange was a voluntary organization, like the innumerable clubs and lodges which had become a tradition of the "nation of joiners" since the Revolution. Its purpose ran directly counter to the national trends of urban growth and big-business power. The Grange was the first widespread, grass roots business organization in America.

As Grangers became more explicitly political and economic in the 1870's, they sought to retain local control of credit institutions (banks were traditionally the most controlled of American business institutions), of transportation facilities, and of other public utilities (like grain elevators and agricultural warehouses), through local governments and state legislatures. The Grange encouraged farmers to form cooperatives for marketing their produce and buying necessary goods, in order to gain leverage with railroads and get greater profits in markets. The Grangers did not attempt to organize political parties because rural populations comprised the normal voting majorities of the parties that existed. The Grangers battled against what they saw as the old wolves—monster bankers and monopolistic corporations—in the new sheep's clothing of great railroad systems and factories.

Their short-lived triumph came in 1877, when the U.S. Supreme Court (in *Munn v. Illinois*) affirmed the tradition of the local regulation of business and applied it to the big railroads. Farmers did not want to work on the railroads; they did not want jobs from big businesses. They were trying to stay in business themselves, and use the railroads and regulate them locally for the common benefit.

The Grangers—and the many others who protested against the big railroads and the methods and growth of big business—were not radicals. As the Ohio Supreme Court said, in an 1892 ruling against Standard Oil's monopoly:

> Experience shows that it is not wise to trust human cupidity where it has the opportunity to aggrandize itself at the expense of others. . . . Monopolies have always been regarded as contrary to the spirit and policy of the common law. . . . A society in which a few men are the employers and the great body are merely employees or servants, is not the most desirable in a republic; and it should be as much the policy of the laws to multiply the numbers engaged in independent pursuits or in the profits of production, as to cheapen the price to the consumer. . . .

Most of those who fought big business in the late nineteenth century were conservative, trying to preserve an entrepreneurial world, trying to prevent big-business revolutionaries from turning everyone into an employee and a consumer of cheap goods.

But the leaders of big business were not content with affirming their considerable skills as businessmen. As Henry Demarest Lloyd wrote in *The Atlantic Monthly* in March 1881: " Their great business capacity would have insured the managers of the Standard success," but they conspired with the big railroads to achieve monopoly. "Our hold on this trade," John D. Archbold of the Standard Oil Trust told a House of Representatives investigating Committee in 1888,

> is . . . the result of the application of better methods and of better business principles than have been brought against us. . . . The people who come to tell you differently tell you that which is false. . . . They are people who have failed under any circumstances. They are soreheads and strikers.

Farmers were not the only "soreheads and strikers" who organized and did battle. Many tradesmen after the mid-nineteenth century formed unions of their local trade associates—typographers, hat makers, stonecutters, cigar makers, iron molders, machinists, blacksmiths, shoemakers—and joined city, regional, and sometimes federated organizations. Their efforts were to keep their businesses in their own hands, set fair prices (and fair wages for their apprentices and skilled laborers), develop cooperatives, and prevent the use of machines (and factories) in their trades. Membership in such unions peaked in the 1870's at about three hundred thousand (about five percent of the total nonfarm working population).

Those early unions frequently took the form of fraternal lodges, as the Grange did. Between 1863 and 1873, they were joined by three fraternal orders, formed by employees of railroads but modeled on the guilds of skilled, entrepreneurial tradesmen—the Brotherhoods of Locomotive Engineers, of Railway Conductors, and of Firemen. These three organizations were made up of people who viewed themselves as businessmen who opposed the big businessmen. The number of workers who were employees of the big railroads and big businesses was rapidly increasing, and the organized opposition to big business, at least until the end of the 1870's, came from traditional business people—from farms, towns, and cities—who did not want to be inexorably caught up in a process of industrialization and urbanization from which there was no escape.

The financial panic and depression of the mid-1870's was accompanied by increasing urban and industrial unemployment, unevenly expanding agriculture, and disruptive movements of population. Immigrants poured into the United States. There was active warfare against Indians on the Plains (George Armstrong Custer and 272 officers and men of the Seventh Cavalry Regiment were killed by a large force of Sioux at the Little Big Horn in June 1876). Blacks in the South were being forced into agricultural, social, and political peonage. Tens of thousands of Americans were moving West each year to homestead, to raise cattle or sheep, to make their fortunes in the goldfields or silver mines.

The corporate battles involved in railroad and big-business consolidations and growth, for markets and resources, intensified in the late 1870's. Labor violence in the western Pennsylvania coalfields involving a secret miners' organization called the Molly Maguires brought convictions and hangings in 1875 and 1876. And in 1877 a general strike of railroad workers, incensed at wage cuts, affected all the major Eastern railroads, resulted in riots in Baltimore, Chicago, and St. Louis, and violent pitched battles with federal troops in Martinsburg, West Virginia, and in Pittsburgh (where twenty-six were killed, and railway tracks, machine shops, and the Union depot were destroyed).

Even as some workers were gradually becoming aware that they were not in business for themselves and had interests opposed to those of their employers, the efforts of the Grangers and of the old-style trade unionists were clearly failing. By the beginning of the 1880's, the federal courts effectively set aside *Munn v. Illinois,* and big corporations corrupted local governments and eroded the local control Grangers depended upon. The railroads continued to consolidate, extend their lines, and attract increasing investment. The large industries, growing rapidly, used the railroads to foster their growth. As they broke into and captured more and more local markets, profits and savings—which they almost always reinvested in their own growth—increased.

At the same time, others in American society—writers and intellectuals, particularly—became more aware of the revolutionary nature of the rapid development and spread of big business. Mark Twain (with Charles Dudley Warner) published *The Gilded Age* in 1873 and not only gave a name to the times but satirized the corruption and oppression of big businesses. In 1880, Henry George (a newspaperman, economist, and lecturer) published *Progress and Poverty*, an enormously influential appraisal of industrialization and big business which pointed out that "the enormous increase in productive power . . . has no tendency to extirpate poverty or to lighten the burdens of those compelled to toil." Poverty increases with modern business production, George wrote.

> The "tramp" comes with the locomotive, and almshouses and prisons are as surely the marks of "material progress" as are costly dwellings, rich warehouses, and magnificent churches. Upon streets lighted with gas and patrolled by uniformed policemen, beggars wait for the passer-by, and in the shadow of college, and library, and museum, are gathering . . . more hideous Huns and fiercer Vandals. . . .

George admitted the argument, frequently made by apologists for industry and big business, that "the poorest may now in certain ways enjoy what the richest a century ago could not have commanded," but, he insisted, "this does not show improvement of condition so long as the ability to obtain the necessaries of life is not increased." And that ability, he argued, had decreased with industrial employment. George proposed a tax which would confiscate all "rent" (all increases in the value of land) as a solution. The tax to be collected by existing governments was to be spent to improve the lives of all the poor. The "single tax" movement of the 1880's and 1890's widely popularized George's ideas, and was one focus of the growing and popular protest against the development of big business.

By the late 1880's and after, much of the popular literature of protest came to accept industrialization, and the growth of big businesses. In 1888, Edward Bellamy published *Looking Backward,* a popular, "science-fiction" novel about a young man who slept from 1887 to the year 2000 and awoke to find himself in a world characterized by amazingly productive industry, armies of workers, and a distribution system which provided for the needs and wants of everyone. He was told that, early in the twentieth century, all the industry and commerce of the country "were intrusted to a single syndicate representing the people, to be conducted in the common interest for the common profit." The whole nation was "organized as the one great business corporation" which was the sole owner of all property, the sole employer, and "the final monopoly" in whose profits and economies all shared equally. Bellamy's book accepted the growth of the great corporations as well as the growth of great unions in opposition to them. Its message was that big-business growth was inevitable and good; it had brought a "prodigious increase of efficiency," "vast economies effected by concentration of management and unity of organization," and an increase in the "wealth of the world" at a "rate before undreamed of." The problem, as Bellamy saw it, for American society was to make the advantages of big business equally available to all.

Henry Demarest Lloyd's *Wealth against Commonwealth* (1894) argued in a similar vein that the growth of big business was "logical" and "inevitable," but that American democracy and the ideal of the commonwealth had to be asserted against the great concentrations of wealth in the hands of corporate big business and its leaders.

The dilemma of those who opposed the big-business revolution—Grangers, intellectuals, early trade unionists—was that almost all of them were in favor of traditional business, of the freedom of the entrepreneur, of the independence Americans had long thought could be found in the marketplace by business activity, yet they felt there was something seriously wrong with big business. Almost all of them felt there were great advantages to machinery, industry, railroads, and the "efficiencies" or the "progress" that seemed to come with big business—yet they felt that its wealth was in the wrong hands. Almost all of them—like local businesses which wanted to compete with a big business—were forced to create large-scale, national organizations, if they wanted to succeed: the scale of the marketplace (and the nature of

American society) had changed. The nationalism generated by the Civil War had been given economic form by the big railroads and big businesses. Those who wanted to preserve democracy, equality, individualism, and business based on local commonwealths and markets had to confront a new and growing national economy.

A New Nation

In the last thirty years of the nineteenth century, and throughout the twentieth century, the advocates of big business took their logic, their rationality, and their business principles into politics and the courts. There they fought the traditions of governmental regulation of business. They sought to establish a new structure of government which would support and encourage the development of the national market which big businesses created and exploited. Corporations sought to establish in law privileges and freedoms identical to those of individuals.

The Civil War had changed popular perceptions of the acceptable relative power of local, state, and federal governments. In general, the war affirmed the power of a national government over state governments, and it cast general doubt on the propriety of state control of social and economic affairs of importance to the whole nation. The postwar amendments to the Constitution (particularly the Fourteenth Amendment) seemed explicitly to have limited state governmental powers. Combined with growing popular nationalism during and after Reconstruction (which ended entirely by 1877), these shifts in belief underlay the gradual acceptance of the new legal arguments of big business.

In 1868, Thomas M. Cooley published *A Treatise on the Constitutional Limitations which Rest upon the Legislative Power of the States of the American Union.* It provided the ammunition used by increasing numbers of attorneys for corporate big businesses who went to courts to free their clients from the regulation and control of local and state governments. Cooley was a teacher of law, former dean of the Michigan Law School, and a judge on the Michigan Supreme Court when his book was published; he remained on the Michigan Court until 1885, when he became a lecturer on political science at Johns Hopkins University. He became president of the American Bar Association in 1894. His *Treatise,* several further books, and his 1890 *Principles of Constitutional Law* were used all over the country in the training of lawyers; Cooley was an excellent speaker and publicist, and by the end of the century he had become "the most frequently quoted authority on American constitutional law." Cooley's arguments were based on a strong belief in natural rights and property rights, and rested on the repeated assertion—which lawyers later tied to the Fourteenth Amendment—that states had no right to legislate or enforce legislation to regulate prices, rates, profits, wages, or market conditions for goods or labor. States and their local governments had long exercised such a right, and long enforced regulatory legislation. But Cooley maintained that the liberty guaranteed to every individual placed severe substantive limits on the ability of state governments to control the activity, the business, or the property of anyone.

Cooley's principles began to appear with great frequency in legal arguments, especially concerning the Fourteenth Amendment, which provided that "no state shall deprive a person of life, liberty or property without due process of law" or deprive any citizen of a state of "the privileges and immunities" of citizens of the United States. In 1873, the first such cases reached the U.S. Supreme Court. In the *Slaughterhouse Cases,* John A. Campbell of Alabama (a former Supreme Court Justice) argued that the Fourteenth Amendment had abolished state sovereignty and made the United States government a central, national (not a federal) government. Furthermore, he believed the amendment "was designed to secure individual liberty, individual property, and individual security and honor from arbitrary, partial, proscriptive, and unjust legislation of state government."

The individual liberty which was protected from state legislation, Campbell argued, was the freedom of a business corporation to make contracts as it pleased and to combine with others for profit. The individual and the business corporation were assumed to be identical in all the arguments business attorneys made before the courts. In the case of *Santa Clara Co. v. Southern Pacific Railroad* in 1887, the U.S. Supreme Court decided that corporations were legal "persons" under the Constitution, entitled to all the civil rights and legal protections of individuals in law.

The business attack on the power of state governments to regulate was not confined to the Fourteenth Amendment. Cooley's laissez-faire ideas were applied in legal argument to the Constitution's interstate-commerce clause as well. In 1875, in *Welton v. Missouri,* under the interstate-commerce clause, Mr. Justice Field's opinion, according to James Willard Hurst's *Law and the Conditions of Freedom in the Nineteenth Century United States,* "declared the positive responsibility, as well as authority, of the central government to fashion the legal conditions of a free national market." States were prohibited from acting in any matter which could be considered interstate commerce, and the Court ruled that congressional inaction—the lack of legislation by the federal government—"is equivalent to a declaration that inter-State commerce shall be free and untrammelled." In 1886, the Court decided (in *Wabash, St. Louis & Pacific Railway Co. v. Illinois*) that businesses had a "right of continuous transportation from one end of the country to the other" without restraints from state governments. This decision resulted in the creation of the Interstate Commerce Commission in 1887.

The contract clause (which prohibits states from "impairing the obligations of contracts") and the "liberty" of the due-process clause were gradually made equivalent by the Supreme Court under the influence of Cooley's assertions and the hundreds of legal arguments, briefs, and articles based on his opinions. By the end of the nineteenth century, the individual's liberty which was protected by the Constitution also permitted a business corporation to make any contract necessary to its happiness anywhere in the nation without being subject to state regulation or control, and with the possibility that not even the federal government could legally regulate such contracts. The courts had become the refuge of big businesses from democratic control and governmental regulation.

The practice of corporate law had become the most remunerative and most popular of the specialties available to American attorneys. Christopher Teideman (another legal theorist and teacher) wrote a justification of the identification of corporate freedom with individual freedom and of the reduction of state powers in his *Treatise on the Limitations of the Police Powers* in 1886. "The conservative classes," Teideman wrote, "stand in constant fear of the advent of an absolutism more tyrannical, more unreasoning than any before experienced by man, the absolutism of a democratic majority." It was to counter the regulation of business by that democratic majority that liberty was redefined by the courts so that, in Teideman's words, "private rights" were protected "against the radical experimentation of social reformers."

But the legal theorists, lawyers, jurists, and big businessmen who won acceptance of the new legal definitions (and the more general definitions of big business as the logical outgrowth of American democracy and as the epitome of independent individualism) were hardly conservatives. They were men bent on the radical transformation of the political, social, and economic worlds into which they had been born. The big businessmen created a national market; the lawyers provided it with a legal and political foundation. Together, they made corporate big business capable of controlling mass production, masses of workers, and national markets. In the process, they transformed the ideals and beliefs of the nation to conform to their desires.

These men called their opponents "radical social reformers," "experimenters," "soreheads and strikers," and other names designed to throw the popular onus of change and revolution on those who opposed big business, and leave big-business leaders with the image of being "conservatives," defenders of traditional freedoms and democracy. Big business has continued to assert its beneficial nature, the essential democracy of its production, and the contribution mass production and mass sales have made to the independence, happiness, and welfare of every American. Public relations and "the corporate image" (as it has come to be called in the second half of this century), the gradual development of welfare capitalism, and consumer-oriented advertising and sales are the modern capstones of the big-business revolution. All are based on the logic that big businesses are, like Vanderbilt's New York Central, "useful benevolent institutions."

Big Business Established

Between the great depression of the 1890's and the great depression of the 1930's, the essential structures for financing and managing nationwide big businesses were put into place. Giant corporations were formed, many out of smaller companies (between 1895 and 1904, one-third of all existing companies disappeared into mergers). Corporate operations were integrated and standardized. Big business gradually became the domain of trained, expert managers. The great private fortunes—like Rockefeller's, Carnegie's, McCormick's, and others—began to become independent of the business corporations (as entrepreneurs and their families realized their fortunes through sellouts and mergers), and much private wealth was directed into educational and social philanthropy. The great corporations were constantly expanding plants, production, and markets as they reinvested vast savings and profits. The great and growing national market provided more and more of the capital necessary to expand markets and investment abroad as well as to develop new products and greater consumption at home.

Big business after the Civil War had, of course, required a great deal of available capital—hundreds of millions of dollars at a time when the dollar would buy many times more than it will today, and when the economy was still quite "undeveloped" in modern terms. Financing the Civil War had created a $1.8 billion federal-government debt. By 1866, eighty-two percent of that debt was owed to wealthy people and to institutions that purchased government bonds in lots of over $10,000. Between 1866 and 1893, the Federal Treasury paid interest and repaid the principal on those bonds until all were retired. Between 1866 and 1879, the government paid an average of $150 million per year in gold on the interest and principal payments; it spent an average of $192.5 million per year on all other expenditures. For fifteen years after the Civil War, the federal government was, in effect, making very large quantities of capital, in gold, available to large-scale investors; considering that Rockefeller capitalized Standard Oil in 1870 for one million dollars and it took Jay Cooke $100 million to buy up the Northern Pacific, $150 million per year of new capital available for investment was significant indeed.

Big business and big banking—investment banking and commercial banking—grew together, each supporting and encouraging the rapid growth of the other. Great banks and the other financial institutions—exchanges, clearinghouses, insurance companies—grew large in the movement of available capital from the U.S. government, from foreign investors particularly eager to profit from U.S. railroads and lands, and from domestic investors, to railroad construction, land exploitation, and from the 1890's on, to industrial big business. By the beginning of the twentieth century, J. P. Morgan &

Company dominated the American investment banking business, centered in New York City. (The other large investment banking firms were First National Bank of New York, National City Bank, and Kuhn, Loeb & Company in New York; and Lee, Higginson & Company, and Kidder, Peabody & Company in Boston.)

Morgan had built his bank—as had the other big investment bankers—on the capital flow from the federal government, on the early establishment of extensive operations in Europe and facilities for the easy movement of capital, cash, and securities across the Atlantic, and on the development of close connections with large investors and large businesses in the United States. The Morgan bank was affiliated, through shareholding and interlocking directorates, with large commercial banks, which added capital to its investment pool (amounting to $632 million by 1913). It held huge investments in railroads, public utilities, insurance companies, and big industrial businesses, and through those investments controlled still more capital ($2.1 billion by 1913). It, and the other banks like it, provided financial services which were essential to the rise and continued growth of big business. Investment banks provided or arranged for capital investment and company expansion; they helped provide cash and working capital in large quantities; and they helped companies and businessmen personally with the reinvestment of the very large sums of money which big businesses were making available.

The profitability and growth was surprising. It took a number of years for bankers and investors to believe that the great industrial corporations were permanent and that the growth of their assets was a sustained phenomenon. By 1906, for example, Standard Oil's assets had grown from the initial one million dollars to $359 million, and profits were an average of twenty-four percent per year. By the late 1880's, investment banks began cautiously to offer capital to big businesses that wanted to grow bigger or combine with other, similar businesses. After the panic and depression of the 1890's, which seemed in part caused by massive speculation in railroad stocks, investment bankers were much more willing to capitalize and create giant industrial businesses.

Between 1897 and 1903, there were 276 big-business combinations—corporations which were holding companies owning and controlling the operations of other corporations—created in America, with a total capital of slightly more than $6 billion. Many of those combinations brought together very large companies built by single entrepreneurs or small groups of entrepreneurs and their families, and gave businessmen and their families the opportunity to leave active management and devote themselves to lives of ease, wealth, and visible social usefulness. The largest and yet typical early-twentieth-century combination was the United States Steel Corporation.

U.S. Steel was created in 1901, a New Jersey holding-company corporation, with a capital of $1.4 billion. It controlled, when it was created, at least eight hundred major plants representing sixty percent of American iron-and-steel-producing capacity. Among the major steel companies which were combined to form U.S. Steel was the Carnegie company, which had become the country's largest single steel producer under the control of Andrew Carnegie and Henry Clay Frick. Carnegie had started in the steel business with a capital of $700,000 in 1873 and was joined by Frick, who had acquired control of coke production (coke was a major ingredient in steel making). Together they built a very large business which controlled mines and ore reserves, railroads, Great Lakes shipping lines, coal mines and coke plants, and iron and steel mills in the vicinity of Pittsburgh. In 1892, wage cuts ordered by Carnegie himself had brought a great strike to the Carnegie Homestead Steel plant, during which strikebreakers from the Pinkerton Detective Agency had been hired. Violence ensued, and Frick was nearly assassinated before the strike was broken. Carnegie sold his steel interests to U.S. Steel for nearly $400 million in cash and U.S. Steel bonds. The Morgan bank, and its agent, Elbert H. Gary, realized more than $62 million profit from underwriting, syndicating, and promoting the financing of U.S. Steel. Gary became the Steel Corporation's first president.

Giant combines were created to control markets. Investment in such companies was more profitable because of the scale of their operations and the efficiency of their management. Big businesses pushed very rapidly into markets outside the United States almost as soon as they achieved some control over the national market. Exports of American manufactured goods increased steadily throughout the late nineteenth and early twentieth centuries, especially in oil, iron and steel, copper, lumber and wood, agricultural implements, and automobiles. Investment in overseas businesses, banks, and other properties also increased, most of it "portfolio investment" controlled by banks.

Most of the direct investment abroad by American big businesses—the active creation and management of operating businesses in foreign countries—was in the Western Hemisphere before 1920. The greatest part was in America's two immediate neighbors: Canada and Mexico. Investment close to home was attractive because most big businesses had been created on the American rail and telegraph network. Expansion to Canada and Mexico was easy and logical. James J. Hill, the great railroad "Empire Builder," had come from Canada and built his first successful railroad from Minneapolis to Winnipeg, for example. On the other hand, foreign companies and foreigners controlled overseas transportation, port facilities, and most domestic railroads. Big-business leaders, accustomed to controlling their transportation (and accustomed to its being rail transportation), were, perhaps unconsciously, less willing to hazard extensive investment overseas where they could not—at least not immediately—acquire control of essential transportation and thus control the flow of goods, as they did at home.

By 1897, American companies controlled eighty percent of all Mexico's railroads, and despite the nationalization started in 1906, in 1920 they still controlled nearly eighty percent of Mexico's railroads. American companies controlled Mexican mining, and until the 1930's they controlled seventy percent of Mexican petroleum production. Americans owned millions of acres of Mexican agricultural land producing chicle, sisal, sugar, tobacco, and fruit. Most Mexican power plants, street railways, telephones, and telegraphs were also controlled by American companies. Direct investment in Canada was primarily in manufacturing, and giant American industries in electricity, agricultural implements, rubber, flour milling, paper making, and automobiles dominated Canadian production and Canadian markets.

In Central America, the United Fruit Corporation (a big-business combine formed in 1890) dominated American investment. By 1914, of the total American investment there of $93 million, United Fruit controlled $73 million—half in fruit plantations and half in railroads, shipping, and port facilities. In South America, American big-business direct investment before 1920 tended to concentrate on companies exploiting resources—copper mines and refineries and nitrate mines in Chile, precious-metal mining in Peru, petroleum companies in Venezuela and Colombia, and rubber plantations in Brazil.

The sprawling scope of these great corporations—controlling the intercontinental movement of resources and manufactured products, developing the efficient mass production of complex goods in huge plants involving thousands of machines and processes along with thousands of working human beings, financing and investing tens of millions of dollars, developing new products and markets and processes, expanding and financing sales—required complex decision-making based on expert knowledge and experience. The people who built great corporate combines and made them work acquired the necessary knowledge and experience as they put their businesses together. But the preservation and growth of existing big businesses could not depend forever on the experience and knowledge of those who built them. Young people had to be taught how to deal with new problems, not the old ones of mechanization. Young people, in ever greater numbers, had to be trained in the special skills demanded by the bureaucracies of business—in engineering, in accounting, in marketing, in advertising, in law, in selling, in production, in sciences. The demand for professional experts and for trained business managers grew as rapidly as big businesses grew.

The Massachusetts Institute of Technology had been established in the 1860's, as had the Columbia School of Mines and the Sheffield Scientific School of Yale University, to provide training in the principles of machinery, mechanics, and the application of science. (Engineering training before the Civil War had been a matter of apprenticeships and practical experience for most, although military academies—including West Point—had taught surveying and civil engineering.) The early engineering schools were endowed by wealthy businessmen and from the beginning maintained close relationships with big businesses. In the 1880's, a new university in California—the Leland Stanford Junior University—was established by a wealthy big businessman and named in memory of his son. It was almost entirely devoted to the teaching of engineering, mining, and other practical studies (one of its early graduates was a young Iowan, Herbert Hoover, who, before he was elected President of the United States, became a wealthy professional engineer and manager). Mechanical-engineering training was applied to the problems of factories, of mechanized systems, of the flow of manufactured products—all problems in big-business management—and a Society of Mechanical Engineers was organized to exchange professional information and ideas on business management and accounting as well as on mechanical design.

In the 1880's, the Wharton School of Finance and Economy was established at the University of Pennsylvania to provide professional training in accounting, an increasingly important aspect of big business. It was not until 1898 that a School of Business, supported by John D. Rockefeller to train professional business managers, was established at the University of Chicago. In 1902, Rockefeller also established the General Education Board, which used, ultimately, millions of his dollars to encourage colleges and universities to establish practical courses—in medicine, in science, in engineering, and in business. The Harvard Graduate School of Business Administration, supported by big-business endowment, was established in 1908. Such professional higher education, supported and financed by big business and the fortunes of big businessmen, became characteristic early in the twentieth century.

In 1902, for example, three cousins—Alfred, Coleman, and Pierre du Pont—took control of their family's long-established firm (started during the Revolution), the E. I. Du Pont de Nemours Company of Wilmington, Delaware. It was primarily concerned with the manufacture and sale of explosives—gunpowder and blasting powder. Two of the du Pont cousins had been in the steel and street-railway business together; the third had been in the family firm. They were determined to make Du Pont an efficient high-volume manufacturing and mass-market selling organization by the application of modern production and management techniques. All three had been educated at the Massachusetts Institute of Technology.

Professional, "scientific" management was what the three du Ponts intended to bring to their company. (*Scientific Management* was the title of an 1895 book by Frederick W. Taylor, the best-known industrial engineer, whose introduction of time and motion studies and the careful analysis of every element in a manufacturing process to make it more efficient, less expensive, and better controlled made him as hated by industrial workers as he was admired by big-business managers.) "Their aim," according to Alfred D. Chandler, Jr., in *The Visible Hand*, "was to dominate the industry by running the most efficient mills as fully and as steadily as possible and so to reduce their unit costs to levels that small competitors could not achieve." They bought control of the resources and raw-materials refineries the company used, and created a traffic department staffed by engineers to manage the flow of materials to their manufacturing plants, and from the plants to the customers. They "quickly transformed the new consolidation into what might be considered," Chandler wrote, "an ideal type of integrated, centralized, functionally departmentalized enterprise."

Aside from integrating the *operations* of the company into specialized, professionally directed departments, the du Ponts created a company headquarters centered on an executive committee made up entirely of salaried, professional managers (most big businesses were still run by unsalaried directors and stockholders, many of whom were not professionals). The executive committee had a development department and a financial department reporting to it. In the course of their reorganization, the du Ponts added an engineering department, a chemical-research department, a real-estate department, and a personnel and pensions-policy department to company headquarters in order to provide professional management and advice for the executive committee.

By 1920, successful American big businesses were, like the Du Pont Corporation, "integrated operating companies," according to Chandler's *The Visible Hand*, which "used capital-intensive, energy-consuming, continuous or large-batch production technology to produce for mass markets." A big business like Du Pont, Chandler wrote,

> flourished when its markets were large enough and its consumers numerous enough and varied enough to require complex scheduling of high-volume flows and specialized storage

and shipping facilities, or where the marketing of its products in volume required the specialized services of demonstration, installation, after-sales service and repair, and consumer credit. It remained successful because administrative coordination continued to reduce costs and to maintain barriers to entry.

Organizing Big Business's Work

During the last two decades of the nineteenth century and the first two of the twentieth, the patterns and the beliefs on which industrial work in America is based were hammered out in conflict between big businesses and their managers on the one hand and growing armies of employees on the other. Business leaders, in their drive to achieve maximum control over work, its products, and the markets, emphasized strong traditions of community and commonwealth, as well as traditions of the "natural" leadership of successful men. Workers and employees, on the other hand, emphasized the traditions of individual independence (in the marketplace as well as outside it) and equality of opportunity in their efforts to achieve a livelihood and liberty in the circumstances of industrial work and urban life. There were intense conflicts between individual and community, between self-interest and the common weal, between coercion and voluntarism, between free market and control, among businessmen and among employees as well as between the different groups.

Big businesses, for example, have argued in their defense that they are the apotheosis of individualism. They seized, in the late nineteenth century, on the newly popular scientific Darwinism and insisted that big businesses were the "fittest" survivors of fierce natural competition among independent individuals. "Individualism, Private Property, the Law of Accumulation of Wealth, and the Law of Competition," Andrew Carnegie could write in the *Gospel of Wealth* (1889) (in a style taken from Darwin), "are the highest result of human experience, the soil in which society, so far, has produced the best fruit." Yet, much later, A. A. Berle and Gardiner C. Means wrote, in *The Modern Corporation and Private Property* (1932), that the development of big business corporations "created economic empires" and "delivered those empires into the hands of a new form of absolutism," which was quite the opposite of traditional individualism.

> The recognition that industry has come to be dominated by these economic aristocrats must bring with it a realization of the hollowness of the familiar statement that economic enterprise in America is a matter of individual initiative. To the dozen or so men in control, there is room for such initiative. For the tens and even hundreds of thousands of workers and owners in a single enterprise, individual initiative no longer exists. Their activity is group activity on a scale so large that the individual, except he be in a position of control, has dropped into relative insignificance.

While some leaders, like John D. Rockefeller, admitted that individualism in business was gone by the end of the nineteenth century, replaced by "combination" and "co-operation," most continued to insist that individual enterprise, free enterprise, and big business were synonymous terms.

The group activity which characterizes mechanized industry of all kinds as well as big business had few available models other than households, slavery, and the coercion of the poor in workhouses. Americans were, however, from the beginning of European colonization, inveterate and idealistic builders of communities. Many towns and settlements were deliberately planned, cooperative efforts based on strong ideals and the shared desire to pool the work, energy, and products of everyone in order to achieve social harmony, common belief and predictable behavior (law and order), and the continued existence and prosperity of the community. Although the post-Revolutionary emphasis on individualism had added a powerful countercurrent to community ideals, and made many communitarian efforts seem utopian or ridiculous (as in the popular response to some religious communities, or the Brook Farm community of intellectuals, in the middle years of the nineteenth century), nevertheless communities continued to be planned and built in America.

Since the beginning of the nineteenth century—starting with Robert Owen's idealistic efforts in New Harmony, and continuing in "more practical" manner in Lowell, Lawrence, Holyoke, Manchester, and dozens of mill and factory towns—deliberately planned industrial communities had combined the community ideal with an effort to solve the problems of the organization of industrial life and work.

In 1880, George Pullman, the designer, manufacturer, and operator of Pullman Palace Cars—the majority of the sleeping, parlor, dining, and private railroad cars in the United States—started building a new factory and a complete industrial community just outside Chicago. Consolidation—the integration of many machines and processes, the efficient fitting-together of many functions in one space—was an obsession of Pullman's, one he shared with many other businessmen. By 1884, the new town of Pullman had a population of more than 8,500 people, who lived in identical houses which had been partially prefabricated in the new factory. In the center of the town was a square-block Arcade building containing every shop, a theater, and a library. A large Market Hall provided for the sale of all fresh produce. The town was built around a park and a lake (which was a cooling basin for the factory power supply), next to the carefully designed Pullman factory. The entire factory was powered by the great Corliss engine which had run every machine in the 1876 Centennial Exposition in Philadelphia, and become a symbol of progress to much of the nation. A Pullman farm on the outskirts of town used the town's sewage for fertilizer and was a profit-making operation which sold its produce in the Market Hall. A single church was provided at high rent (it was a large building) to serve all Christian denominations. For nearly a decade, town and factory were believed to form a productive, happy industrial community—the living embodiment of the American ideal of community life in a profitable, industrial setting.

Pullman's purpose was to provide up-to-date surroundings and housing for workers who were expected to be hardworking, productive, moral, disciplined, and happy as a result. The town itself was run by the Pullman company. It was expected to make a profit from the rents on housing, shops, church, and the market, as well as from the operation of the farm and the hotel. George Pullman did not approve of company-operated stores, so the shops were rented to entrepreneurs. For ten years, the Pullman company realized an average annual profit of three percent on its investment.

Pullman's solution to the problem of how to coordinate and direct the disciplined work of large numbers of employees who operated a complex system of production was to integrate work and living, factory and community, into one centrally controlled operation. His workers not only were dependent on machines for their productivity, on overseers, managers, and corporate rules for their training and discipline, and on the company for their pay, but were also dependent on the company for all their social and communal lives. In the logic of Pullman's belief, work in the factory was inseparable from life in the town. Yet Pullman's experiment collapsed—in part because the employees balked at the company's control of community life and invasion of their individual freedom, but in great part because the company insisted, when economic crisis threatened, that town and company, community and employment, were, after all, separate.

As the depression of the 1890's became increasingly severe, the Pullman car business fell off. In 1893, the company laid off seventy-five percent of its workers, and then severely cut wages before it rehired half of those laid off. The company refused to reduce rents for its houses, however, and it hired only men who lived in the town of Pullman. When it refused to discuss rents with the workers, they went out on strike under the aegis of the American Railway Union. The strike spread to the nation's railroads as ARU members boycotted Pullman's cars. President Cleveland ordered federal troops to ride the trains to get the mails through (although union workers offered to move the mails so long as they were not carried on Pullman's cars, but the railroads refused), and violence marked the strike in Chicago and elsewhere in the nation—as well as in Pullman. The strike was broken in August 1894. Pullman reopened its factory and hired only men who were not union members—a thousand union members turned in their cards and got jobs. The company's actions and the strike destroyed the town as a model of industrial organization and of big-business social responsibility. In the years following the strike, the company sold all the buildings and the town land.

Questions concerning community responsibility and company autonomy became paramount in the course of the strike. The appeal to "business principles" and the continued use of an accounting system which separated town and factory finances despite the putative "integration" of the two, along with the determination of the company to pay a dividend even in hard times and the desire to control the organization of the workers, proved stronger than its desire for a happy, harmonious, and prosperous community. Ironically, it was the workers who insisted that the relationship between work and town be continued and that the community be preserved by company policies which coordinated wages and rents. But the workers' search for independence of the company undermined their insistence on the preservation of community.

The failure of the community did not prevent other businesses in the twentieth century from building industrial communities: U.S. Steel built Gary, Indiana, and a chocolate company built Hershey, Pennsylvania, years after Pullman ceased to be a company-owned and -operated town. The problem Pullman was trying to solve remained: how to get large numbers of Americans to tolerate the coercion, regimentation, and harsh discipline of mechanized industrial work, and at the same time achieve and maintain the large-scale labor force necessary to big businesses.

Part of the "search for order" which has characterized big business (particularly between 1877 and 1920, according to the book of that title by Robert H. Wiebe) has been the effort to reconcile Americans to the dependency and regimentation of industrial work. In the twentieth century, some companies have built worker housing, stores, schools, and libraries; others have established profit-sharing, stock-ownership, group insurance, pension and medical programs; some have encouraged religious, temperance, and moral-reform programs; and a few have sponsored unions. While all such welfare capitalism, as it has been called, has been part of efforts to achieve control and discipline of the work force, it has also been motivated by businessmen who want to create communities, participate in their government, and win the approval of community members.

Organizing Employees

Between the 1880's and the 1920's, the majority of productive work in America came to be done by employees in national businesses organized without reference to local or regional markets, control, or communities. The traditional ideal of the working American remained the achievement of individual independence, happiness, and success through the sale of products or services in a marketplace. The tensions created between realities and ideals, especially among city workers of agrarian background, proved very nearly unbearable.

By 1900, more than sixty percent of the American working population was employed—dependent, working for wages or salaries—by industrialized businesses. Those workers were in a market from which they could not withdraw (withdrawal was, according to Adam Smith, an essential criterion for the proper functioning of a free market); they were entirely dependent upon the industrial marketplace. "Economic growth," according to James Willard Hurst in *Law and the Conditions of Freedom in the Nineteenth Century United States,*

> tied the lives of an increasing proportion of people to the market and the division of labor; they were either wage or salary earners, or small producers or traders in specialized ranges of goods or services. Theoretically, buyers consent to the practical compulsions of the market in which they buy; if they do not consent, they stay out. But men who find their whole livelihood in the market are too vulnerable to stay out.

From the 1880's to the 1920's, the real wages of industrial workers increased very little and very slowly, while the average salaries of "white-collar" employees (and the number of white-collar jobs) increased somewhat more rapidly. Nevertheless, by the beginning of the twentieth century, the great majority of working Americans were no longer in business and no longer able to choose to be in business. They were employees.

Subtly and without any widespread consciousness of the process, being an employee had taken on a kind of heroic status in American life. In the popular literature of the late nineteenth century (and throughout the twentieth), the heroes were employees. Cowboys, for example, were the heroic figures of the dime novels and pulp magazines which were first published during the Civil War. Cowboys were direct descendants of earlier American frontier heroes (who were not employees): they lived in the Far West, they had a symbiotic relationship with Indians, they were fighters for civilization and law 'n' order, and they were visibly part of the living world (Buffalo Bill Cody, the archetype of the early dime-novel hero, ran a Wild West Show which brought cowboys and Indians to nearly every American community of any size before he died in 1917). Cowboys appealed to Americans because they were adventurers, still seemingly independent, sometimes "loners" who rode off into the sunset. Nevertheless, real cowboys were always hired hands, and cowboy heroes generally worked for large ranches, towns, governments, and sometimes even for big businesses like cattle companies, railroads, or mining corporations. Cowboys, and their adventurous twentieth-century cousins, detectives, showed their urban-employee readers and admirers heroic possibilities, despite being employees.

Another set of heroes consistently celebrated as employees, who reflected the traditional virtues of mobility, independence, and individuality, were Horatio Alger's plucky young men. Alger's novels and stories sold tens of millions of copies and created a mythology which many today believe characterizes the rise of big business and industrialization, the rise "from rags to riches." Every one of Alger's heroes was employed. None was an entrepreneur. Every one of his heroes, furthermore, achieved success by "rising" in a modern urban environment of cities, large stores, great commerce, offices, and many organized employees. The "riches" Alger's heroes achieved were jobs in offices at "good" salaries. Alger's heroes, like the cowboys, were employees in a big-business, industrial world—and they made being an employee look like the epitome of American success and of traditional American individualism.

"I say that you ought to get rich, and it is your duty to get rich," Russell Conway preached in his famous sermon-lecture "Acres of Diamonds." Conway gave that lecture more than six thousand times to large audiences in the first two decades of the twentieth century. "Money is power," he said,

> and you ought to be reasonably ambitious to have it. . . . Money printed your Bible, money builds your churches, money sends your missionaries, and money pays your preachers, and you would not have many of them, either, if you did not pay them. . . . The man who gets the largest salary can do the most good with the power that is furnished to him.

The money which gave power to individuals in modern society was money earned as salary or wages—by employees, part of organized businesses in an industrial world.

Yet there were few Americans by the early twentieth century who were reconciled to permanent employee status, however inescapable or heroic that status was supposed to be. Conway's injunction to get rich did not seem to apply in any realistic way to the majority of working Americans. "The working class and the employing class," the Industrial Workers of the World said in 1919,

> have nothing in common. There can be no peace as long as hunger and want are found among millions of working people, and the few, who make up the employing class, have all the good things of life.

Not only did the employing class seem to have all the good things of life, but the big businesses, because of their effective national organizations, were able to control the conditions of work as well as wages and salaries. The businessmen who owned and managed big businesses, and the professionals (industrial engineers like Frederick Taylor or Frank Gilbreth) who designed, used, and managed their machines and factories, all thought of mechanized production, and modern factories, as labor-saving. They expressed their admiration of machines in terms of the number of men whose work a machine could do. Machines and factories meant getting rid of workers (much as mergers and combinations meant getting rid of small businesses and competitors). They made business more efficient and therefore better. More machines meant fewer workers. Machines were assets, as were factories, to be paid for and cared for. Workers were liabilities, to be paid as little as possible and eliminated as much as possible. The productivity of workers was (and is) measured by comparing the amount invested against the profit earned by the goods produced. Scientific management was a technique for eliminating the "waste" of worker movements and time in order to make workers more like machines.

As such attitudes directly affected the lives of increasing numbers, employees began to create national organizations of their own, controlled by workers, in order to defend their interests and independence. In 1878, the Knights of Labor became the first national workers' union which accepted mechanized industry and the dependence of workers on wages from employers (despite its rejection of the idea that there was a separate class of workers). Under the leadership of Terence Powderly (the mayor of Scranton, Pennsylvania, when he became head of the union), the Knights of Labor grew in the 1880's to nearly six thousand locals and a membership of over 700,000. The Knights successfully used boycotts and negotiations in preference to strikes to win shorter hours and better work conditions. The Knights used the old fraternal-organization technique, but they strongly emphasized solidarity among all employees, skilled and unskilled, and they urged the formation of cooperatives among their members. The Knights were strongly opposed to the old trade unions—the organizations of craft guilds, which they viewed as business, entrepreneurial unions of employers. They attempted to form industrial unions, of all who were employed (skilled or not, members of crafts or not) in one industry.

In the early 1880's, the Knights achieved some remarkable

successes in negotiations and in organizing workers. However, a disastrous general strike in Chicago in 1886, combined with a bomb explosion during a labor rally in Haymarket Square there which killed seven policemen and injured seventy people, brought strong public reaction against the Knights and labor organizations in general. After that strike, there were many who began to agree with the widely accepted view that labor unions were conspiracies of dependent, often foreign and therefore inferior people, and were a danger to public order and economic prosperity.

Growing industries continued to need large numbers of workers, however. And opposition to the appalling conditions of industrial labor and to the businesses which imposed those conditions remained near the level of violence. A new national alliance of labor unions, the American Federation of Labor, was formed in 1886. The A F of L was violently opposed to the Knights' national industrial organizations, however, and it campaigned to destroy the Knights. It emphasized the skills of members of trades, reverting to the older guild-apprenticeship-master model, but it was more willing than the Knights to accept the idea that there was a class of industrial employees and that workers were entitled to a greater share of the profits their work produced. The ideal of industrial unions as a direct counter to the nationally organized industries—which the Knights had espoused—was taken up in turn in the 1890's by the socialists, by the Industrial Workers of the World (the IWW, or the "Wobblies") in 1905, and again, and much more successfully, by the Congress of Industrial Organizations (the CIO) in 1935 and after.

The A F of L used strikes and other pressures from skilled workers to gain better hours and better wages. But the industrial workers they excluded from membership and many other of the employees of big businesses continued the public attacks on big businesses and railroads as the nation slid into depression in the 1890's. In 1890, in response to public demands, Congress had passed the Sherman Antitrust Act, which outlawed "conspiracies in restraint of trade" and pushed big businesses to find new legal devices for their organization. Anti-trust legislation was used against labor unions, as conspiracies, before it was effectively used against big businesses.

In 1892, farmers' alliances and labor organizations joined to create the People's Party. The Populist platform stated bluntly that "we meet in the midst of a nation brought to the verge of moral, political, and material ruin." The Populists argued that, as a result of the growth of big business,

> . . . the people are demoralized . . . public opinion silenced, business prostrated, homes covered with mortgages, labor impoverished, and the land concentrating in the hands of capitalists. The urban workmen are denied the right to organize for self-protection, imported pauperized labor beats down their wages. . . . The fruits of the toil of millions are boldly stolen to build up colossal fortunes for a few . . . and the possessors of these, in turn, despise the Republic and endanger liberty. . . . We breed the two great classes—tramps and millionaires.

The new party advocated the government ownership and operation of the railroads, telegraphs, and telephones; the establishment of various guarantees of an adequate money supply and a safe banking system; the limitation of immigration; the ending of land grants and other subsidies to corporations; and a variety of political reforms aimed at making government and politics more democratic and more responsive to popular desires.

While the Populists did not elect enough people to office to become a permanent political party, they were throughout the first half of the 1890's an influential political presence, and were forceful in opposition to big business, big railroads, and big financiers. In 1896, thirty-six-year-old William Jennings Bryan of Nebraska won the Democratic Presidential nomination with a speech (which was to become famous as his "Cross of Gold" speech) centered on Populist issues:

> ... the great cities rest upon our broad and fertile prairies. Burn down your cities and leave our farms, and your cities will spring up again as if by magic; but destroy our farms and the grass will grow in the streets of every city in the country.... Our ancestors, when but three millions in number, had the courage to declare their political independence of every other nation; shall we, their descendants, when we have grown to seventy millions, declare that we are less independent than our forefathers? ... Having behind us the producing masses of this nation and the world, supported by the commercial interests, the laboring interests, and the toilers everywhere, we will answer their demand for a gold standard by saying to them: You shall not press down upon the brow of labor this crown of thorns, you shall not crucify mankind upon a cross of gold.

Bryan did not win election in 1896 (and not in 1900 or in 1908, when he was also the Democratic nominee) and the Populist Party disappeared after that election, but the popular desire to control big businesses in the interest of "the working man" and of the commonwealth grew.

The majority of industrial workers in the twentieth century effectively rejected the idea that there was an identifiably separate "working class" in America, permanently established and with interest exclusive to it. But workers nevertheless continued to establish national union organizations, and nationwide strikes affecting entire industries became more frequent in the twentieth century than they had been in the nineteenth. Strikes in steel, coal, the railroads, automobiles, and other industries demonstrated that workers were increasingly aware that they were "vulnerable" in the national marketplace created by big business. But they have never been completely convinced that national organization was the only way to achieve independence. In the 1980's, fewer than one-quarter of all workers in America belong to unions.

Belief in traditional individualism—with its new employee-heroes—and in the traditional democracy where government was the most effective protector of the commonwealth has appealed more strongly to Americans in general than worker organizations and new political parties as the best devices for the control of big business. The progressive political and social reforms of the early twentieth century, designed to make governments at all levels more responsive to the people and designed to bring business excesses under federal government control were generally more successful than unions and strikes. After the establishment of the Interstate Commerce Commission and the Sherman Antitrust Act in the late nineteenth century, twentieth-century reforms aimed at business regulation and control picked up momentum. The Clayton Antitrust Act, the Pure Food and Drug Act, the Federal Reserve Act, the Federal Trade Commission, the Budget Act of 1922, much of the legislation of the 1930's, and a majority of federal legislation since the 1930's have been directed to creating control in the national market of the sort that had once existed in localities and states. The employees of the twentieth century—a majority of the American population—have depended in large part on democratic and political organization to control big business, rather than class, or protest, or union organization.

World War Business

When World War I began in 1914, American agriculture and industry outproduced every other nation on earth. Corporate big business dominated production to a degree not true of business in any other nation, especially in the most rapidly growing parts of the economy: chemicals, steel, foodstuffs, and petroleum. American businessmen were accustomed to dealing with foreign governments without interference from the government in Washington. While the federal government had long been of help to the growth of big business, and a cooperative relationship had developed between business and the agencies of the federal government in the first two decades of the twentieth century, nevertheless businessmen rarely served in the government, and they very seldom called upon the government for aid or assistance in markets outside the United States. By November 11, 1918, the end of the world war, the United States had become the financial capital of the world and the assets of big business had vastly increased. Americans were convinced that the war had been won by American wealth, power, productivity, management, and know-how.

War raged in Europe for two and a half years before the United States abandoned official neutrality and entered it on the side of the Allies. Business was involved in the war, however, from its beginning. Arms and munitions makers did ever-increasing business—the *Lusitania,* a British liner sunk by a German submarine in 1915, was carrying American rifles and ammunition. American cotton and grains found ready markets in Britain and France. As the Allies bought more and more goods in America, some manufacturers engaged their entire production in war goods, while others reasoned the war could end at any time, and refused to invest capital or engage in production for an uncertain market.

The Allied need for money to support the war effort made increasing demands on—and possibilities for profit for—American banks and financial institutions. The Morgan bank became the Allied governments' purchasing agent and the chief Allied loan agent in the United States—taking commissions on hundreds of millions of dollars' worth of goods purchased, and on billions of dollars' worth of investments transferred and loans arranged. Between 1914 and 1918, $2.5

billion of loans were floated for Allied governments, and over $3 billion of European investments in the United States and Latin America were sold and the proceeds transferred or used to purchase war supplies. By 1918, the United States had ceased to be a debtor nation—with European investments in America of greater value than American investments in Europe—and had become the creditor of the world.

In 1915, the Wilson Administration established an Industrial Preparedness Committee whose responsibility was to find out what America's industrial capacity was, and what could be produced in the event of war. Howard E. Coffin, the vice president of Hudson Motors, an automobile manufacturer, was asked to chair the committee, and a survey of twenty thousand manufacturers was immediately instituted. In 1916, Congress established a Council of National Defense to prepare the legislation and plan the administrative agencies that might be necessary if the United States entered the war. An Advisory Commission to the Council was created, staffed almost entirely by people from big businesses.

The Advisory Commission developed plans and drafted legislation for the establishment of military conscription, for the provision of essential industrial labor, for war financing, and for the establishment of agencies to control food, fuel, production, transportation, and information. Big businessmen were accustomed to making strategic decisions and planning for the allocation of resources, the establishment of priorities, the large-scale flow of materials, products, and people through complex spaces, and for the organizational structures to administer national and international operations. No other Americans had such training and experience. As a result, the transport section of the commission was headed by businessman Daniel Willard, of the B & O Railroad, the munitions section by Howard Coffin, the supplies section by Julius Rosenwald, of Sears, Roebuck & Company (already the largest retailer of consumer goods in America), the raw-materials section by Bernard Baruch (a commodities and stocks broker and investor), and the labor section by Samuel Gompers, the president of the American Federation of Labor.

When the United States declared war on the German and Austro-Hungarian empires in April 1917, military conscription was immediately instituted. In the eighteen months remaining of the war, more than two million men were drafted, equipped, trained, supplied, and more than a million of them sent to Europe to fight. The techniques of regimentation developed by big businesses were applied to military problems (as they were to industrial war workers) to bring about effective and rapid mobilization.

Four large government agencies were created to support, supply, and move the military forces. All the agencies called upon business leaders and managers to lead and staff them. Many businessmen volunteered to serve, some without pay. A Food and Fuel Administration was created, headed by Herbert Hoover, who had already made a reputation directing the massive program early in the war for the relief of the Belgian people. Hoover introduced the latest management techniques to supplying food and fuel to the military and to the people at home, without causing undue hardships and without introducing elaborate rationing programs. A War Labor Policies Board was created, headed by Harvard law professor Felix Frankfurter, who worked closely with Samuel Gompers and other labor leaders. Under Labor Board policies, many workers established the eight-hour day as the norm in their industries (the great steel strike in 1919 was in part caused by the return of the steel industry to the fourteen-hour day after the wartime eight-hour shifts). The United States Railroad Administration, directed by William G. McAdoo (a California railroad and oil man who had been Wilson's Secretary of the Treasury, and became Wilson's son-in-law), took control of all the railroads in the United States throughout the war.

The War Industries Board, headed by Bernard Baruch, supervised the organization of war production. Hundreds of businessmen worked in the sixty sections of the WIB, including leaders like Robert S. Lovett, the chairman of the Union Pacific, and Alexander Legge, the general manager of International Harvester. The WIB set prices of goods purchased by the government, it supervised contracts for war matériel, and it encouraged businesses—with high prices, liberal contracts, and cartel arrangements—to produce quantities of goods as rapidly as possible and move them quickly to where they were needed. WIB policies made it possible for large-scale, efficient producers (most of the big businesses) to make extraordinary profits.

Many of the businessmen who moved into government for the duration of the war attempted to achieve the necessary production voluntarily. Through publicity and public-relations programs and by propaganda, wartime agencies tried to get people to volunteer for the armed forces, voluntarily to take industrial jobs and work longer hours, voluntarily to give up certain foods or reduce their use of them, voluntarily to buy Liberty bonds. Businessmen were asked to volunteer their services. However, coercion was used: conscription, imprisonment of conscientious objectors (and of outspoken opponents of the war), publicity about people who did not buy bonds, refusal of government contracts to businesses unwilling to obey WIB guidelines. "The ideology of voluntarism," as Robert D. Cuff pointed out in his article about it, was expected to appeal generally to Americans in the tradition of voluntary collective efforts by free, independent individuals. Voluntarism functioned "to close off questions about the ambiguities and contradictions that emerged in practice" about coercion, central control, and regimentation. The fact that businessmen served voluntarily, without being paid, in the government's war effort was intended as a public demonstration of the social consciousness of American business.

The assumption made by businessmen, and by much of the general public, when World War I ended, was that America had won the war in great part by its voluntary willingness to fight and produce and work extraordinarily hard for freedom and democracy. When the war ended, all the effort ended: the "boys" were brought home and the military disbanded, the government agencies closed their doors (some people actually left their jobs on November 11, 1918—they simply left their government offices on news of the Armistice and never went back), and the contracts for war goods were canceled. But the memory of the great effort, of the voluntary cooperation between government and business—and its effectiveness—remained. "If we had a Government business manager with a free hand to run the business side of Government, as free as Baruch had in the War Industries Board," a business leader said in the 1920's, "we should have a successful Government of business." A federal government of business had become a part of the experience of American business.

Consuming Business 1900-1984

The consumer society is a creature of our time. In this century, businesses and their managers have turned their attention and inventiveness to the distribution, marketing, and consumption of goods—away from the almost exclusive nineteenth-century focus on resources, processing, manufacturing, and production.

Big businesses today justify their great power, their continued existence, and their growth on the argument that they do the productive work of the society: they *do* produce. Work is their moral justification. They supply the goods of the good life. Their publicity concentrates on the creation rather than on the marketing of those goods, on the elaboration of the moving assembly line and mass production, on the productive use of great energy sources, on huge plants, on armies of workers, and on images of endless, effortless production speeded along by automation and the recent applications of computers. And, in reality, big businesses have devised increasingly ingenious and frequently more efficient ways to produce more and more products. But the very productivity they have created has forced them to seek newer, more efficient means to market goods and to assure themselves of growing markets.

In the modern industrial economy, as Bruce Barton (a leading advertising executive) pointed out in the 1920's, the supply of manufactured goods always exceeds the demand. (Barton was deliberately contradicting the "law" of supply and demand discovered by businessmen in the second half of the nineteenth century.) The business problem in the twentieth century, Barton pointed out, was to create demand for goods already in supply. Since production is ever-renewing, the ideal market must be ever-renewing as well. Twentieth-century manufacturers have tried to create a market which consumes—uses up—manufactured goods and therefore always needs more.

Many American economists and political leaders as well as employees and business managers have come to believe that the consumer market is the logical, inevitable outgrowth of industrialization and mass production. Yet that market was invented in America. The consumer marketplace did not become a major part of industrialized business in any other nation until long after it had been created and developed in America.

It was not easy. Although the egalitarian ideal on which the consuming society is based had long been strong in America, old and enduring attitudes had to change for people to be able to accept the idea of consumption. Traditionally, for example, we had concentrated on the making of durable, crafted goods which would last a lifetime. American mass manufacturing has not always lived up to that ideal, but a consumer market requires attitudes which run counter to tradition. Using up goods, consuming durable, crafted products had to become a virtue.

Americans had long believed that independence—and therefore the social worth of any individual—was measured by the work of the individual. Work, industry, and saving were the visible, social measures of individual success. Conspicuous consumption was justified, generally, by the argument that the well-to-do and ostentatious had worked exceptionally hard and had earned what they consumed.

To make consumption a virtue, a countermyth was required. Society had to be convinced that spending was more virtuous than saving, that individual labor need not produce a socially valuable product but rather spendable money. The worth of the individual in a consumer society is not measured by what he or she does or saves. Rather, it is measured by what he or she spends, by what goods are possessed and used up. Conspicuous consumption needed to be available to all, and acceptable by all, in America's egalitarian society. If a "rising standard of living" was the goal of American progress, then the standard of living needed to be defined as visible consumption.

If big businesses wanted to have mass markets of consumers—and in the twentieth century they have come to depend on them—then they had to provide the means, the dollars. They were the major producers of wealth; they had to see to it that consumers had enough money to consume.

Few big-business leaders or advocates in America have realized the importance of business in the distribution of wealth to consumers. Believing that their rational self-interest lay in accumulating assets as rapidly as possible, and acquiring and retaining control over all the wealth they could, they resisted most efforts to wrest money from them. It has taken strikes, great and small, depressions and recessions, financial crises and collapse, the increasing power of the federal government, world war, and half a century of political coalitions, protests, voters, and consumers ranged against them to bring businesses to a recognition that their interests lay in adequate money in the hands of masses of consumers. The growth and activity of unions, the creation of facilities for consumer credit, the establishment of minimum-wage levels and the principle of collective bargaining, the increasing effort by the whole society to provide employment for all, and the development of wage, pension, and insurance agreements in major industries have—while not consciously seeking the goal—all been part of the uneven development of the consumer society.

Many business leaders in the twentieth century have believed they were an elite band fighting the good fight against dark forces—like democracy, big government, liberalism, ungrateful workers, communists, and foreigners—bent on destroying all that business had built. The battle to preserve and protect a big-business civilization has paralleled the construction of the consumer society.

At the same time, populist views of business have remained alive. As attacks on big businesses have increased, business has been forced to justify itself to the American public. Unions and workers have fought long, violent battles to achieve national organizations, to acquire access to the power and protection of the federal government comparable to big business's access, and to force more money and material benefits for workers out of the coffers of the great corporations. The long depression of the 1930's spread distrust of and disillusionment with the morality and efficacy of big business. And while the generally increasing prosperity of the years since World War II has revived popular acceptance of business, it has not destroyed a pervasive assumption that the big boys, the fat cats, the Wall Street bankers, and the great corporations are out to exploit the consumers, corrupt the government, and grab every buck and every privilege they can.

As Americans have come to recognize their increasing dependence on big businesses for goods, jobs, money, success, mobility, and security, they have become more widely determined to control and regulate business. Part of that effort has been the conscious and unconscious building of "countervailing powers" (in unions, pressure groups, and governments) to counteract the power of management. Part has been the continuing reinforcement of distrust and dislike of big business in popular culture, in education, and in social analysis. With heavy irony, C. Wright Mills wrote in *The Power Elite:*

> Of all the possible values of human society, one and one only is the truly sovereign, truly universal, truly sound, truly and completely acceptable goal of man in America. That goal is

money, and let there be no sour grapes about it from the losers.

Another part of the effort to control has been the development and encouragement of collective action by consumers to protect their own interests by using governments, courts, and public media (as big businesses do) to affect the marketplace and their position in it.

The justification for business—the logic of the consumer society—is based in large part on the argument that it *does serve* the common good and the commonwealth. Big businesses, that argument goes, do important work for the society; they are industrious, frugal, and hardworking; they are, therefore, good and moral. They create wealth; they produce goods; they provide jobs and work for millions. Through wages, salaries, and employee benefits (as well as through the goods they produce), they distribute wealth. They serve the commonwealth.

Business defenders extend the logic to make big businesses the personifications of American ideals: they incorporate the work ethic. Individualism is also incorporated in big businesses: they are fierce competitors; they demand independence and autonomy; they resist and defy authority and government; and they have their peculiarly American legal standing as "persons."

The argument which ultimately justifies big business in the consumer society is that it serves Americans' dreams. The big companies provide ladders to success, status, and wealth. The Horatio Alger dream is made more available to more Americans as businesses proliferate and grow larger and wealthier. *Time* magazine, in a January 1984 cover story, reported that "a number of company founders" have become, "overnight, some of the richest people in the U.S.," all in the Alger tradition.

> The winners . . . include a Korean immigrant, a former disc jockey, a onetime airplane mechanic, a theater critic-turned-

> stock analyst, a college dropout, an engineer-turned-stock analyst-turned-financier, and a molecular biologist.
>
> Most of the new multimillionaires come from middle- or lower-middle-class families, and few showed much early promise. Several had indifferent school records and drifted until some spark propelled them toward supersuccess. Yet all were independent enough to start or finance a new venture and canny enough to find fields ripe for development.

When Henry Ford said he wanted to make a "family horse" that every working person could afford, he was expressing the peculiarly American dream of being independently mobile (as well as the dream of riches to be made by successful dream-merchants).

In the course of the creation of the consumer marketplace, businesses have devised new structures of management aimed at improving productivity and providing control over conglomerate corporations. They have made increasingly sophisticated efforts to control markets and manipulate consumers and governments to their advantage through advertising and the mass media. Multinational corporations seek to create a global market. Like the interstate, national big businesses of the late nineteenth century, multinationals are working to break down the powers of "local" governments to control and regulate business, its resources, growth, profits, management, and behavior.

The consumer society has become the most effective social support for business growth and power at home and abroad. Modern American big-business leaders do not see themselves as revolutionaries. Rather, they believe they are conservatives, preserving business civilization. They have created a consumer marketplace and given shape to a consumer society in America in order to win democratic consent and egalitarian participation in a civilization they dominate.

Henry Ford and the Automobile

Henry Ford was born in 1863, in the midst of the Civil War. He died in 1947, after the end of World War II. He started life on a farm, appropriately enough for a mid-nineteenth-century American, and he was the son of an immigrant. He became imbued with the spirit of manufacturing at an early age, which was also appropriate. By 1891, he was an engineer with the Edison Illuminating Company in Detroit, working with electricity, the power which would shape the world of twentieth-century business. He was also tinkering with the possibility of a "horseless carriage." In 1896, he drove the first car he ever built. By that time he was Detroit Edison's chief engineer. Shortly thereafter, he left electricity and helped form the Detroit Automobile Company. It failed. But he designed and built a winning race car, built some other cars, and in June 1903 helped form the Ford Motor Company, of whose one thousand shares he was allotted 255. He was forty years old, the century had barely begun, and he had a business idea which would change the world.

Ford did not invent the automobile, nor did he build the first one. The American system of manufacturing had long been based on the assembly of interchangeable parts. Ford transformed the system; he hired engineers from arms manufacturers to help him design a moving assembly line: the modern mass-production equivalent of the old American system. He was not the first American businessman to distrust bankers (and the management of production based solely on considerations of money flow and profit), and not the first to try to keep control of his own company. Myths about Ford became current during his lifetime because he was a superb publicist—a mythmaker himself—and because he became a symbol to the consumer society. It was easy and logical for twentieth-century Americans to believe that Henry Ford invented the car, mass production, and mass consumption.

Ford's earliest experiences convinced him that racing—and winning—was good publicity; it would sell cars. But he wanted to go further. He wanted, he said, to make a "family horse," a car anyone could use and everyone could buy. It was not simple to develop a cheap, lightweight, sturdy, easy-to-build, easy-to-drive-and-maintain car. Several of his associates in the Ford Motor Company were opposed to the idea. The short automotive tradition was against it. Successful early automobiles were heavy, like the Oldsmobiles and Cadillacs, or they were heavy, expensive, and lavishly hand-worked like the French Panhards, Delahayes, Renaults, and Peugeots, the German Daimlers, the British Wolseleys and Napiers. Cars were high-profit items. They sold to the same well-to-do people who owned horses and carriages.

But in October 1908 Ford made his Model T, the "Tin Lizzie," available to the public. It was built in a new factory at Highland Park, just outside Detroit, specially designed to produce the Model T. 1908 was also the year William C. Durant put together a holding company he named General Motors.

Ford designed the Highland Park plant to make, with specially designed machinery, nearly all the parts needed for an automobile; to move all those parts in the sequence needed to be assembled into components (sub-assembly lines for sub-assemblies); and to move the components in proper sequence to a moving assembly line where men and machines put components together to make an automobile. By 1912, the entire moving assembly line was in operation, and mass production became a reality. Ford produced 170,000 cars in 1912, and became the leading manufacturer of automobiles in the world. The plant—considered a miracle of engineering and business genius—was open to visitors from all over the world. Other American automobile manufacturers seized upon Ford's ideas, but it was years—in many cases, decades—before the moving-assembly-line idea spread to other kinds of manufacturing.

Profits were high from the very beginning in 1903. In 1908,

when Ford had become the majority stockholder, dividends in cash and stock amounted to $2.5 million. By 1913, when mass production was in full swing, $11.2 million were paid in dividends. In 1914, Henry Ford started building himself a new, $2 million home in Dearborn on the river Rouge. By that time, the company was worth tens of millions of dollars, all of it generated from corporate profits and savings. When he died in 1947, Henry Ford was still majority stockholder, and his estate was estimated to be worth on the order of $2 billion.

Ford's idea was to provide every American with that "family horse." His intuition, his shrewd sense of where profits lay, his fascination with machines and mechanical processes, his delight in wheels and motion, along with his desire to "make it big" all coincided with American egalitarianism (only the well-to-do could afford horses, carriages, and the freedom and mobility which they provided) as well as with the intense desire for mobility—the symbol of quintessential American independence. It was the power and realization of those widespread desires for independence, material success, and mobility that created the market for vast numbers of Fords—and other mass-produced American cars. In order to sell more cars, Ford reduced prices. The Model T roadster sold for $680 in 1910. The price was reduced to $525 in 1912, and to $440 in 1914. There was no comparably priced car in the entire world—and only other American car manufacturers attempted to price for sales to a mass market. In 1914, Ford also decided that the more than nine thousand men and women who worked in his plants should be paid enough so that they could afford to buy a car. The company reduced the work day to eight hours (ran its plants with three shifts) and raised all wages to a minimum of $5 per day. Ford workers could buy Ford cars on such wages. Company sales and profits grew.

In 1914, Ford stopped trying to fit production to estimated sales; the company simply produced all the cars it could.

They were sold: 300,000 in 1914; 500,000 in 1915; 700,000 in 1916. Others copied Ford; the American market seemed inexhaustible. Over one million automobiles—Fords and others—were made and sold in the United States in 1916, the first year that happened (much more than the annual production of all the rest of the world). Except for a brief dip during World War I (1917–18), and the stoppage of production in World War II (1942–46), at least one million cars were made and sold in the United States every year since 1916. In most years, several million were sold. In 1980, there was a car on the road for every second man, woman, and child in the United States.

Sales and distribution networks capable of moving millions of cars into the market every year were developed by Ford, General Motors, and the other mass auto makers. Large profits gave the auto companies the leverage to establish quotas and service standards for dealers. The distribution of parts and the need to provide services for these complex machines gave dealers more opportunities for profit, and the companies more leverage to maintain strong, centralized control over dealers. By the 1920's, automobile dealers had a new kind of spin-off market—the used-car market—which provided them some profit independent of auto-company control.

In the 1920's, General Motors' Alfred P. Sloan, Jr., introduced a sales technique (also a production technique) which encouraged people to consume automobiles. Most Americans thought of cars as long-term investments, possibly durable for a lifetime. But General Motors began changing the appearance, the styling of its cars, each year. New models made it possible to sell to the same person again and again—made it possible for the buyer to "use up" a car and get a new one. General Motors' sales began to exceed Ford's by the 1920's because Fords were cheap, standardized, and uniform—you could buy a Model T in any color you wanted as long as it was black. Eventually, in 1928, Ford brought out the Model A to meet the growing demand for a change—the consumers wanted, or had been persuaded, to consume.

The sixth automobile made by the Ford Motor Company in 1903 had been exported and sold in Canada. In 1904, Ford established the Ford Motor Company of Canada. In 1911, Ford of Great Britain was started, to bring Ford production and sales to British and European markets. Ford, General Motors, and other American auto companies founded subsidiary manufacturing and selling companies all over the world after World War I. These companies, started with American capital, using American engineering, manufacturing, and management techniques, made the auto companies multinational.

After World War I, General Motors took a major step in the creation of the consumer society. It created a subsidiary corporation, the General Motors Acceptance Corporation, to lend customers the money to buy its cars. The cars themselves were security for loans—they could be repossessed if necessary and sold in the growing used-car market. GMAC became a very large-scale lending company which was not subject to banking regulation and was therefore able to charge highly profitable rates of interest. Now GM earned a profit on the car and on the loan; credit was made available to consumers in a new way. Consumer credit, a partial and unconscious solution to the problem of the maldistribution of wealth, not only made it possible for Americans to buy cars (symbols of mobility, affluence, and success) but also gave them a sense of "commanding" credit and being independent in ways hitherto only available to the rich and successful. While big businesses only slowly began to invest in and develop consumer credit in the 1920's, and did little to encourage its growth during the Depression and World War II, since the 1950's the idea of consumer credit (and investment in it) has become essential to big business as well as to the consumer.

When Henry Ford died in 1947, Michigan Senator Arthur H. Vandenberg said that Ford's career was

> the vivid epitome of what one man can do for himself and for his fellow men under our system of American freedoms. Through his own irresistible genius and courage he not only rose from humble obscurity to fame and fortune, but he also founded a new national economy of mass production which blessed his hundreds of thousands of employees with his wages and his millions of customers with low prices.

As Sigmund Diamond has pointed out in *The Reputation of the American Businessman,* the nearly universal verdict of the American press at Ford's death was not only that he had created the assembly line and mass production, "democratized" American business, and made the egalitarian consumer society, but that he had been the very epitome of American individualism and at the same time a common man, a representative of the American system and the American character. Furthermore, he was not a robber baron. Most agreed that Ford had been driven by a desire to serve his society and his nation. His profits and his fortune, like the man himself, were products not merely of American business but of the system and the nation. Ford's life and work seemed, according to some, successfully to have reconciled big business and the values basic to American society. The consumer society, which Ford helped create, was the modern, big business-embroidered version of that society. Even United Auto Workers President Walter Reuther, barely ten years after bitter strikes and conflicts at Ford, wrote—in the company newspaper—that Henry Ford had been a great man and that part of his

> greatness arose from his willingness to pioneer. . . . He recognized that increased purchasing power in the hands of the workers meant more contented workers and a greater potential market—a greater America. . . . His mistakes were never mistakes of the heart.

By 1947, purchasing power was at the heart of the consumer society.

Creating the Consumer Marketplace

America did not become a consumer society overnight. The mass production of automobiles and the widespread distribution of electrical power to household users—both essential to the consumer society and both well established in mass production by the end of the second decade of the twentieth century—began to make it obvious to a few that markets to consume those goods had to be created. For most Americans, however, especially the millions trying to survive in turbulent, expanding cities, it was not a matter of choosing what goods to buy but rather whether they would be able to buy enough food, shelter, and clothing to survive. The inequitable distribution of the growing wealth of the country was their concern, not consuming mass-produced goods.

Businesses had to create the marketplace, convince the masses that they ought to buy, and make it possible for them to pay for the goods being produced. The desire for goods, even for food to consume and clothes to wear, is never, in any society, simply the desire for necessary material things. Food, clothes, houses, possessions of all kinds, along with their use and consumption, have always carried symbolic, social, ritualistic meanings which appear to be at least as powerful in motivating our behavior as material necessity. (The enormous popularity of fast-food chains in America in the 1980's, for example, seems to depend as much upon the sense of independence and freedom they give their millions of patrons as on the fact that they purvey food.)

The earliest big-business effort to make it possible for more consumers to buy more goods was to lower prices. As big businesses became capable of creating goods in ever-increasing quantities, they sought ways to make their production techniques "more efficient" and thereby lower their unit costs. Lower costs could mean lower prices, and therefore increased sales—so producers believed. Most business leaders did not believe (as Henry Ford did in 1914) that increased workers' wages meant increased markets. Generally, they believed that demands for higher wages and improved working conditions did not lead to decreased costs and business efficiency. Even Ford was convinced, by the 1920's, that resisting demands for higher wages kept control of his business where it "belonged"—in his hands. It became a truism of management that the interests of the firm were best served by more efficient production (firmly under management control) rather than by the uncontrolled market benefits that might be gained from higher-paid, happier workers. Productivity—ever-cheaper goods in ever-larger quantities—was the big-business contribution to the commonwealth, so businessmen argued. High wages and the distribution of wealth in the society were not, by the same logic, the responsibilities of businesses.

Early in the twentieth century the focus of most big businesses was on production. The automobile companies were unusual with their dual focus on production techniques and consumer marketing. While producing and wholesale distributing companies were—like the meat packers, the flour millers of Minneapolis, and giant corporations like National Biscuit and United Fruit—interested in attracting consumers to markets, they did not deal directly with consumers.

The earliest large-scale businesses to operate directly in a consumer market were department stores, mail-order companies, and chain stores. None of these businesses was a producer. But the collection and marketing techniques they developed in the nineteenth century and improved in the twentieth were based on the growth of mass production and were applied to consumer marketing by all big businesses in this century. Their experience is the foundation of our consumer society.

Many of the original department stores have remained in business for over a century, although the first of them—Alexander T. Stewart's—died not long after he did in

1876. Most big department stores grew out of dry-goods establishments; some of them started from wholesale businesses. Marshall Field, Wanamaker, Arnold Constable, Lord & Taylor, Macy, Abraham & Straus, B. Altman, Best & Company, Stern Brothers, Jordan Marsh, R. H. White, Carson, Pirie, Scott, Hutzler, Woodward and Lothrop, E. J. Lehman, The Emporium, J. L. Hudson, F. & R. Lazarus, John Shillito—all started in the department-store business between 1870 and 1890. Adam Gimbel created a chain of department stores, starting in the 1870's in Vincennes, Indiana, and then in Milwaukee, Philadelphia, and New York. Gimbel came to New York City in the first decade of the twentieth century, and Bullock's opened in Los Angeles, Rich's in Atlanta, and Neiman-Marcus in Dallas. These stores offered clothing for men and women, furs, carpets and rugs, upholstered goods and furniture, silverware, parasols and umbrellas, jewelry, hats, shoes, toys, books, stationery, china and glassware, crockery, flowers and feathers. Their aims were high volume, high turnover, often at low prices and low margins. They employed hundreds of salespeople and dozens of buyers, and did thousands of transactions per day. Their emphasis on volume and turnover made it standard practice to mark down the prices of slow-moving goods, to advertise extensively, and to have periodic sales. The bargain basement, where unsold goods were offered at exceptionally low prices in order to move them, was a twentieth-century innovation by Filene's in Boston. Department stores integrated the management of the sales of a great diversity of manufactured goods with the controlled activity of large numbers of employees. They were reflections, in retailing, of the factory in manufacturing: they depended on increasingly available machine-made goods in the national market, and on cities for an adequate pool of low-cost employees—as well as for increasing numbers of consumers.

Department stores were joined by increasing numbers of large, high-volume stores selling women's ready-to-wear clothing at the beginning of the twentieth century. These stores—like Peck & Peck, Henri Bendel, Bonwit Teller, Franklin Simon, Bergdorf Goodman, and Lane Bryant in New York—were aimed at attracting the growing numbers of women in the rapidly expanding urban middle classes. They emphasized conspicuous consumption, rapid and seasonal fashion changes, and made available mass-produced clothing to a new, large, and important group of consumers. Women's clothing stores and department stores borrowed marketing techniques from each other and are the basis of the values conditioning the purchase and use of clothing in America today.

Aaron Montgomery Ward formed the first mail-order company in Chicago in 1872. Its business was based on catalogues sent primarily to farmers and farm organizations—the Grange was instrumental in building Ward's business—and on railway express delivery of goods from Chicago. By 1887, its catalogue listed more than 24,000 items. Like department stores, it, too, depended on volume sales and rapid turnover for its profit. Sears, Roebuck & Company entered the mail-order sales field in 1887, selling only watches. But, with new capital and new partners, Sears expanded rapidly in the late 1890's, and made the decision to sell everything that department stores were selling, as well as nearly everything manufactured in the United States that could be sold directly to consumers. By the 1920's, Sears was America's largest retailer and one of the biggest corporations.

Chain stores, too, had been established in the latter part of the nineteenth century, but their success in the mass market began to come in the 1920's. The Great American Tea Company, founded in New York City in 1859 by G. F. Gilman and G. Huntington Hartford, changed its name in 1869 to the Great Atlantic and Pacific Tea Company. A & P spread its chain geographically and expanded the variety of products it sold. By 1900 it had nearly two hundred stores. And by that time the forerunners of Grand Union, Kroger, Jewel Tea,

American Stores, and First National Stores were all established as chains in the grocery trade. Variety chain stores also started: Woolworth from Pennsylvania was first, followed by McCrory in Pennsylvania, Kress in Tennessee, and Kresge in Michigan. While these chains, along with United Drug and United Cigar, did become national in their operations by the 1920's, most chains were local and regional until after World War II.

Chain-store supermarkets began to appear in the 1920's. They combined chain-store supply and management techniques with department-store display, marketing, service, and packaging know-how. Sears and Ward's both established large chain-store retailing operations in order to get a firm grasp on urban markets. Retailers began aggressively to expand into suburbs in the 1920's. Grocery retailers experimented with a marketing system which opened the shelves to the consumers and made the customer select the goods and do the work of the store clerk in assembling individual orders—a process which gradually appealed to the ideal of individual independence. The supermarket, to be profitable, had to have a large available population because it depended upon very high volume and turnover. It had to have large retailing spaces, in order to display large varieties and quantities of goods, and it required a transportation system which was available to large numbers of people. The depression of the 1930's and World War II slowed the process of supermarket development, but growth was explosive after the war.

Modern supermarkets and shopping malls depend principally on highways, trucks, and automobiles (as department stores had earlier depended on railroads, trolleys, and subways). The goods for supermarkets are assembled at warehouses and distribution centers run by chain-store companies and are distributed by truck to the supermarkets and malls. The supermarkets and malls depend on automobiles to bring them customers (and to take away the goods sold). Packaging of goods for individual consumers has become an essential of modern consumer retailing techniques.

The effect of the big retailers was to acquaint the growing population with the quantity and diversity of goods available. Furthermore, department and chain stores in urban areas, and mail-order businesses in rural and early suburban areas, accustomed individual Americans to buying goods in large, impersonal marketplaces in which they could feel themselves to be free agents acting independently. They were not, it is true, selling in those marketplaces, and customers were not haggling and bargaining—but they could at least find "bargains" and make economic decisions. In short, the great retail merchandising centers and stores which became characteristic of twentieth-century American cities helped ordinary Americans believe they were still operating in a marketplace and expressing freedom and independence there.

Retailers, following the lead of the auto companies, began to introduce installment buying and consumer credit early in the 1920's. "A dollar down and a dollar a week" and "layaway" plans encouraged those with low wages as well as the rest of the population to participate in consumer retailing. Not until after the end of World War II, however, did large-scale investment in consumer credit and widespread affluence make mass participation in consumption possible. In 1950, Diner's Club, a credit organization devoted to consumption, introduced the use of a plastic card. The credit card rapidly became a symbol of consumer credit and of the consumer society, and plastic (like copper, bronze, silver, gold, and paper before it) became a form of money.

With money and credit gradually becoming available, excursions into the great emporia of the cities—or into the hundreds of pages of goods illustrated in the catalogues—brought increasing numbers of people to the conclusion that they needed to use and consume an increasing range of available goods. The process was simple, fashionable, and democratic. Consumer businesses appealed to conflicting American values. "Everyone has one" and "Only the fashionable have them" were statements equally appealing to democratic Americans. "This is unique and exclusive" was as powerful an inducement as "This is our best seller" to Americans with credit, eager to be upwardly mobile and popular.

Americans have become willing members of a consumer society in part because they are convinced that consumption is an indication of national progress, of a high standard of living, and of social good. The individual pushing a cart through the supermarket, picking from a wide variety of goods, finding bargains, making decisions, and driving away with the goods is achieving freedom, independence, and mobility in an egalitarian marketplace. For most Americans, that conviction justifies business. Consumption has come to signify virtue, social standing, reward for work, and usefulness to the society—for individuals and for big business.

Informing the Consumer

Advertising as a separate enterprise was developed to market consumer goods. When, early in the nineteenth century, all markets were local, a merchant could simply inform potential customers by public announcement—by crier possibly, certainly by posted bill, flyer, or newspaper—that certain goods were available for sale. The assumption was that those who sought or needed the goods (the existing "demand") would, when informed, seek out the supply. By the second half of the nineteenth century, as railroads and growing industries expanded the quantity and variety of goods available, the need to inform potential customers grew. The desire to induce new customers to buy, and to induce them to change their "custom" from one store or variety of goods to another, brought increasing business attention to the means of attracting customers and convincing them to buy.

In 1865, the year the Civil War ended, American businesses spent about $6 million to advertise their products. By 1880, $200 million was spent annually. By 1904, the figure had reached $800 million a year—approximately four percent of the gross national product. Advertising costs have remained about four percent of the GNP throughout the twentieth century. The numbers of large advertising companies, staffed with artists, writers, social scientists, and business managers, developing advertising "campaigns," labels, images, polls, market research, and mythmaking in the national (as well as global) market have grown from one in the 1870's to hundreds a century later.

As production, businesses, and markets grew, advertising developed specializations. But even where customers were very limited, efforts to sell through the media were modeled on the ways of winning individual consumers for mass-produced products. Advertising in the consumer society is aimed primarily at the individual and the family.

The early-nineteenth-century distinction between public (and economic) life on the one hand and private (and family) life on the other was blurred both by the production of goods for individual consumption, and by growing business awareness of the marketing possibilities which lay in individual and family purchasing power. Catalogues for mail-order companies were among the earliest to invade our privacy with mass-produced goods. They were followed by magazines and newspapers, which, by the beginning of the twentieth century, were themselves mass-produced, increasingly dependent upon advertising revenues for their support, and dependent upon mass sales for those revenues. Chains of newspapers, owned by publishers like William Randolph Hearst and Joseph Pulitzer, had from their inception the dual role of attracting customers to the products of big retailing and producing businesses as well as informing readers about public events.

Radio (as an important medium for the broadcast of public information) in the 1920's was made possible by the availability of electricity to urban America and by mass production. Like the great metropolitan daily newspaper chains, radio became a "mass" medium as a result of advertising. Commercial radio broadcasting began in 1924. By the 1930's, national networks made national advertising possible: it was possible for a single advertising agency to control every aspect of an advertising program or campaign as it reached millions of potential consumers. Radio was used primarily to gain consumers for packaged, brand-named, mass-produced, nationally distributed goods. Advertising agencies created and owned the programs, as well as the commercials—the people who read or sang commercials and tried to attract consumers to the products being advertised were also part of the show. Jack Benny and Jell-O became equally well known, as did Edgar Bergen, Charlie McCarthy, and Chase & Sanborn Coffee. Old Ma Perkins and Oxydol, Jack Armstrong (the All-American Boy) and Wheaties (the Breakfast of Champions) were deliberately identified by the advertising agencies so that positive feelings about programs, performers, and characters would be automatically associated with specific products. Well-conceived radio commercial slogans, songs, and labels, with their associations of pleasure, have lasted decades in the memories (and consuming behavior?) of many Americans.

The movies in America did not become a significant medium for the sale of products. Movie commercials were not—as they were in many other countries—used to reach mass audiences. The lack of movie commercials was due to the American advertising desire to appeal to the individual sense of independence, which was more readily accessible at home, in private, than in large audiences in movie theaters.

Advertising has been the most obvious and visible big-business means of informing and winning consumers, but the effort to generate public support and popularity went further. Like most Americans, business people wanted to be liked. They never doubted (as Richard Tedlow wrote in *Keeping the Corporate Image*) that "the locus of power lay with public opinion," and through increasingly elaborate public-relations programs they have sought public support for their wealth, their control, their great size, and their continued existence.

The big railroads of the late nineteenth century courted public opinion by giving free passes to opinion leaders and politicians. Railroadmen also talked to newspapermen, tried to get their views widely published, and even bought newspapers (Jay Gould backed Whitelaw Reid's purchase of the New York *Tribune*, Henry Villard bought the New York *Evening Post*, and later *The Nation*) in an effort to win public support. In the twentieth century, public relations became a specialized and separate business (like advertising) created to cultivate and encourage public support of big business.

In 1906, the Pennsylvania Railroad hired Ivy L. Lee, one of the earliest public-relations professionals, to publicize the railroad's charitable contributions, to get publicity for the railroad's "happy family," and to justify in public media—through news releases, leaflets, speeches, and bulletins to newspapers—the railroad's effort to charge higher rates. In the next decade, American Telephone and Telegraph, Standard Oil of New Jersey, U.S. Steel, Bethlehem Steel, and Du Pont all hired public-relations firms or established corporate departments for public relations, in order to cultivate a favorable image. Public-relations departments have since become standard. Governments—in America and abroad—as well as other large bureaucracies have learned from big business that it is advantageous to "sell" to the public not only goods and services but ideas, justifications, rationalizations which can bring public support or win public tolerance.

Despite the evidence of their successful advertising campaigns, mounting sales, increasing profits, and vast assets, big businesses and their leaders throughout the twentieth century have felt a continuing need to gain acceptance. Business leaders almost universally feel that public opinion has "turned against them," and that the public is being misled into hostility by union organizers, government officials, politicians, social workers, do-gooders, and other "radicals." They have tried, through their advertising and public relations, to "tell their story." But the battle has been uphill, in part (as Douglas Dickson pointed out in the 1984 book *Busi-*

ness and Its Public) because business, especially big business, is generally blamed "for whatever economic ills trouble America," and in part because business people dislike and distrust any elements of change which are outside the normal business environment of markets, competition, technology, and resources, or outside their control. Informing consumers about available products and influencing them to buy has not—so far—created general public confidence in the morality of big businesses and their leaders.

Critics and Defenders of Business Civilization

The year 1929 was not a good year for American business. Late in October, recession led to panic among speculators and investors; the stock-market crash became a spectacular prelude to deepening depression. Yet in March 1929 Herbert Hoover, a leading proponent of business, a successful financier, and the epitome of the progressive, professional business manager, had been inaugurated President of the United States (the only man to become President as the result of a career based entirely on business success and efficient bureaucratic management). And, also in 1929, an eminent American historian, James Truslow Adams, published *Our Business Civilization,* in which he asserted that America "has come to be almost wholly a business man's civilization." For many Americans, the ten years of terrible depression that followed 1929 seemed to prove the weakness and failure of such a civilization.

Adams wrote *Our Business Civilization* during a stay in England, and in it he compared English society to American. "England has always been a great commercial and . . . manufacturing country," he wrote, "yet English civilization . . . is not as yet a business man's civilization in the same sense as is America's." In England, the landed gentry, the established Church, the powerful civil service, and the military all provided rewards, power, and alternatives to business careers. In America, the Revolution and nineteenth-century expansion had "swept away" all "other orders in society," so that "a business career" was "the sole one that leads inevitably to power when successful." "The prizes for a successful business career" in America, Adams wrote, "have been such as are undreamed of in European business."

Adams did not like America's business civilization. He devoted most of his book to demonstrating that businessmen were "blind to the aesthetic quality in life." The result of businessmen having made America "an economic civilization in which efficiency is the one great god," he said, was that Americans generally had ceased to be concerned about serving society, no longer cared about the ultimate effects of present profits on future generations, had no concern for beauty, for "sanely occupied leisure," or for the benefits of liberal education and gentle behavior. "Profit first, and then, perhaps, as much service as is compatible with profit," had, he wrote, become the fundamental social value. Happiness in such a society was found only in material things. The corporate form of business had destroyed individuality, he believed, so that "among the workmen, executives, and stockholders in the modern corporation there has ceased to be personality anywhere." Businessmen had only "short views" and no long-term understanding of the effects of work, profits, or production. Monthly, quarterly, and annual sales, production, and profit figures were the meaningful limits of business vision, as described by Adams.

Adams's complaints were similar to those of Henry Adams, who, a generation earlier, in *The Education of Henry Adams,* had railed against the decline of the power of established, educated, gentlemanly families (like the Adamses) in the face of the raw power and wealth of big businessmen. But Henry Adams had frankly worshipped the "dynamo" which symbolized for him the energy and creativity of big businesses. James Truslow Adams, on the other hand, regretted the disappearance of energetic robber barons, and attacked the insidious values of "Babbitts," who were not giants of enterprise who imposed themselves by sheer force on the society, but near-professionals intensely absorbed in business affairs, Horatio Alger climbers, small-town philistine boosters whose crass materialism was on a lesser scale (but more prevalent in the society as a whole) and therefore less romantic and praiseworthy than that of the robber barons.

Our Business Civilization was an extensive summary of the academic, literary, and journalistic attack on the virtues and values of the business civilization which was publicly very prominent by the beginning of the 1920's. Sinclair Lewis's popular novels (for which he was, ultimately, awarded the Nobel Prize), among them *Babbitt* (1923), were in the forefront of that attack. In them, Lewis had identified the values of the modern business civilization Adams described—judging all on the basis of profit, seeing the world as a marketplace, assessing the value of individuals on the basis of their incomes and the goods they possess, requiring that any worthy social act make a material addition to the society. Such identification became extremely popular in the 1920's and 1930's in literature, movies, stories, and newspaper and magazine articles. Those traditional small-town business values were often portrayed in sharp contrast with modern urban, aesthetic, and individualistic ones. Traditional America, according to many urban writers and publicists, was a business civilization in which a great majority of people accepted the values of the marketplace, were entrepreneurs and businessmen, and judged everything in their lives on the basis of profit and material wealth. In place of that traditional, rural, small-town "Gopher Prairie" life, Lewis, Adams, and many others advocated urban life, the big city with its openness, its glittering opportunities, and its intellectual freedom.

The Babbitt imagery and small-town values were often explicitly attached to big-business people and big businesses. Henry Ford, for example, was portrayed by critics as a foolish, sometimes pernicious, "traditional" small-town mechanically minded businessman who, like all entrepreneurs and boosters, liked to do things big. They thought it was funny that Ford, who had given Americans wheels, had sent a Peace Ship in 1915 to Europe to try to bring World War I to an end, and that he tried to collect as many artifacts as possible of the American past. They also thought it terrible that he exploited the working people of Detroit. John D. Rockefeller was, to most such critics in the 1920's, a vaguely distasteful old duffer who gave shiny dimes to people and was typically small-town in his enthusiasm for the Baptist Church and his philanthropy. Rockefeller's children and grandchildren were much more acceptable to such critics because they were obviously modern and urban (urbane as well), educated, interested in art and architecture, and less likely to be members of the local Rotary Club.

The big-business revolutionaries of the nineteenth century and their modern apologists had argued that they were expressing the values—independence, entrepreneurship, individualism, enterprise, social service—of the American business civilization which had grown up after the Revolution. By identifying the more modern values of big business with the traditional American small town (long the American model of democracy, community, and commonwealth), the critics of the 1920's and 1930's were *giving* big-business apologists the ground they had always claimed. The critics left themselves very little tradition to appeal to once they had given up community and commonwealth ideals, along with independence, individualism, and marketplace activity. They emphasized the attractive economic opportunities offered by cities. They emphasized that the city provided the individual freedom from the prying and cloying values of small towns. But their rejection of traditional community left them only the remote federal government to appeal to if they wanted democratic community action for the common good. By implication, their enthusiastic acceptance of big cities meant acceptance of the big businesses, national markets, and corporate organizations upon which and with which those cities had grown.

The defense of America as a business civilization used the same values of freedom, individual autonomy, and profitable abilities. President Coolidge's famous assertion that "the business of America is business" was an affirmation of the goodness of a business civilization. Herbert Hoover—in the twenties as Secretary of Commerce (1921–28), in the thirties as President (1929–33), and for three decades before he died in 1964—made himself the foremost public defender of the values of business as the values of "traditional" American individualism. He argued frequently and persuasively that modern big-business insistence upon laissez-faire merely asserted long-established principles of American freedom, independence, and individualism. He advocated efficiency based on modern business-management techniques; he brought standardization and uniformity, through the offices and resources of the federal government, to a great variety of industrial products, thereby making big businesses and mass production more efficient; he developed federal programs which subsidized the growth of big businesses in new industries and which helped rescue some threatened by the panic of the Depression. Hoover's defense of big business, and his justification of federal support for it, asserted the "traditional" place of big business in American life, identical in all respects with the small-town values and behaviors which the critics were attacking. It was ironic (an irony not apparent at the time) that rural, small-town America was being defended in the name of the big businesses whose organization, techniques, and growth had destroyed it.

Finally, in the depression of the 1930's, the attack on America's business civilization shifted. For many, the idea that business made America strong, wealthy, and prosperous was no longer acceptable. It was the national and social utility of big business which the Depression called into question—particularly for urban people who were totally dependent on businesses for their jobs and for the necessities of life. The lesson of the Depression, for millions, was that the traditional business virtues—hard work, frugality, entrepreneurial effort—had failed. Business civilization had failed. The massive unemployment, the disastrous decline in wages, the collapse of the banking and financial system, the contraction of large-scale production and the "rationalization"—i.e., the elimination of small entrepreneurs, family businesses, and small-scale producers—of many sectors of the economy, all seemed to prove that business could not deliver on its promises of freedom, independence, individual success, and prosperity for all.

Furthermore, by the 1930's, fewer and fewer Americans believed that just because big businesses did the productive work of the society they were ipso facto socially responsible, useful, or necessarily responsive to the needs of the common welfare. Many believed that business had to be regulated and controlled in order to make it socially useful and beneficial, and that only the federal government directed by a responsive President seemed able to provide for the common good. President Franklin D. Roosevelt in his 1936 campaign called big businessmen "economic royalists," and the implication was that royalists were opposed to a proper democracy of suffering "little people." The federal government became, in the rhetoric of the New Deal and the beliefs of its millions of supporters, the republican preserver of the commonwealth, the democratic advocate of the common good, and the regulator of big business in the interest of the consumer.

The Depression and World War II convinced Americans that consumers, not big businesses, made markets. Consumers could, therefore, rightfully demand the regulation of business for the common good. Consumers, not entrepreneurs, not big businesses, provided the energy and drive and power that made the economy go. It was therefore logical that consumers be protected and that government at every level be involved in supporting the economy by providing monies, subsidies, legislation, and aid, not to business (as governments in the past had done), but rather to the consumers. "Priming the pump" of the American economy and providing for the common welfare—so Presidential advisors, political and economic pundits argued—required getting money to the consumers, from whom it would "trickle up" to businesses, rather than getting money and credit to businesses, from whom it could "trickle down" to consumers.

Defenders of free enterprise and advocates of American business civilization argued that the focus on consumers was a radical change from the past, a distortion or abandonment of fundamental beliefs and ideals. Franklin D. Roosevelt and the New Dealers, Keynesian economists, union leaders, government officials generally, and later consumer advocates like Ralph Nader, were lumped together by business defenders as "socialists" determined to replace "traditional" freedoms with state control, independence with regimentation, and free enterprise with government bureaucracy. Business advocates began to postulate a golden age of laissez-faire which was being destroyed forever by un-American leaders. Ironically, widespread public belief in that golden age of business freedom also grew as popular historians and journalists wrote about the fascinating evils of robber barons and laissez-faire: Matthew Josephson's widely popular *The Robber Barons: The Great American Capitalists, 1861–1901* was published in 1934—the same year Senator Nye's committee reported on the "merchants of death" and the role of freewheeling big businesses in World War I.

The striking parallels between the actions of the federal government in the 1930's and the role of state and local governments a century earlier were hardly noticed. The provisions, for example, of the Norris–La Guardia Act of 1930 (which Senator George Norris of Nebraska proudly called labor's Magna Charta), of Section 7a of Part I of the National Industrial Recovery Act of 1933, of the National Labor Relations Act of 1935 (sponsored by Senator Robert Wagner of New York), of the Employment Act of 1946, and even of the Taft–Hartley Act of 1948, which protected, regulated, and encouraged the large-scale, national industrial organization of employees into big unions, were comparable in purpose to the early-nineteenth-century establishment and encouragement of corporations. So, too, were the determined and detailed efforts of the federal government to regulate the national financial, agricultural, and industrial marketplaces in order to provide for the good of all rather than the perceived privileges of a few. In the nineteenth century, nationalism and big businesses had destroyed the power of state governments to intervene to protect and provide for the common welfare. In our century, the federal government has been pushed to encourage, to police, and to control economic activity in a consumer society.

War and Consuming Success

World War II brought revival to the economy, victory to the military, and renewed esteem to American business. War brought full employment to a nation which had suffered a minimum of ten percent unemployment for nearly ten years. It brought the consumption of manufactured and agricultural goods at a rate unknown in American experience.

War brought federal regulation and direction of business on a scale much greater, and of longer duration, than in World War I. It brought business leaders and managers, engineers, accountants, and business professionals into the federal government at all levels. It vastly expanded the bureaucracies of government under the direction of many of those business people, and created a permanent interplay between government and businesses. The war brought management techniques—especially in allocation, strategies, and planning—to the federal government. It gave business leaders experience in large-scale mobilization of populations, in logistical traffic management, and in the uses of well-funded research and development programs.

The war moved the federal government into unprecedented control of the national market. Government agencies controlled prices and wages, allocated people to jobs, rationed foodstuffs and manufactured goods, and directed the use of resources. Government bureaucracies, staffed or led by business people, not only planned and regulated production but also controlled the behavior of millions of consumers.

World War II became the great American success story for the majority of those who lived through it. At the end of the war, Americans were determined that never again would the economy collapse into depression, never again would people suffer want and be deprived of the food, clothing, houses, and goods that business could produce and market so well. Yet many were fearful that the end of the war would bring economic collapse and renewed depression. Americans wanted to preserve, protect, and extend the success the war had brought.

Therefore, the years after the war brought a determined and extended search for an economic equivalent of war. For many, it was a search for the reproduction of wartime experiences, or for the continued application of techniques, practices, or "lessons"—by government, by people, by businesses—which they believed had come out of the war. There was near-universal insistence, for example, that the federal government plan and provide not only for the demobilization of soldiers but for their training for productive tasks in society. The GI Bill and its extensions and reenactments in the years since 1945, along with more general programs for job training and education, were all intended to extend the benefits of the war. So, too, were the demands for planning for the conversion of war production to peacetime consumer production through extensive government aid. Businesses continued after the war to seek and welcome government support: contracts, subsidies for capital, funds for research, and funding for the development of potentially profitable ventures, processes, and techniques. They sought to extend the profitable and successful relationship with government. In the postwar world, while some business leaders automatically reverted to the prewar adversarial relationship with government, many (whatever their rhetoric) supported the continuation of government involvement in scientific research and development, in communications, in fuels and minerals and chemicals, in electronics and aviation, because Washington provided lucrative contracts and very often the capital necessary for business expansion. While much of this was reminiscent of the long-standing relationship between the federal government and the arms industry, and even reminiscent of the Jeffersonian willingness to use the federal government's power for the perceived immediate benefit of the commonwealth, few post–World War II Americans were aware of the historical closeness of government and business enterprise. Businesses actively sought to continue the exchange with government agencies which had developed during the war, but they did it believing they were acting in an extraordinary way justified only by extraordinary crisis.

In the years immediately following the war, the threat of economic chaos and return to depression seemed real. The shift of millions of veterans into the labor market, the dislocation of industrial production, the hundreds of strikes and thousands of labor disputes as wartime controls were removed, the threat of inflation as price controls were dropped, all combined to create the terrifying possibility of economic disaster. To avert it, business, government, and the whole society turned to the successful experience of the war as a model: goods must be produced as rapidly as possible, as many people employed and as much money distributed to them as possible, and the goods produced must be consumed as rapidly as possible to make room for more goods and more consumption.

Directly out of the war experience came new techniques of mass consumption. Packaging for individual consumption and "throw-away" or consumable utensils and containers, for example, transformed the manufacture of durable goods, retailing enterprises, marketing techniques, and the attitudes of millions of consumers in the years after 1945. "Planned obsolescence" also became an acceptable way of massively increasing consumption. "Don't fix it, throw it away and buy a new one" gradually became the prevailing attitude. Increasingly, the practice of changing fashions, models, and specifications prevailed. "Durable" goods and machines were less well made and became consumable.

The wartime propaganda which loudly and convincingly emphasized the unique ability of American business to produce—as in the great assembly lines at Ford's Willow Run factory or the remarkable building of Liberty ships in a matter of days at Kaiser's shipyards—became the folklore of the postwar period. Americans could outplan and outproduce everyone on earth. After the trauma of depression, businesses and their managers were eager to maintain the level of wartime production—but they feared that the massive consumption of the war could not be continued. The problem in the postwar world was to continue the fabled production (with its profits and growth for business), be free of wartime government control, and still maintain the high levels of consumption that only war had brought.

After the war, most Americans actively looked to business for personal, individual economic security and success. Yet there remained widespread ambivalence about business. The big businesses offered money, goods, jobs, the possibility of success; they offered security and pensions and insurance; they were symbols and realities of power, wealth, and affluence. On the other hand, those same businesses were personified as tyrannical, exploitative, and greedy; they regimented and oppressed individuals, manipulated and sought control of consumers and employees alike; they were insatiable seekers of power and money; they proclaimed free enterprise, free markets, and individualism in order to delude and destroy freedom and democracy.

A literature reflecting this ambivalence grew in the 1950's and after. Novels such as Frederic Wakeman's *The Hucksters* (1946), Sloan Wilson's *The Man in the Grey Flannel Suit* (1951), Cameron Hawley's *Executive Suite* (1952), Ian Fleming's James Bond fantasies (which came from Britain in the 1950's), Joseph Heller's *Catch-22* (1961), and the more recent popular television serials—*Dallas, Dynasty,* and *Falcon Crest,* for example—all show the powerful, continuing attraction of big business and what it seems to offer Americans. At the same time, they reveal the distress Americans feel over the perceived loss—in independence, idealism, personal liberty, and happiness—which big business exacts. That ambivalence—as well as evidence of the widespread, continuing belief in the centrality of big business in American life—is reflected as well in more intellectual and scholarly works exploring the same themes: C. Wright Mills, *The Power Elite* (1956), David Riesman et al., *The Lonely Crowd* (1950), John K. Galbraith, *American Capitalism* (1952) and *The Affluent Society* (1958), Vance Packard, *The Hidden Persuaders* (1957).

The economic lesson Americans learned from the war was the necessity of consumption. Many businesses encouraged government to continue in the war market—or in defense spending, as it came to be known after 1947. War and defense justified government spending for jobs, public works, education, and scientific development. It justified high costs and inefficient use of capital by businesses: the purpose was to produce an article to war or defense specifications, even if research and development costs were very high. The interstate highway system, built between the late 1950's and the late 1970's, for example, started as a defense measure and provided tens of thousands of jobs and billions of dollars of expenditure by federal and state governments. It indirectly provided a much-improved network to serve suburbs, supermarkets, the trucking and warehousing businesses, and the automobile business. Government contracts for military and defense measures have poured hundreds upon hundreds of billions of dollars into the economy since the late 1940's, providing employment, capital investment, business profits, research and development costs, and untold spin-off benefits. The careers of military officials, government bureaucrats, and big-business managers have become so interlocked that movement from one sector to another has become widely accepted. Government spending for war and defense remains a central part of the success of many (if not of all) American big businesses, and a vital part of the employment, the production, and the distribution of money which maintains the mass-consumer marketplace.

On January 17, 1961, President Dwight D. Eisenhower made a farewell broadcast before leaving the White House. Eisenhower, a symbol of the victory and successes of World War II, pointedly warned of the dangers of continuing the connections between business and the military:

> ... We have been compelled to create a permanent armaments industry of vast proportions. ... We annually spend on military security more than the net income of all United States corporations.
>
> This conjunction of an immense military establishment and a large arms industry is new in the American experience. The total influence—economic, political, even spiritual—is felt in every city, every state house, every office of the federal government. We recognize the imperative need for this development. Yet we must not fail to comprehend its grave implications. Our toil, resources, and livelihood are all involved; so is the very structure of our society.
>
> In the councils of government we must guard against the acquisition of unwarranted influence, whether sought or unsought, by the military-industrial complex. The potential for the disastrous rise of misplaced power exists and will persist.

> . . . We should take nothing for granted. Only an alert and knowledgeable citizenry can compel the proper meshing of the huge industrial and military machinery of defense with our peaceful methods and goals. . . .

The dangers inherent in the model of wartime success which supports the military-industrial complex in the consumer society have not disappeared. In March 1984, for example, an ad appeared in *The Washington Post* under a headline in bold type reading "Defense Entrepreneurs":

> Want your own business? Can you command any defense contracts? If you leave Government, will you leave friends behind? If so, we'll set you up as a division of a national corporation and give you equity, as well as a top salary with tax sheltered benefits!! Curious? For a luncheon discussion, send a brief letter stating your current position, field of interest and home telephone number. We'll take it from there.

It was a *world* war which brought overwhelming success to modern big business, to American consumption, and to the national economy. It also brought a large measure of public praise and acceptance to big business, after years of criticism and outright opposition. The wartime and postwar experiences changed the views of many business leaders: they accepted the consumer marketplace and the need to serve and encourage consumption; they accepted the necessity (and welcomed the public approval which it brought) of large-scale defense spending—a new social justification for big business; and they even came to accept active federal-government encouragement and support of consumers (although not government regulation of businesses in the interest of consumers). Many younger business leaders in the postwar world simply accepted the complex of federal laws and regulations, taxes and agencies, as part of the fascinating game of business. And American big business in general became engaged in the search for success, profits, and growth outside the United States which some had long been involved in.

Conglomerates, Multinationals, and the Global Market

Most American big businesses did not adopt either conglomerate or multinational corporate structures and management techniques until after World War II. However, those structures and techniques were first developed early in the 1920's. They were created by the managers of a few giant corporations—Du Pont and General Motors foremost—who sought new ways to govern their diverse operations.

The first to develop a new structure was General Motors. The second, later in the same year (1921), was Du Pont. The Du Pont company had purchased a 27.5 percent interest in General Motors in 1917, and in 1920 Pierre du Pont had become president of GM (his brother Irenée was president of Du Pont). However, despite the connections, the reorganizations of the two companies took place independently (at GM, based on recommendations by Alfred P. Sloan, Jr.; at Du Pont, on recommendations of several Du Pont managers).

The new structure sounds simple and obvious, since its complexities have been analyzed and carefully explained by business historian Alfred D. Chandler, Jr. At General Motors it became clear to the new, postwar managers that there was no central planning, no overall direction, and no rational resource allocation for all the many nearly independent operating companies and divisions that made up the corporation. At Du Pont, management saw a clear need to integrate diverse divisions created or enlarged by the war, and to provide overall strategies for new products and continued company growth after the war. Both companies created a general corporate headquarters charged with responsibility for all corporate strategy. The general headquarters, the executive committee at the center, and the officers who staffed the headquarters, were removed from all operational decision-making and physically removed from production and sales operations. The general headquarters was provided with a large staff of specialized bureaus—legal, development, research, services, traffic, advertising (and later, personnel, public relations, international)—which provided advice, information, and expertise for corporate decision-making. Under the direction of the chief executive officer (CEO, usually the president) of the company, there were also decentralized operational divisions functioning quite separately. Such divisions were, in essence, similar to the traditional centralized corporation. The new general headquarters provided overall supervision of the top officers of each division, but the day-to-day operations and tactical decision-making of a division were entirely in the hands of divisional managers.

This structure permitted specialization. Each division managed its own resource acquisitions, its own manufacturing or processing, its own sales and traffic flow within the resources allocated to it and the guidelines established by headquarters.

This new structure made it possible for corporations built on the national market, and successful in that market, to invest in and control other businesses. As Chandler wrote:

> As the enterprise reached the limits of the existing market set by available consumer income, the state of technology, and the location of population, and as it came to the limits of cost reduction through rational and systematic integration and use of its resources, its senior executives began to seek new markets or new lines of business where they might apply some resources only partially used or where existing ones might be employed more profitably. . . . Not only did they seek these overseas but they also took their enterprises into new lines of businesses that were similar enough to . . . existing activities to permit a transfer of resources. . . . Finally, those companies that did develop new markets or new products then had to reshape the channels of communication and authority within

> the enterprise. Otherwise, the offices managing the several functional activities lost contact with the new and even the old markets, and the senior executives had increasing difficulty in allocating intelligently the expanded and more varied resources at their command.

The structure established by Du Pont in 1921 is still the structure of that corporation. General Motors' structure, too, although somewhat more complex, is still very much the one established, modified, and settled on by 1924. As Chandler has pointed out, Sears, Roebuck, the largest single retailing corporation in America, and Standard Oil of New Jersey (now Exxon), the largest petroleum and gasoline corporation, also adopted similar structures in the 1920's. It was the full experience of complex, predominantly consumer, national mass-market operations that brought some brilliant managers into these very large firms to create structures in which planning for corporate growth and resource allocation were combined with effective centralized control over decentralized operations. The result was a conglomerate corporation capable of growth into diverse businesses, diverse markets, and operations all over the world, limited only by the resources available.

Most established big businesses did not follow these few giants. In the 1920's, most corporations seemed to believe that "we must be doing something right" and felt little need for structural changes. During the Depression and World War II, most were reluctant to make important internal changes in the face of the radically changed conditions outside company control. Changes in big-business structures took place very tentatively in the late 1940's and gained momentum in the 1950's and after. Other giant corporations began the process of diversification and conglomeration across the world after 1945, so they created structures of centralized corporate government adaptable to diverse markets and decentralized operations. They thus adopted or developed structures very similar to those invented at GM and Du Pont in the 1920's.

The experience of business in World War II helped create a willingness to seek markets—for resources, for production, for sales, for profits—outside the United States. Many businesses had been selling in overseas markets for a very long time before World War II, and for a few of them those markets had been important. Fewer companies had been in resource-extraction businesses outside America, and fewer still in manufacturing and production overseas. But military expansion into the rest of the world during and following the war, the governing of Japan by Americans, the active participation in the government of Germany, and active American leadership in the world since 1945 were reflected in businesses and encouraged by business people. The markets of the world became much more visible and tangible than they had been to Americans before World War II.

The growing emphasis on consumers in the national market which "took off" after 1945 also encouraged businesses to seek new resources, new plant capacity, and new markets. Increased profits and assets at home combined with wartime destruction in the rest of the world meant opportunities for American firms to move into markets that had been supplied by others before the war. Businesses expanded, invested overseas, and bought up other companies both at home and abroad.

The rapid postwar spread of a global transportation, communication, and information network—made possible by airplanes, radios, electronics, and computers—made effective management of global firms possible. American firms began to conglomerate—buy companies that were operating profitably, but not necessarily in the same markets in which the purchaser was operating. They began to diversify—create conglomerates as a matter of conscious policy. And they began deliberately to make themselves multinational corporations—operating fully in multiple national markets under the laws of other countries. The corporate structure created in the twenties by Du Pont, General Motors, Sears, and Standard of New Jersey had led the way.

The responsibility for world leadership which became central to the American government's foreign policy after 1945 increased cooperation between the federal government and big businesses operating outside the United States. Multinational oil companies were used by the government to establish American power and presence in Europe, the Middle East, and elsewhere. The companies' frustrated desires to maintain autonomy were made bearable by trade-offs: acquisition of wartime government investments in Mideast petroleum-production facilities was made easier and there was less anti-trust prosecution.

American companies acquired manufacturing and distributing companies in all the markets of the world. Initial investments were often quite small, but sufficient in postwar hard times to acquire control or a large interest in a foreign operation. As times improved in the foreign market—very often helped by aid and loans from the American government—earnings rose and were reinvested. Foreign subsidiaries American companies had owned before World War II also grew from reinvested earnings. As a result, multinationals often required very little capital from the United States.

In European, Asian, African, and Latin American markets, American companies often found customers with no dollars to buy their goods. To enter such markets, companies often acquired foreign manufacturers already in the markets. Further, American purchases of foreign goods, American military spending overseas, and foreign aid rapidly built up dollar balances in the rest of the world. Continued government spending overseas and the near-insatiable American consumer market has maintained a very high flow of dollars to the rest of the world. American multinationals have also helped open the American market to foreign companies, and they have pressed for American participation in the General Agreement on Trade and Tariffs in order to assure an adequate flow of dollars. Since the 1960's, many multinational big businesses have even argued for free trade—the movement of goods and companies and profits without national control or restriction—as essential to worldwide operations.

Americans have moved into every available foreign market since 1946. For at least two hundred years before that, Great Britain had been the major world investment and selling power. But by 1960 the total British private overseas investment was $26.4 billion, including portfolio investment, while just the direct investment of American companies overseas was $31.8 billion (without counting billions more of portfolio investment).

The global market of multinational business is quite different from the traditional international marketplace which the British did so much to create in the eighteenth and nineteenth centuries. And it is different from the American national marketplace created in the nineteenth and early twentieth centuries. Multinational companies attempt to avoid the surveillance and control of any government, including their own (much as big businesses evaded and fought state and local regulation in the nineteenth century). They have invaded national markets in an effort to create a global market, but they have not developed effective techniques for controlling that market.

"I'm much more frightened today than when I came back from the war and faced up to what had to be done," Henry Ford II told a magazine interviewer in May 1981 (referring to his return from World War II in 1943 to take charge of the Ford Motor Company from his grandfather). "You can't be afraid of the [national] marketplace if you have any intuition about it and you are confident about what you should do," he continued. "But when you're fighting in a world marketplace dictated by forces over which you have no control, it's quite different. It's like playing football with only one arm."

The control American business leaders have been seeking during the past century still eludes them. The ability of a limited cartel of oil producers (OPEC) to manipulate the world price of oil and create shortages despite the theoretical opposition of the largest petroleum-producing country in the world—the United States—is one visible danger in the new global marketplace. The multinational oil corporations, strongly based in national markets, seem unable to control (although they can profit from) their resources, their production, and much of their global marketing. It is an open question—"like playing football with only one arm"—whether multinational corporations will prove adequate to the new marketplace their managers are trying to create.

The Consumer's Business Person

The nineteenth-century robber barons have disappeared. The entrepreneur-founders of the great twentieth-century corporations have died, leaving unspectacular, less conspicuous, less wealthy professional managers in charge of the companies that have become symbols of what Americans mean by "rugged individualism" and "free enterprise" and efficient, productive, independent business. IBM, Exxon, Mobil, Ford, General Motors, Chase Manhattan, Citicorp, General Dynamics, Boeing are representative entrepreneurs of modern business civilization.

The consumer society, with its emphasis on giant corporate businesses, mass production, egalitarianism, and mass consumption, has transformed the general American perception of the very rich, of business success, and of the utility of great accumulations of wealth. Wealth is still believed to be the goal of individual success, and Americans continue to believe that new big businesses are the result of individual entrepreneurial efforts. But popular beliefs about the uses to which great wealth ought to be put—whether the wealth is individual or corporate—have changed.

The Astors, the Vanderbilts, the Carnegies, and many of the great robber barons were conspicuous consumers. They used their wealth to build great mansions, to eat, dress, and entertain lavishly, and to accumulate enormous collections of expensive things. Their wealth and its conspicuous consumption were believed to be the rewards of work, industry, and success.

In the modern consumer society, the palaces and playgrounds of the very rich have become less visible and less exclusive. The rich—especially the newly rich—are now "trendsetters." " 'I can smell the Ferrari now,' chants a fresh crop of instant multimillionaires," in a 1984 *Time* magazine headline—in a society in which nearly every adult owns a mass-produced automobile. Wealth in the consumer society is still believed to be the reward for individual success; a degree of conspicuous consumption is tolerated (consuming is what the society is "all about"!), but there are very strong pressures on the wealthy, on business people, on corporate managers, on political leaders, to make wealth visibly useful.

The multimillionaire children and grandchildren of the Rockefellers, the Harrimans, the Fords, the Annenbergs, the Kennedys, the Watsons, to name but a very few, have become high-ranking public servants—ambassadors, cabinet secretaries, governors, senators, and even Presidents. Houses and buildings, collections of objects and art, accumulations of archives of the very rich have been opened or given to the public. Much of the wealth earned by individuals, inherited by families, or accumulated by corporations has been turned over to foundations which, in turn, grant large sums for publicly visible, socially desirable or useful purposes. All this demonstrates the social value of money and of the individuals (and big businesses) who created it.

Business success still brings personal fortune—and great corporations, it is widely held, add to the efficiency and wealth of the society of consumers. Thomas J. Watson and the creation of IBM, J. Paul Getty and the creation of Getty Oil, exemplify success, and stories about them are still being told in consumer America late in the twentieth century. Those stories resemble the earlier success stories, and they are taken as demonstrations of the continuity of America's business civilization. But they incorporate new elements—big business corporations, national and global market operations, and service in a consumer society—which (while present-day listeners and readers simply expect them to be there) demonstrate a new logic, and new implications, very different from those in the stories of successful businessmen like Girard, or Astor, or Colt in an entrepreneurial society.

The story of Howard Hughes—probably the richest man in America when he died (as Girard, Astor, Vanderbilt, Carnegie, and Ford had been in their day)—is a cautionary tale. Hughes was undoubtedly very successful in business; he was almost a caricature of the "rugged individual"; yet something went "wrong" with his career which leaves Americans uncomfortable in using him as an example of modern business success.

Hughes started out in business in 1923, at age eighteen, when he convinced a Texas court to give him full control of the Hughes Tool Company left to him by his father's sudden death. The multimillion-dollar company made and leased oil-well drilling bits and other well machinery. Hughes Tool became the holding company and capital supplier for all of Howard Hughes's business ventures.

At nineteen, Hughes married and moved from Texas to Hollywood. He created a movie company and produced pictures. In 1930 he both produced and directed *Hell's Angels*, a multimillion-dollar extravaganza which made a star of Jean Harlow but really featured airplanes—Hughes's lifelong obsession. Not long after, Hughes took a brief job as a co-pilot on American Airlines to learn something of commercial passenger flying. In 1934 he created Hughes Aircraft Company and gathered a team of mechanics and designers to build a racing airplane. In 1937 he bought control of Transcontinental & Western Air, a passenger airline called TWA, which he later renamed Trans World Airline. In 1938 he flew his own plane around the world, and was welcomed in New York as a hero. Through the 1940's, World War II, and after, he made, developed, and produced military aircraft on government contracts, and built TWA into a world airline.

Always personally erratic, a "loner" with a mind for detail and the ability to absorb complex technical and business situations almost instantaneously, Hughes grew increasingly wealthy and involved in a bewildering complexity of business, finance, and publicity. His youth, wealth, and romantic connection with Hollywood, movies, beautiful stars, and with flying all combined to make him widely known. His own desires to be perfectly free, mobile, and private seemed contradicted by his conspicuous seeking of publicity and his flair for public display. He publicly rejected the egalitarianism along with the mass publicity of the consumer society, yet he justified his great wealth and the power it gave him on the basis that his laboratories, Hughes Aircraft, and TWA all served that society and its defense needs. He battled with the Congress and agencies of the federal government, and ultimately exiled himself from America. Long before he died, he lost control of the airline he built. He became a billionaire and a recluse, moved "offshore," died a lonely death, and left his fortune for a multitude of claimants to squabble over.

"That we have made a hero of Howard Hughes," Joan Didion wrote in *Slouching Towards Bethlehem,*

> tells us that the secret point of money and power in America is neither the things that money can buy nor power for power's sake . . . but absolute personal freedom, mobility, privacy. It is the instinct which drove America to the Pacific, all through the nineteenth century, the desire to be able to find a restaurant open in case you want a sandwich, to be a free agent, live by one's own rules.

In a consumer society which "increasingly appears to prize social virtues," Didion concluded, Howard Hughes was "not merely antisocial but grandly, brilliantly, surpassingly, asocial." He was, she wrote, "the last private man, the dream we no longer admit." What was inadmissible about Hughes, however, was not his privacy, his individual independence, his wealth, or his conspicuous use of his wealth for personal gratification: the wealthy, conspicuous "stars" of the consumer society are all encouraged to fulfill public fantasies about the meaning of individual independence. It was Hughes's role as a businessman who refused to be responsible to the society that made his dream inadmissible.

In the 1980's, there are many stories told of the success of individual entrepreneurs who build or expand great combines of business across the country and around the world. Almost all the metropolitan daily newspapers devote considerable space to stories of businesses and business people (the national-circulation daily *The Wall Street Journal* is entirely devoted to business); there are numerous magazines and periodicals (led by *Forbes, Fortune,* and *Business Week*) devoted to such stories; and there are television documentaries and dramas which are about the conduct and success of business. The range of public interest and awareness, of discussion and opinion—itself a phenomenon of the consumer society—acts as a constant pressure on business people to be responsive to social expectations.

Some of the stories, on the surface at least, seem more appropriate to the nineteenth than to the twentieth century: such as the recent attempt of the Hunt brothers to "corner" the world's supply of silver. Hunt family holdings, based on the fortune built by Dallas oil man H. L. Hunt before he died in 1974, were estimated to be worth at least $5 billion by the beginning of the 1980's. They included, according to a *New York Times* article (January 6, 1980),

> one of the largest independent oil companies in the country, the Placid Oil Company; Penrod, the largest privately held drilling contractor, with 100 rigs; probably the biggest hoard of silver under a single individual's control; the largest sugar

> beet refiner in the nation; possibly the largest amount of acreage in the United States held by one family; some 2.5 million tons of coal reserves, and the largest string of thoroughbred race horses held by any American. Even they make money, according to their owner, Nelson Bunker Hunt.

Those were only the holdings directed by Nelson Bunker Hunt and Herbert Hunt, and did not include holdings based on "80 percent of the original Hunt Oil Company" controlled by other Hunts and their family trusts.

In 1980, the effort of the two Hunt brothers to acquire nearly all the available silver in the world and drive the price very high collapsed—with considerable loss to the Hunts, and serious disruption of some of the world's commodity and money markets. When, in the 1870's, Jay Gould's effort to corner the American gold market collapsed, a financial panic and a serious depression had ensued. The magnitude of the growing global market in the 1980's as compared to the nascent American national market in the 1870's is made clear by the relatively small effect the collapse of silver had on world finance or the world economy. The scale of the Hunt family fortune is of a different order from the money available to Gould; the Hunt resources enabled them not only to make the attempt, involving billions of dollars, but also to survive the collapse without losing all or even a large part of their assets.

Even the Hunt brothers, who are known as "old-fashioned" individualistic wheeler-dealers, behave like egalitarian members of the consumer society. Both brothers, according to the *New York Times* story,

> are listed in the Dallas phone book. . . . Bunker doesn't smoke or drink, favors inexpensive, chocolate-brown suits, and in the words of one Texas editor and Hunt-watcher, "is the kind of guy who orders chicken-fried steak and Jell-O, spills some on his tie, and then goes out and buys all the silver in the world."

> Herbert lives in a middle-class neighborhood . . . "just like everybody else." . . . Neither man has a driver, and during last summer's gasoline crisis Herbert, one of the world's oil moguls, was spotted in a two-hour gas line, waiting patiently with his wife and his dog.

The family gives tens of millions to modern religious causes which seek mass participation, and is actively involved in political organizations.

Such family business combines, based on but not limited to corporate big businesses, are an increasingly important aspect of business control and entrepreneurial behavior in the modern consumer society. In March 1984, for example, a family named Pritzker bought and restarted the bankrupt, two-years-grounded Braniff airline. The Pritzkers are, according to an article by Marilyn Bender (*The New York Times*, February 26, 1984), "a tightly knit clan of amiable financiers" who display "a genius for spotting undervalued businesses and nursing them back to robust profitability." They "prefer to operative privately," according to Bender, "hiding their interests in a maze of holding companies, operating companies and corporate shells" which make it impossible to calculate the extent of their fortune. The Marmon Group of companies is "the family's industrial empire," and it "brings in nearly $3 billion a year in revenues. Marmon averaged a 20 percent return on equity during the last decade," according to Bender's article, and it is a "sprawling and diverse holding company for some 65 domestic operating units and another 16 affiliated foreign companies." "H Group Holdings" is another Pritzker "umbrella company" which contains Braniff, gambling casinos, and "the 41,000 room chain of luxury Hyatt hotels." The Pritzkers also own extensive real-estate and farming interests, *McCall's* magazine, and investments in publicly held companies "such as the Levitz Furniture Corporation."

"Basically what we have is an entrepreneurial approach," Bender quoted Thomas J. Pritzker (thirty-three-year-old president of Hyatt Corporation) as saying. The family lives "well, but unostentatiously." One Pritzker and his wife "occasionally touch base with the jet set. But the family uses its own jets sparingly, even for business."

The family firm has an office in Chicago, in which lawyers and accountants "occupy themselves with Pritzker deals and philanthropies." The Pritzkers are not conspicuous consumers, and, according to the Bender article:

> The Pritzker wealth is visible mostly through largess. The Pritzker Foundation supports educational, cultural, religious, welfare and scientific institutions: a $12 million gift to the University of Chicago for its medical school, $1.4 million for ecology studies to the Illinois Institute of Technology. . . . The A. N. Pritzker Youth Foundation spends $50,000 a year on an after-school program for the elementary school he attended on the North Side of Chicago. The Hyatt Foundation awards an annual prize of $100,000 for architectural distinction.

The Pritzkers, like the Hunts, the Kennedys, the Rockefellers, and many other families of great wealth, are managers of investments rather than of corporate operations (although when they engage in corporate management it is with the single purpose of making corporate operations produce revenue and profit). High-volume, high-cash-flow big businesses based on mass consumption are most favored for investment, because they accumulate assets, savings, and profit most quickly; smaller producing units, with limited markets, high production costs, or low volume are frequently "spun off" by investors, sold or left (as John D. Rockefeller left the ownership of oil wells) to individual entrepreneurs and small companies willing to work and risk for comparatively low levels of turnover and profit.

Individual entrepreneurs still build big businesses in America. They start small, build their businesses into the national market, and expand to the global market in their own lifetimes. Some even continue the tradition of John Jacob

Astor and Andrew Carnegie, immigrants with few assets but intelligence, ambition, and entrepreneurial skills who were determined to make their fortunes in America. But the new builders of big businesses conform to the demands of the consumer society. They build their businesses amid the pressures of national and global markets, competing very often with established big businesses. They operate effectively with complex, constantly changing scientific knowledge, developing technologies, governmental specifications and regulations, and growing public pressures for visible social responsibility and service.

One such individual entrepreneur, An Wang, is, according to a 1980 *Time* article, "the premier peddler of the new machines showing up in business offices." Wang started in the electronics business in 1951,

> . . . in a dingy room above an electrical fixtures store on Boston's Columbus Avenue. The firm engineered one-of-a-kind products to fill special customer needs. One result was the first digital scoreboard, built for the opening of New York's Shea Stadium in 1964.

By 1980, Wang's company—Wang Laboratories, Inc.—was producing "state-of-the-art equipment for the office of the future," and it dominated the market for "integrated information systems." By 1981, Wang Labs' annual profits were over $90 million on sales of $1 billion.

An Wang was born in Shanghai, China, in 1920, and received a Bachelor of Science degree from Chiao Tung University in 1940. He was an engineer for the Chinese Central Radio Works through World War II. He came to the United States in 1945 to do advanced work in applied physics at Harvard, from which he received a Ph.D. in 1948. His thesis was "An analysis of the two-terminal non-linear oscillator with applications to frequency multiplication and division." It was in fact the invention of the magnetic core memory, "a tiny, doughnut-shaped storage element" which was the basis of all computer data storage until the introduction of the semiconductor at the beginning of the 1970's.

Wang sold the magnetic-core patent to IBM early in the 1950's. In 1955, he became a U.S. citizen, incorporated his laboratory, and moved his operations to Lowell, Massachusetts (the city which had been designed in the 1820's by Francis Cabot Lowell's associates as the first urban creation of America's business). In 1979, a fourteen-story Wang tower became company headquarters in Lowell.

Wang developed and introduced the first electronic desktop calculator in 1964. He set up a direct sales force to get his calculators into business offices, and his company began to "take off." The company lost the calculator business in the early seventies when Texas Instruments introduced smaller calculators based on new technology. Wang then developed word processors, using microprocessors from Intel, and introduced the screen readout. "Most of the industry now does it Wang's way," *The New York Times* said in 1980, "and Wang is second only to IBM in word processors." "Wang seems to have an almost uncanny ability to be where the action is," Jeff Blyskall wrote in *Forbes* (February 15, 1982). "An Wang is clearly an innovator. Now you will see if he's equally good at marketing." By 1980, one-third of all Wang sales were in Europe, and An Wang was completing negotiations with the People's Republic of China to operate a small, computer manufacturing joint-venture in Nanjing. By 1983, Wang profits were in excess of $152 million on sales approaching $2 billion.

"The doctor [An Wang] is the dominant force" in Wang Labs, according to a (January 1980) *Forbes* report, "but he is surrounded by strong managers and a young, aggressive staff." In 1983, one of those managers, John F. Cunningham, became president and chief executive officer of the company, while An Wang remained chairman and chief executive, and Frederick A. Wang (Wang's elder son) became executive vice president and chief development officer. Wang has taken care to keep control of the company in his and his family's hands. Although the company has borrowed heavily to expand, and increasing numbers of shares have been sold publicly, Wang has issued two classes of stock (voting and nonvoting), enabling the Wang family to retain ownership of nearly half the voting stock. "We want to concentrate on building our company," *The New York Times* reported An Wang saying in February 1980. "We do not want to be distracted by fighting takeovers and that sort of thing."

Wang Labs has developed a reputation for being a good place to work, high on the lists of young university graduates looking for jobs in "high-tech" companies. The company even bought a country club in Groton, Massachusetts, and has made it a recreational facility for employees. In the late 1970's, Wang created the Wang Institute of Graduate Studies (he is listed in *Who's Who in Finance and Industry, 1983–84*, as "bd. regents, bd. dirs., trustee, pres. Wang Inst. Grad. Studies") in order "to be sure of getting good people" (according to *Forbes*). Wang donated $4 million of stock to start the institute. "I want to give back something to the community that has given me so much," *The New York Times* reported him as saying. The report continued:

> In setting up the Institute, Mr. Wang, as usual, went it alone. He did not even approach his alma mater, Harvard, or the nearby Massachusetts Institute of Technology.
>
> "They," he said, apparently unaware of the irony in his remark, "would want to do things their way."

The big-business entrepreneur in America still wants to do things his or her way, and part of that way has become visible service to the consumer society.

The Big and the Small

The American national market and the new global market are dominated by very large firms with massive resources, thousands of employees, and billions of dollars of income. Great size has become characteristic of American business. And since the beginning of the twentieth century when John D. Rockefeller told the United States Industrial Commission that "the day of the combination is here to stay" and the du Pont cousins began to introduce scientific management techniques to the old family business, modern American corporations have rejected individualism in favor of predictable behavior, cooperation, teamwork, and company loyalty. While giant corporations view themselves as (incorporated) individuals, nevertheless they require people to behave like properly regimented employees, part of a collective team of business experts. The "entrepreneurial" behavior most Americans today associate with business is the behavior of multinational corporations or very large family combines. Yet what might be called "classical" entrepreneurial business—small individual proprietorships operating in limited markets—still flourishes in America.

Big businesses dominate the economy. They provide all the "economic indicators" which describe and measure the health of a consumer economy. They do the bulk of the nation's business. Nevertheless, four to five million individual proprietorships, small-scale partnerships, and small corporations make a product or provide a service in the American economy every year (as compared to seventy-five thousand medium-sized businesses, and about one thousand big businesses). Those small businesses keep alive and prevalent belief in individual enterprise, entrepreneurship, and classical Adam Smith-type market activity.

"In small business and large," Ross M. Robertson states in *The Vital Majority: Small Business in the American Economy* (a federal government publication marking the twentieth anniversary in 1973 of the Small Business Administration),

> . . . the ultimate success is achieved by men and women who have a special talent . . . for undertaking ventures. These are the gifted few who do more than the humdrum chores of

> administration, who risk everything, on their own or with somebody else's capital. . . . They shoot craps in the full understanding that a wrong turn of the dice brings ruin. They play for enormous stakes and sleep well nights while waiting for news of an uncertain outcome. . . .
>
> It is precisely this kind of thinking that relieves the burdens of the world, that lightens the darkness of mediocrity in any kind of endeavor. So long as the *possibility* of success remains for those who just *may* have the trading temperament, who have the courage to risk life itself in the hope of gain . . . the American business system will retain . . . support for its centuries-old role.

The idea that there is a special entrepreneurial talent, a "trading temperament" possessed only by a few, is part of the general admiration for the successful entrepreneur (and helps fuel the ambitions of the many who start businesses each year). Americans also believe that anybody can (and ought to) go into business. "Unlike sports or the arts," Eric Sevareid wrote in *Enterprise*, business

> . . . seems to demand no exceptional innate talent. Unlike science or medicine, it doesn't necessarily require extensive education. And unlike a politician, an entrepreneur does not need to find satisfaction in being a public figure. The opportunities afforded by business, moreover, are varied. People uncomfortable with a large business can start a small one; people unhappy with Wichita can move to San Diego. There is no single center of action, and there is no single track to success.

Small business people, millions of them, have kept business beliefs and talents alive in our time by visibly providing goods and services in local markets.

Consumers who expect standardized products and uniform services at uniform prices (the result of big-business mass production and mass marketing) have created local markets where wages, prices, and standards of service are variants on national norms rather than independently arrived at. No longer are small entrepreneurs and their customers free to haggle (as Adam Smith prescribed) in the modern consumer society. The growing effort to protect consumers and public health in the twentieth-century urban world has brought local and state regulations of increasing stringency on businesses having to do with foodstuffs, public health, and safety. Minimum standards of quality and honesty, to protect consumers and increase consumption, have been created and enforced not only by local governments but by chambers of commerce, better business bureaus, service organizations like Rotary and Kiwanis, as well as by reform and consumer-protection groups.

While consumer regulation has been a "positive market force" which has generally increased confidence in the goods and services of local, small businesses and has, therefore, increased their consumption, it has also tended to increase the investment necessary to enter or continue in a consumer business. As a result, regulation (whether local, state, regional, or national) has tended in the course of the twentieth century to reduce the number of businesses in a particular market and increase their size.

Mass consumption has invaded small-business markets and practices since the end of World War II in the form of cooperative and franchise chains. In the cooperative chains, stores are locally owned and operated, and supplied by a central warehousing organization. The franchise chains, many of which deal in fast foods (like McDonald's or Kentucky Fried Chicken) or in hotels and motels, are big business organizations which require investment of capital by their retailers but control all supplies, advertising, design, and operations. The requirement of investment by the local franchise-holder, however, puts the local outlets in the category of small business.

In 1900, thirty-six percent of the American work force was self-employed—entrepreneurs in small businesses. By 1960, although the work force had nearly doubled in size, only sixteen percent of it was self-employed. In the 1980's, the percentage is slightly lower. In the consumer society, most working people are employees. Many of them, although not the majority, are employed in small businesses. And, in fact, small business accounts for the majority of new jobs created in the United States every year.

Small businesses tend to be labor-intensive; people with little capital invest their work and expand by hiring others "willing to work."

Jobs are lost, and workers unemployed, as businesses grow larger. Big businesses are often formed by the merger of two or more companies which are "reorganized" in order to acquire "efficiencies of scale"; the result is fewer employees. As businesses grow, their efficiencies often take the form of increased mechanization (including automation).

Most small businesses fail. Many cease to do business at the death of their proprietors. In the consumer society, the temptation to proprietors or partners in a successful small business to realize the accumulated capital in the business is very great. Very often, they sell to "get their money out" in order to invest in something else, or have the money to spend. Even more frequently, small businesses collapse, go "under," stop doing business, or go bankrupt. Ordinarily, the demise of a small business is simply assumed to be "one of the breaks of the game." There might occasionally be local concern; sometimes local communities or their governments try to help. But while the collapse, or threatened collapse, of a big business—such as Lockheed Aircraft, or Chrysler Corporation—forces public concern and brings demands for massive government aid, only rarely are small businesses rescued. The "message" of such behavior, clear to most Americans, is that big businesses are vital to the consumer society, they are essential parts of America's business; and small businesses, successful individual entrepreneurs, are not.

On September 29, 1982, an advertisement appeared in *The New York Times,* "one of a series of messages in support of a brighter future for America" from Amway Corporation. Its large headline was "Hooray for the Yankee Peddler" and there was a sketch of a peddler's cart in the center of the ad. It exhorted Americans to revere the tradition of the independent contractor, the self-employed. We are, Amway claimed, the lineal descendants of the individuals who made America what it is today. Amway distributors, modeled on early-twentieth-century door-to-door Fuller Brush salesmen more than on Yankee peddlers, may look and feel like individual entrepreneurs, but actually they are distributors of products made or assembled or wholesaled by a very large corporation. The existence of such distributors, along with several million small businesses and individual entrepreneurs, keeps alive the belief that all American businesses are competing in a fierce marketplace of supply and demand and freedom. But in truth, if "every American created his or her own business," as Amway advocates, there would be no one to run the great bureaucracies, the offices, the factories, on which all modern business depends. Small businesses today do take risks, develop new products, establish new businesses, and provide considerable employment, but few believe they are central to the economy.

The dream of the independent entrepreneur, which was fundamental to the strength and effectiveness of American business civilization in the early nineteenth century, is gone, a nostalgic vision of a Yankee peddler long dead. While the business of many Americans who are not employees today is undoubtedly entrepreneurial, the majority of Americans are employed by corporate big businesses. America's business is big business, supported and supplemented by a few million constantly changing small businesses.

Is Business Still America's Business?

Over many years the patterns of doing business and the ideas underlying producing and taking goods, resources, services, and labor to market and exchanging them there for money and profit have become generalized and idealized in America. Wealth, social position, class, power, deference, and individual success or failure are all measured by reference to business. We trace our ancestry to and identify the aristocrats by business success. Business, not warfare, not birth, not inherited class, not chivalry, services, examinations, mandarins, governments, or parties, provides the structure of American society. In that sense—and it is a very far-reaching sense—America today continues to be a business civilization.

Yet today's is a very different kind of business civilization from the one which grew early in the nineteenth century, based both on the revolutionary ideals of individualism, independence, and democracy and on the actual, direct participation of most working Americans in markets as entrepreneurs. Most of us today are not entrepreneurs. Few of us produce goods directly, or take them to market, haggle with possible buyers and sell them. We participate, indirectly, as employees in the market process. But doing business has become so large-scale that few can feel a sense of direct participation. Americans today are employed by businesses, some of them run businesses, a few build or create businesses, but very few are in business.

And there is increasingly persistent questioning, among Americans, of the benefits of business.

We have come a long way since William Bradford and the Plymouth colonists tried to grow a little extra corn to sell, or William Fitzhugh shipped a hundred or more barrels of tobacco at one time to his merchants in England. It took generations of colonists reluctantly producing for markets to come to the conclusion that wealth, success, and high social position might be acquired (rather than inherited) through wheeling and dealing, risking, adventuring, and laboring in a boisterous, exciting, crowded, heart-stopping, sometimes terrifying physical place full of real people called a market.

The circumstances of American life have changed since Benjamin Franklin, Alexander Hamilton, Thomas Jefferson, and the Revolutionary generations wove business, democracy, and independence so permanently into the fabric of America's culture. During the first half of the nineteenth century most working Americans became involved in markets willy-nilly. Economic choices were limited: either a person "opted out" and tried to live, literally, off the fat of the land (which could indeed produce an adequate hand-to-mouth living), or one went to market with the products of one's labor in order to acquire more than life's necessities, build an estate, and gain independence and success in the eyes of the community. There were few patterns of predictability or long-standing institutions in post-Revolutionary America. It is little wonder that Americans seemed obsessed with making communities and systems, creating immortal organizations like corporations, building monopolies which had some measure of security, banding together in groups of mutual interest for mutual benefit, and seizing upon all possibilities for eliminating work, forcing others to do it, or making machines that could do more work more systematically than humans ever dreamed of. The exciting ideals of individual liberty, independence, equality, and democracy combined with the availability of land to maintain a dynamic tension between individualism on the one hand and corporate life on the other.

The big-business revolution of the late nineteenth and the twentieth century, which created the national market and is in the process of creating a global market, was for many the realization of a dream. It brought massive, productive, working systems of business into existence which seemed permanent and profitable. They employed entire communities, created vast national wealth, and unified the nation. Yet the impact of big business was devastating to the markets and the business activity of earlier, entrepreneurial America. In the enormous, complex national market, it was impossible for all or even a majority of working Americans to participate. Entrepreneurs had to create great corporations in order to survive in the national market. Great corporations are the units of national markets, the operators in those markets, and there is no remote similarity between them and the entrepreneurial, market activity on which Adam Smith based his economics or Thomas Jefferson his politics. The big business corporation has become, according to economic historian Edward S. Mason,

> . . . so much our most important economic institution and it is so thoroughly integrated into our business culture that to suggest a drastic change in the scope or character of corporate activity is to suggest a drastic alteration in the structure of society. . . . We are now a nation of wage and salaried employees and, in the main, we work for corporations. The days of Jeffersonian democracy are over and nothing can be done to resurrect them. . . .

What price are we paying for our business civilization? is a question more and more Americans ask. What world have we lost in order to live as we do today?

Control of the work and products of factories, machines, and people is the purpose of the big business corporation. Power, not individual independence or liberty, is big business's goal. Growth—of cash, assets, market control, profits—is the ideal, not community standing and not benefit to the commonwealth. The "market pressures" to which big businesses respond are rarely identified with the interests of a community, or of the nation. Only when community or national interests are accompanied by power—often but not always expressed through governments—do big businesses feel it necessary, or in their interest, to respond. While most business leaders agree with the idea expressed by Charles Wilson in the 1950's (he was former president of General Motors, and Secretary of Defense) that "what is good for General Motors"—or any other big business—"is good for America," there are few who think that what is good for Americans in general, or for particular communities, groups, or interests, will be good for business. As General Motors Chairman Roger B. Smith and President F. James McDonald put it in their letter to stockholders in the 1982 Annual Report, the corporation was dedicated "to serve the customer better than anyone else," it was determined to serve stockholder interests and committed to "social responsibilities," but its ultimate "goal" and "pledge" was, they said, "simple." It was "to keep General Motors number one."

But have we lost the lead? Is America—and American business—no longer "number one"? Is that bad?

We Americans, with approximately five percent of the world's population, still consume more than seventy-five percent of the world's manufactured goods, produce more food than any other nation on earth, and use the great majority of the world's raw materials and natural resources every year. But many Americans today doubt the efficiency and the productivity of big business. Our machines and factories consume quantities of nonrenewable resources every year. In the process they have altered the nature of the four ancient elements—air, water, fire, and earth—with which all human beings must live.

Has it all gone too far? Can we afford to clean up the air and the water? stop raining acid on ourselves, our forests and earth, our neighbors? Can we still eat if we stop plowing, leaching out the soil, dumping chemicals on it? Can we any longer afford the kind of mass production and mass consumption we have developed? Can we possibly change?

Extremes of modern big-business logic and practice have only become obvious as the result of the continued expansion of big business throughout the twentieth century. Those extremes have become possible because the community controls which were woven into the patterns of expectation and behavior in the old entrepreneurial civilization were unraveled by big business as it created national and global markets. New controls, based on consumer demands, consumer organization, and consumer protection, as well as on federal government power, regulation, and enforcement, have only slowly and imperfectly developed. Indeed, as James Cook pointed out, for example, in a 1980 *Forbes* article, "organized crime is the logical extension of business." Organized crime has become big business in the modern consumer society; it has used both the markets and the techniques of corporate big business as it has grown. "It is sharp practice turned murderous," as Cook wrote, "tax avoidance made systematic, competition followed to its logical conclusion." The effect, in modern America, of the visible growth of organized crime has been to cast doubt on business as a whole.

If the logic of big business carried to its extreme leads to organized crime, then should the business of America be business?

At the other end of the logical spectrum, the consumer society encourages a big-business variant of entrepreneurship in which it is possible to build very large businesses, borrow enormous sums of money, manipulate the stocks, credit, and asset values of big business corporations, ultimately to buy and sell those very corporations. Big corporations are the units of the national market, and in the global market such corporations have become the commodities of modern entrepreneurs—like the products of farms and manufacturing, or like the public lands of the nineteenth century. Giant corporations, themselves multinational conglomerates containing other corporations, are bought and sold, parts of them "hived off" and sold, other parts reorganized, consolidated, and sometimes also sold. For example (picked at random from *Who Owns Who in America, 1980*):

> Long Life Pen Company
> is owned by Aljac Corporation, which
> is owned by Anja Engineering Corporation, which
> is owned by Scripto Incorporated, which
> is owned by Wilkinson Sword (USA) Incorporated, which
> is owned by Wilkinson Match (North America) Limited, which
> is owned by Wilkinson Match, Limited, United Kingdom, which
> is owned by Allegheny Ludlum Industries Incorporated
> 2 Oliver Plaza, Pittsburgh, Pennsylvania 15222

Growth, control, and assets—like production and markets—have all become abstractions, seemingly divorced from real people, real places, real markets. It is impossible to determine who owns such corporate units, just as it is impossible to determine to what commonwealth, community, or nation they belong.

Business is still the name of the game in America (we have had an immensely popular game called Monopoly for fifty years). American political leaders are sometimes businessmen, always surrounded by business people. American ambassadors have traditionally been wealthy business people, because there are few wealthy enough to be ambassadors who are not business people. To members of the ruling establishments in other countries, it seems obvious that the American establishment is a business establishment. The American government is filled with business people. Before World War II, American businesses were far more aggressive than the American government and its ambassadors in the affairs and markets of other nations. Since 1945, the expansion of American business and the growth of a global market based on American businesses has accompanied the role of world leadership taken on by the United States. To foreigners, even American unions, labor leaders, and workers seem willing participants in business. Despite the eager imitations of the consumer society by other nations since 1945, despite the great successes of Germany and Japan and other nations in the global market, America is still the preeminent business nation in the world.

But if the business of America continues to be business, is it possible that business has a central responsibility for the nation? Is the business of business America?

Americans ask such questions and worry about whether big business is a good thing, or whether it has failed. We are employees and consumers in an economy built on big business. Many work in the massive bureaucracies of multinational corporations, and all of us require the products of big businesses in order to lead satisfactory lives. We have hesitantly, and not unanimously, come to accept some of the institutions of a consumer society—labor unions, consumer credit, government regulation, even (more reluctantly) defense spending and the military-industrial complex it has spawned, to name a few—because we want to benefit from the perceived advances of modern progress, balance the power of big businesses, and help assure the distribution of goods and services.

We are, however, still Americans. We try to find jobs with good pay, security, health and pension plans—so we can have the goods and leisure which mark our liberty, our industry, our independence, and our mobility. We look forward to retirement, which (if we're lucky) will remove us from the control of bosses, and provide us "independent means" (something only the wealthy used to be able to hope for). We "moonlight," so we can rise faster, be more independent, and get more of "all the things money can buy." We find an expense account, a company car, a WATS line all to be signs of individual progress, of rising and success, of independence. We still dream of going into business—and fantasize about making a million—but few of us do. Periodically, newspaper headlines remind us that "A Pioneer Spirit Sweeps Business" (*The New York Times* Sunday Business Section, March 25, 1984), so we know that our business is still peculiarly American.

But most of us do not find liberty, mobility, and independence in business directly. We find them instead in our automobiles and in the supermarkets. Individual control, power, choice are all there, physically and symbolically. In mass-produced, consumer-marketed, credit-purchased cars all of us can go places, be mobile, display our prowess and success, choose our companions, be safe and entertained in a hostile world, serve our families, our car pools, and our communities, and even transport goods to and from the market.

Phyllis Rose, in a *New York Times* article (April 12, 1984), clearly and humorously characterized the active, meaningful sense of engagement in America's business that comes from the supermarket:

> Last year a new Waldbaum's Food Mart opened in the shopping mall. . . . This is the wonderful egalitarianism of American business . . . the same chain stores with the same merchandise from coast to coast. . . .
>
> Another wonder . . . is Caldor, the discount department store. . . . I go to Caldor the way English people go to pubs: out of sociability. To get away from my house. To widen my horizons. For culture's sake. . . .
>
> It is a misunderstanding of the American retail store to think we go there necessarily to buy. Some of us shop. There's

> a difference. Shopping has many purposes, the least interesting of which is to acquire new articles. We shop to cheer ourselves up. We shop to practice decision-making. We shop to be useful and productive members of our class and society. We shop to remind ourselves how much is available to us. We shop to remind ourselves how much is to be striven for. We shop to assert our superiority to the material objects that spread themselves before us. . . .
>
> You need the feeling of power that comes with buying or not buying. . . . You need the feeling that someone wants something you have—even if it's just your money. . . .
>
> Caldor, Waldbaum's, Bob's Surplus—these, perhaps, are our cathedrals.

Pushing carts through the aisles of a supermarket, Americans find independence, the individual pursuit of happiness, and satisfying marketplace activity by making choices and decisions, by getting bargains, by keeping up with the Joneses, by checking out the goods and beating out the competition, and above all by serving ourselves. These preeminently consumer activities, in a society dominated by big business and mass production, are the threads which tie us all still to America's business.

Select Bibliography

Because of space limitations, fewer than one-third of the more than one thousand books, document collections, and articles I have used in writing this book are listed here. Under each of the chronological divisions of the book, by major subject headings, I list the works I have quoted; the works from which I have taken ideas and interpretations; and a selection of works which offer insight and substance to a reader interested in pursuing a subject further. I have not included collections of articles and documents, general business histories, or many histories of companies and industries—all of which are valuable and have provided me with substantive information and insight. For those who desire further reading in business history, I recommend the references and bibliographies in the works listed, particularly in the works of Thomas C. Cochran and Alfred D. Chandler, Jr., and the bibliographies included in most general economic histories of the United States.

Books and articles are cited only once, under the subject for which they were first used.

CREATING AMERICAN BUSINESS 1565–1776

General economic and business developments: Richard D. Brown, *Modernization: The Transformation of American Life, 1600–1865* (New York,

1976); Thomas C. Cochran, *Business in American Life: A History* (New York, 1972) and *200 Years of American Business* (New York, 1977); Douglas C. North, *Growth and Welfare in the American Past: A New Economic History*, 2nd ed. (Englewood Cliffs, N.J., 1974), and with Terry L. Anderson and Peter J. Hill, 3rd ed. (1983): Stuart Bruchey, *The Roots of American Economic Growth, 1607–1861: An Essay in Social Causation* (New York, 1965).

The development of the colonial economy: Alice Hanson Jones, *Wealth of a Nation to Be: The American Colonies on the Eve of the Revolution* (New York, 1980); Allan Kulikoff, " 'Growth and Welfare in Early America,' An Essay Review," *William and Mary Quarterly* 39 (1982); Edmund S. Morgan, "The First American Boom: Virginia, 1618–1630," *William and Mary Quarterly* 28 (1971): Thad W. Tate and David L. Ammerman, eds., *The Chesapeake in the Seventeenth Century: Essays on Anglo-American Society* (New York, 1979).

The growth of economic ideology: Louis Dumont, *From Mandeville to Marx: The Genesis and Triumph of Economic Ideology* (Chicago, Ill., 1977); Joyce Oldham Appleby, *Economic Thought and Ideology in Seventeenth Century England* (Princeton, N.J., 1978); J. E. Crowley, *This Sheba Self: The Conceptualization of Economic Life in Eighteenth Century America* (Baltimore, Md., 1974); J. G. A. Pocock, "Virtue and Commerce in the Eighteenth Century," *Journal of Interdisciplinary History* 3 (1972); William B. Scott, *In Pursuit of Happiness: American Concepts of Property from the Seventeenth to the Twentieth Century* (Bloomington, Ind., 1978); Adam Smith, *An Enquiry into the Nature and Causes of the Wealth of Nations* (Chicago, Ill., 1952); William Appleman Williams, "The Age of Mercantilism: An Interpretation of the American Political Economy, 1763 to 1828," *William and Mary Quarterly* 15 (1958).

Trade, merchants, and companies: Bernard Bailyn, *The New England Merchants in the Seventeenth Century* (Cambridge, Mass., 1955); W. T. Baxter, *The House of Hancock: Business in Boston, 1724–1775* (Cambridge, Mass., 1945); William Bradford, *Of Plymouth Plantation, 1620–1647*, Samuel Eliot Morison, ed. (New York, 1952); Wesley Frank Craven, *The Virginia Company of London, 1606–1624* (Williamsburg, Va., 1957); Richard Beale Davis, ed., *William Fitzhugh and His Chesapeake World, 1676–1701: The Fitzhugh Letters and Other Documents* (Chapel Hill, N.C., 1963); James B. Hedges, *The Browns of Providence Plantations* (Cambridge, Mass., 1952); Keach Johnson, "The Baltimore Company Seeks English Markets: A Study of the Anglo-American Iron Trade, 1731–1755," *William and Mary Quarterly* 16 (1959); Aubrey C. Land, *The Dulanys of Maryland: A Biographical Study of Daniel Du-*

lany, The Elder (1685–1753) and Daniel Dulany, the Younger (1722–1797) (Baltimore, Md., 1955); Richard Pares, *Yankees and Creoles: The Trade Between North America and the West Indies before the American Revolution* (New York, 1956); James Wharton, *The Bounty of the Chesapeake: Fishing in Colonial Virginia* (Williamsburg, Va., 1957).

Land and farmers: Robert Beverly, *The History and Present State of Virginia* (1705), Louis B. Wright, ed. (Chapel Hill, N.C., 1947); Paul G. E. Clemens, *The Atlantic Economy and Colonial Maryland's Eastern Shore: From Tobacco to Grain* (Ithaca, N.Y., 1980); Avery O. Craven, *Soil Exhaustion as a Factor in the Agricultural History of Virginia and Maryland, 1606–1860* (Urbana, Ill., 1926); Richard Eburne, *Plaine Path-Way to Plantations* (London, 1624); Robert E. Gallman, "Influences on the Distribution of Landholdings in Early Colonial North Carolina," *Journal of Economic History* 42 (1982); Darrett B. Rutman, "Governor Winthrop's Garden Crop: The Significance of Agriculture in the Early Commerce of Massachusetts Bay," *William and Mary Quarterly* 20 (1963).

Communities and control of business: J. R. T. Hughes, *Social Control in the Colonial Economy* (Charlottesville, Va., 1976); Arthur L. Jensen, *The Maritime Commerce of Colonial Philadelphia* (Madison, Wisc., 1963); Jacob M. Price, "Economic Function and the Growth of American Port Towns in the Eighteenth Century," *Perspectives in American History* 8 (1974); Leila Sellers, *Charleston Business on the Eve of the American Revolution* (Chapel Hill, N.C., 1934); Harry S. Stout, "Religion, Communication, and the Ideological Origins of the American Revolution," *William and Mary Quarterly* 34 (1977).

Social structure and mobility: Linda Auwers Bissell, "From One Generation to Another: Mobility in Seventeenth Century Windsor, Connecticut," *William and Mary Quarterly* 31 (1974); Paul Boyer and Stephen Nissenbaum, *Salem Possessed: The Social Origins of Witchcraft* (Cambridge, Mass., 1974); John Browne, *The Marchants Avizo* (London, 1607); Bruce C. Daniels, "Economic Development in Colonial and Revolutionary Connecticut; An Overview," *William and Mary Quarterly* 37 (1980); John Demos, *A Little Commonwealth: Family Life in Plymouth Colony* (New York, 1970); Jack P. Greene and J. R. Pole, eds., *Colonial British America: Essays in the New History of the Early Modern Era* (Baltimore, Md., 1984); Philip J. Greven, Jr., *Four Generations: Population, Land, and Family in Colonial Andover, Massachusetts* (Ithaca, N.Y., 1970); James A. Henretta, *The Evolution of American Society, 1700–1815: An Interdisciplinary Approach* (Lexington, Mass., 1973); Peter Laslett, *The World We Have Lost* (New York, 1965); Russell R. Menard, "From Servant to Freeholder: Status, Mobility and Property

Accumulation in Seventeenth Century Maryland," *William and Mary Quarterly* 30 (1973).

Work, servants, and slavery: Richard S. Dunn, *Sugar and Slaves: The Rise of the Planter Class in the English West Indies, 1624–1713* (Chapel Hill, N.C., 1972); David W. Galenson, *White Servitude in Colonial America: An Economic Analysis* (Cambridge, Mass., 1981); Edmund S. Morgan, *American Slavery, American Freedom* (New York, 1975); Abbot Emerson Smith, *Colonists in Bondage: White Servitude and Convict Labor in America, 1607–1776* (Chapel Hill, N.C., 1947).

Benjamin Franklin: Benjamin Franklin, *Advice to a Young Tradesman. Written by an Old One* (Boston, 1762?), *Information to Those Who Would Remove to America* (London, 1794); Chester E. Jorgenson and Frank Luther Mott, eds., *Benjamin Franklin: Representative Selections, with Introduction, Bibliography, and Notes* (New York, 1962); Frederick B. Tolles, "Benjamin Franklin's Business Mentors: The Philadelphia Quaker Merchants," *William and Mary Quarterly* 1 (1947).

THE FABRIC OF A BUSINESS CIVILIZATION 1776–1850

General works and comparative developments: Carl Abbott, *Boosters and Businessmen: Popular Economic Thought and Urban Growth in the Antebellum Middle West* (Westport, Conn., 1981); Vincent P. Carosso, *Investment Banking in America: A History* (Cambridge, Mass., 1970); John F. Kasson, *Civilizing the Machine: Technology and Republican Values in America, 1776–1900* (New York, 1976); David S. Landes, *The Unbound Prometheus* (Cambridge, 1969); Jonathan Zeitlin, "Alternative Paths to European Industrialization, 1780–1914," Lectures in the History Faculty, Cambridge University, Lent Term, 1983.

Paying for independence: Lance Banning, "Republican Ideology and the Triumph of the Constitution, 1789–1793," *William and Mary Quarterly* 31 (1974); Robert A. East, *Business Enterprise in the American Revolutionary Era* (New York, 1938); E. James Ferguson, *The Power of the Purse: A History of American Public Finance, 1776–1790* (Chapel Hill, N.C., 1961); Eric Foner, *Tom Paine and Revolutionary America* (New York, 1976); Robert F. Jones, "William Duer and the Business of Government in the Era of the American Revolution," *William and Mary Quarterly* 32 (1975); Ralph Lerner, "Commerce and Character: The Anglo-American as New-Model Man," *William and Mary Quarterly* 36 (1979); Clarence L. Ver Steeg, *Robert Morris: Revolutionary Financier* (Philadelphia, Pa., 1954); Gordon S. Wood, *The Creation of the American Republic, 1776–1787* (Chapel Hill, N.C., 1969).

Business on the land: Joyce Oldham Appleby, "Commercial Farming and the 'Agrarian Myth' in the Early Republic," *Journal of American History* 68 (1982), "The Social Origins of American Revolutionary Ideology," *Journal of American History* 64 (1978), and "What Is Still American in the Political Philosophy of Thomas Jefferson?" *William and Mary Quarterly* 39 (1982); Richard Buel, Jr., *Securing the Revolution: Ideology in American Politics, 1789–1815* (Ithaca, N.Y., 1972); Paul W. Gates, *The Farmer's Age: Agriculture 1815–1860* (New York, 1960); James A. Henretta, "Families and Farms: *Mentalité* in Pre-Industrial America," *William and Mary Quarterly* 35 (1978).

Merchants: Jonathan Goldstein, *Philadelphia and the China Trade, 1682–1846: Commercial, Cultural, and Attitudinal Effects* (University Park, Pa., 1978); Oscar and Mary Handlin, *Commonwealth, a Study of the Role of Government in the American Economy: Massachusetts, 1774–1861* (New York, 1947); Judith McCaw, "Specialization and the Origins of Agribusiness: John Hare Powel and American Livestock Breeding," *The Business History Conference,* March 8–10, 1984 (Hartford, Conn.); James Duncan Phillips, *Salem and the Indies: The Story of the Great Commercial Era of the City* (Boston, 1947); Kenneth W. Porter, *John Jacob Astor, Businessman* (Cambridge, Mass., 1931), 2 vols.

The useful corporation: Joseph S. Davis, *Essays in the Earlier History of American Corporations* (1917; reissue New York, 1965), 2 vols.; Oscar and Mary Handlin, "Origins of the American Business Corporation," *Journal of Economic History* 5 (1945); James Willard Hurst, *The Legitimacy of the Business Corporation in the Law of the United States, 1780–1970* (Charlottesville, Va., 1970); William E. Nelson, *Americanization of the Common Law: The Impact of Legal Change on Massachusetts Society, 1760–1830* (Cambridge, Mass., 1975); Howard B. Rock, *Artisans of the New Republic: The Tradesmen of New York City in the Age of Jefferson* (New York, 1984); Ronald E. Seavoy, "The Public Service Origins of the American Business Corporation," *Business History Review* 52 (1978).

Roads, canals, and early railroads: Ira Cohen, "The Auction System in the Port of New York, 1817–1837," *Business History Review* 45 (1971); Carter Goodrich, *Government Promotion of American Canals and Railroads, 1800–1890* (New York, 1960); Alvin F. Harlow, *Old Towpaths: The Story of the American Canal Era* (New York, 1926); Arthur M. Johnson and Barry E. Supple, *Boston Capitalists and Western Railroads: A Study in the Nineteenth Century Railroad Investment Process* (Cambridge, Mass., 1967); Nathan Miller, *The Enterprise of a Free People: Aspects of Economic Development in New York State during the Canal*

Period, 1792–1838 (Ithaca, N.Y., 1962); George Rogers Taylor, *The Transportation Revolution, 1815–1860* (New York, 1951); Peter Temin, *The Jacksonian Economy* (New York, 1969).

The richest men in America: Donald R. Adams, Jr., *Finance and Enterprise in Early America: A Study of Stephen Girard's Bank, 1812 1831* (Philadelphia, Pa., 1978); Bernard De Voto, *Across the Wide Missouri* (Boston, Mass., 1947); Sigmund Diamond, *The Reputation of the American Businessman* (New York, 1966); Henry Emerson Wildes, *Lonely Midas: The Story of Stephen Girard* (New York, 1943).

The business of working machines: Alfred D. Chandler, Jr., "Anthracite Coal and the Beginnings of the Industrial Revolution in the United States," *Business History Review* 46 (1972); George S. Gibb, *The Saco-Lowell Shops: Textile Machinery Building in New England, 1812–1949* (Cambridge, Mass., 1950); Siegfried Giedion, *Mechanization Takes Command: A Contribution to Anonymous History* (New York, 1969); Constance McLaughlin Green, *Eli Whitney and the Birth of American Technology* (Boston, Mass., 1956); Dolores Greenberg, "Reassessing the Power Patterns of the Industrial Revolution: An Anglo-American Comparison," *American Historical Review* 87 (1982); David J. Jeremy, *Transatlantic Industrial Revolution: The Diffusion of Textile Technologies between Britain and America, 1790–1830s* (Cambridge, Mass., 1981); Jeanette Mirsky and Allan Nevins, *The World of Eli Whitney* (New York, 1952); L. T. C. Rolt, *A Short History of Machine Tools* (Cambridge, Mass., 1965); Merritt Roe Smith, *Harpers Ferry Armory and the New Technology: The Challenge of Change* (Ithaca, N.Y., 1977) and "Technology, Culture, and the First Industrial Revolution," Seminar on American Social and Political History, *American Antiquarian Society*, February 17, 1984; Barbara M. Tucker, "The Merchant, the Manufacturer, and the Factory Manager: The Case of Samuel Slater," *Business History Review* 55 (1981); Caroline F. Ware, *The Early New England Cotton Manufacture: A Study in Industrial Beginnings* (1931; reissue New York, 1966).

The spirit of manufacturing: Donald R. Adams, Jr., "The Standard of Living During American Industrialization: Evidence from the Brandywine Region, 1800–1860," *Journal of Economic History* 42 (1982); Robert F. Dalzell, Jr., "The Rise of the Waltham-Lowell System and Some Thoughts on the Political Economy of Modernization in Ante-Bellum Massachusetts," *Perspectives in American History* 9 (1975); Thomas Dublin, *Women at Work: The Transformation of Work and Community in Lowell, Massachusetts, 1826–1860* (New York, 1979); Benita Eisler, ed., *The Lowell Offering: Writings by New England Mill Women* (New

York, 1978); Paul G. Faler, *Mechanics and Manufacturers in the Early Industrial Revolution: Lynn, Massachusetts, 1780–1960* (Albany, 1981); Constance McLaughlin Green, *Holyoke, Massachusetts: A Case History of the Industrial Revolution in America* (New Haven, Conn., 1939); Herbert G. Gutman, *Work, Culture, and Society in Industrializing America: An Essay in American Working-Class and Social History* (New York, 1975); Eric J. Hobsbawm, *Primitive Rebels: Studies in Archaic Forms of Social Movement in the 19th and 20th Centuries* (New York, 1963); William H. Lazonick, "Production Relations, Labor Productivity, and Choice of Technique: British and U.S. Cotton Spinning," *Journal of Economic History* 41 (1981); Gerda Lerner, "The Lady and the Mill Girl: Changes in the Status of Women in the Age of Jackson," *Mid-continent American Studies Journal* 10 (1969); David Montgomery, "The Shuttle and the Cross: Weavers and Artisans in the Kensington Riots of 1844," *Journal of Social History* 5 (1972), and *Workers' Control in America: Studies in the History of Work, Technology, and Labor Struggles* (Cambridge, Mass., 1979); Edward Pessen, *Most Uncommon Jacksonians: The Radical Leaders of the Early Labor Movement* (Albany, N.Y., 1967); E. P. Thompson, *The Making of the English Working Class* (New York, 1963).

Managing slavery: James O. Breedon, ed., *Advice among Masters: The Ideal in Slave Management in the Old South* (Westport, Conn., 1980); Stuart Bruchey, ed., *Cotton and the Growth of the American Economy: 1790–1860* (New York, 1967); Philip S. Foner, *Business and Slavery: The New York Merchants and the Irrepressible Conflict* (Chapel Hill, N.C., 1941); Elizabeth Fox-Genovese and Eugene D. Genovese, *Fruits of Merchant Capital: Slavery and Bourgeois Property in the Rise and Expansion of Capitalism* (New York, 1983); James Oakes, *The Ruling Race: A History of American Slaveholders* (New York, 1982).

Samuel Colt and the American system: Rex Burns, *Success in America: The Yeoman Dream and the Industrial Revolution* (Amherst, Mass., 1976); Felicia J. Deyrup, *Arms Makers of the Connecticut Valley: A Regional Study of the Economic Development of the Small Arms Industry, 1798–1870* (Northampton, Mass., 1948); H. J. Habakkuk, *American and British Technology in the Nineteenth Century: The Search for Labor-Saving Inventions* (Cambridge, Mass., 1962); Bern Keating, *The Flamboyant Mr. Colt and His Deadly Six-Shooter* (Garden City, N.Y., 1978); *Report of the Committee on the Machinery of the United States of America,* Presented to the House of Commons, in Pursuance of their Address of the 10th July 1855 (London, 1855); Jack Rohan, *Yankee Arms Maker: The Incredible Career of Samuel Colt* (New York, 1935); Nathan

Rosenberg, *Technology and American Economic Growth* (New York, 1972); Carl Siracusa, *A Mechanical People: Perceptions of the Industrial Order in Massachusetts, 1815–1880* (Middletown, Conn., 1979).

BIG BUSINESS AND THE NATIONAL MARKET 1850–1925

General and comparative developments: Thomas C. Cochran, "The Paradox of American Economic Growth," *Journal of American History* 61 (1975); Carl N. Degler, *The Age of the Economic Revolution, 1876–1900* (Glenview, Ill., 1967); David DeLeon, *The American as Anarchist: Reflections on Indigenous Radicalism* (Baltimore, Md., 1978); Daniel T. Rogers, *The Work Ethic in Industrial America, 1850–1920* (Chicago, Ill., 1974); Martin J. Weiner, *English Culture and the Decline of the Industrial Spirit, 1850–1980* (Cambridge, Mass., 1981).

Railroads as big business: Edward Atkinson, *The Industrial Progress of the Nation* (New York, 1890); Alfred D. Chandler, Jr., "The Railroads: Pioneers in Modern Corporate Management." *Business History Review* 39 (1965); Thomas C. Cochran, *Railroad Leaders, 1845–1890: The Business Mind in Action* (Cambridge, Mass., 1953); Albert Fishlow, *American Railroads and the Transformation of the Ante-Bellum Economy* (Cambridge, Mass., 1965); Gabriel Kolko, *Railroads and Regulation, 1877–1916* (New York, 1970); Albro Martin, *James J. Hill and the Opening of the Northwest* (New York, 1976); John F. Stover, *American Railroads* (Chicago, Ill., 1961).

Civil War business: Ralph Andreano, ed., *The Economic Impact of the American Civil War* (Cambridge, Mass., 1967); Russell F. Weigley, *Quartermaster General of the Union Army: A Biography of M. C. Meigs* (New York, 1959).

Big-business revolution: Bruce Bringhurst, *Antitrust and the Oil Monopoly: The Standard Oil Cases, 1890–1911* (Westport, Conn., 1979); Alfred D. Chandler, Jr., "The Beginnings of 'Big Business' in American Industry," *Business History Review* 33 (1959); Thomas C. Cochran and William Miller, *The Age of Enterprise: A Social History of Industrial America*, revised ed. (New York, 1961); Arthur Menzies Johnson, *The Development of American Petroleum Pipelines: A Study in Private Enterprise and Public Policy, 1862–1906* (Ithaca, N.Y., 1956); Edward S. Mason, ed., *The Corporation in Modern Society* (Cambridge, Mass., 1960); Allan Nevins, *Study in Power: John D. Rockefeller, Industrialist and Philanthropist* (New York, 1953), 2 vols.; Ida M. Tarbell, *The History of the Standard Oil Company, Briefer Version*, David M. Chalmers, ed. (New York, 1966), and *The Nationalizing of Business, 1878–1898* (New York, 1936).

Agribusiness: Gilbert C. Fite, *American Farmers: The New Minority* (Bloomington, Ind., 1981); W. Turrentine Jackson, *The Enterprising Scot: Investors in the American West after 1873* (Edinburgh, 1968); Joseph M. McFadden, "Monopoly in Barbed Wire: The Formation of the American Steel and Wire Company," *Business History Review* 52 (1978); Dan Morgan, *Merchants of Grain* (New York, 1979); Donald L. Winters, *Farmers Without Farms: Agricultural Tenancy in Nineteenth Century Iowa* (Westport, Conn., 1978).

Counterrevolution, workers, and protest: Edward Bellamy, *Looking Backward, 2000–1887* (Boston, Mass., 1887); David Brody, *Steelworkers in America: The Nonunion Era* (Cambridge, Mass., 1960); Robert V. Bruce, *1877: Year of Violence* (Indianapolis, Ind., 1959); Michael J. Cassity, "Modernization and Social Crisis: The Knights of Labor and a Midwest Community, 1885–1886," *Journal of American History* 66 (1979); Alan Dawley, *Class and Community: The Industrial Revolution in Lynn* (Cambridge, Mass., 1976); Philip S. Foner, *The Industrial Workers of the World, 1905–1917* (New York, 1965); John A. Garraty, ed., *Labor and Capital in the Gilded Age* (Boston, Mass., 1968); Henry George, *Progress and Poverty* (New York, 1880); James Willard Hurst, *Law and the Conditions of Freedom in the Nineteenth Century United States* (Madison, Wisc., 1967); John H. M. Laslett, *Labor and the Left: A Study of Socialist and Radical Influences in the American Labor Movement, 1881–1924* (New York, 1970); *Report of the Committee of the Senate upon the Relations Between Labor and Capital and the Testimony Taken by the Committee* (Washington, D.C., 1885), 5 vols.; John Tebbel, *From Rags to Riches: Horatio Alger, Jr., and the American Dream* (New York, 1963); James Weinstein, *The Decline of Socialism in America, 1912–1925* (New York, 1967).

Robber barons: John O. Cawelty, *Apostles of the Self-Made Man: Changing Concepts of Success in America* (Chicago, Ill., 1965); E. L. Godkin, "Cooperation," *North American Review* 106 (Jan. 1868), *Problems of Modern Democracy: Political and Economic Essays,* Morton Keller, ed. (Cambridge, Mass., 1966), and "Social Classes in the Republic," *Atlantic Monthly* 78 (Dec. 1896); John N. Ingham, *The Iron Barons: A Social Analysis of an American Urban Elite, 1874–1965* (Westport, Conn., 1978); Matthew Josephson, *The Robber Barons: The Great American Capitalists, 1861–1901* (New York, 1934); Edward C. Kirkland, *Dream and Thought in the Business Community, 1860–1900* (Ithaca, N.Y., 1956); Irvin G. Wyllie, *The Self-Made Man in America: The Myths of Rags to Riches* (New Brunswick, N.J., 1954).

The Constitution and business nationalism: Thomas M. Cooley, *A Treatise on the Constitutional Limitations Which Rest upon the Legisla-*

tive Power of the States of the American Union (Boston, Mass., 1868); Sidney Fine, *Laissez Faire and the General-Welfare State: A Study of Conflict in American Thought, 1865–1901* (Ann Arbor, Mich., 1956); Clyde E. Jacobs, *Law Writers and the Courts: The Influence of Thomas M. Cooley, Christopher G. Tiedeman, and John F. Dillon upon American Constitutional Law* (Berkeley, Calif., 1954); Robert Green McCloskey, *American Conservatism in the Age of Enterprise: A Study of William Graham Sumner, Stephen J. Field, and Andrew Carnegie* (Cambridge, Mass., 1951); Arthur Selwyn Miller, *The Supreme Court and American Capitalism* (New York, 1968); Benjamin R. Twiss, *Lawyers and the Constitution: How Laissez Faire Came to the Supreme Court* (Princeton, N.J., 1942).

Investment, mergers, expansion, and management: Loren Baritz, *Servants of Power: A History of the Use of Social Science in American Industry* (Middletown, Conn., 1960); William H. Becker, *The Dynamics of Business Government Relations: Industry and Exports, 1891–1921* (Chicago, Ill., 1982); Alfred D. Chandler, Jr., *The Visible Hand: The Managerial Revolution in American Business* (Cambridge, Mass., 1977); Sherman Cochran, *Big Business in China: Sino-Foreign Rivalry in the Cigarette Industry, 1890–1930* (Cambridge, Mass., 1980); John H. Dunning, *American Investment in British Manufacturing Industry* (London, 1958); Louis Galambos, *The Public Image of Big Business in America, 1880–1940: A Quantitative Study in Social Change* (Baltimore, Md., 1975); Dolores Greenberg, *Financiers and Railroads, 1869–1889: A Study of Morton, Bliss and Company* (Newark, Del., 1980); Samuel Haber, *Efficiency and Uplift: Scientific Management in the Progressive Era, 1890–1920* (Chicago, Ill., 1964); Helen M. Kramer, "Harvesters and High Finance: Formation of the International Harvester Company," *Business History Review* 38 (1964); Frederic S. Lee, *The Human Machine and Industrial Efficiency* (New York, 1918); Daniel Nelson, *Frederick W. Taylor and the Rise of Scientific Management* (Madison, Wisc., 1980); Ralph L. Nelson, *Merger Movements in American Industry, 1895–1956* (Princeton, N.J., 1959); Frederick W. Taylor, *Scientific Management* (New York, 1947); Mira Wilkins, *The Emergence of Multinational Enterprise: American Business Abroad from the Colonial Era to 1914* (Cambridge, Mass., 1970).

Corporate control and community: Daniel Bell, *Work and Its Discontents: The Cult of Efficiency in America* (Boston, Mass., 1956); Edward D. Berkowitz and Kim McQuaid, "Businessman and Bureaucrat: The Evolution of the American Social Welfare System, 1900–1940," *Journal of Economic History* 38 (1978); Adolf A. Berle and Gardiner C. Means, *The Modern Corporation and Private Property*, revised ed. (New York,

1967); Stuart D. Brandes, *American Welfare Capitalism, 1880–1940* (Chicago, Ill., 1976); Stanley Buder, *Pullman: An Experiment in Industrial Order and Community Planning, 1880–1930* (New York, 1967); Andrew Carnegie, *The Gospel of Wealth and Other Timely Essays* (New York, 1901), and *Problems of Today: Wealth—Labor—Socialism* (New York, 1909); Peter F. Drucker, *The New Society: The Anatomy of the Industrial Order* (New York, 1950); Harold U. Faulkner, *The Decline of Laissez-Faire, 1897–1917* (New York, 1962); Louis Galambos, *Competition and Cooperation: The Emergence of a National Trade Association* (Baltimore, Md., 1966); Louis M. Hacker, *The World of Andrew Carnegie, 1865–1901* (Philadelphia, Pa., 1968); Edward C. Kirkland, *Business in the Gilded Age: The Conservatives' Balance Sheet* (Madison, Wisc., 1955); Thorstein Veblen, *The Theory of Business Enterprise*, 2nd ed. (New York, 1915) and *The Theory of the Leisure Class: An Economic Study of Institutions* (New York, 1934); Robert H. Wiebe, *Businessmen and Reform: A Study of the Progressive Movement* (Cambridge, Mass., 1962) and *The Search for Order, 1877–1920* (New York, 1967); W. D. Rubenstein, "Entrepreneurial Effort and Entrepreneurial Success: Peak Wealth-Holding in Three Societies, 1850–1939," *Business History* 25 (1983).

World War I: Robert D. Cuff, "Herbert Hoover, the Ideology of Voluntarism and War Organization during the Great War," *Journal of American History* 64 (1977), and *The War Industries Board* (Baltimore, Md., 1973); Paul A. C. Koistiner, "The 'Industrial-Military Complex' in Historical Perspective: World War I," *Business History Review* 41 (1967); George Soule, *Prosperity Decade: From War to Depression; 1917–1929* (New York, 1964).

CONSUMING BUSINESS 1900–1984

Consumer society and economy: Daniel Bell, *The Cultural Contradictions of Capitalism* (New York, 1976); Raymond E. Callahan, *Education and the Cult of Efficiency: A Study of the Social Forces That Have Shaped the Administration of the Public Schools* (Chicago, Ill., 1962); Thomas C. Cochran, *The American Business System, A Historical Perspective, 1900–1955* (Cambridge, Mass., 1957); Seymour Martin Lipset and William Schneider, *The Confidence Gap: Business, Labor, and Government in the Public Mind* (New York, 1983); Gardiner C. Means, *The Corporate Revolution in America: Economic Reality vs. Economic Theory* (New York, 1962); Humbert S. Nelli, *The Business of Crime: Italians and Syndicate Crime in the United States* (New York, 1976); J. J. Servan-Schreiber, *The American Challenge* (New York, 1968); Eric Sevareid with John Case, *Enterprise: Doing Business in America* (New York,

1983); Jonathan Steinberg, "Why the Recession May Last Until 1996," *Financial Times* (London, 1982); Charles Wilson, *The History of Unilever: A Study in Economic Growth and Social Change* (New York, 1968), 3 vols.

Ford and automobiles: James J. Flink, *America Adopts the Automobile, 1895–1910* (Cambridge, Mass., 1970); James Foreman-Peck, "The American Challenge of the Twenties: Multinationals and the European Motor Industry," *Journal of Economic History* 42 (1982); Allan Nevins and Frank Ernest Hill, *Ford: I. The Times, the Man, the Company* (1954), *II. Expansion and Challenge, 1915–1932* (1957), *III. Decline and Rebirth* (1963) (New York); John B. Rae, *The Road and the Car in American Life* (Cambridge, Mass., 1971); Alfred P. Sloan, *My Years with General Motors* (Garden City, N.Y., 1964); Mira Wilkins and Frank Ernest Hill, *American Business Abroad: Ford on Six Continents* (Detroit, Mich., 1964).

Consumer marketing and retailing: Boris Emmet and John E. Jeuck, *Catalogues and Counters: A History of Sears, Roebuck & Co.* (Chicago, Ill., 1950); Ralph M. Hower, *History of Macy's of New York, 1858–1919; Chapters in the Evolution of the Department Store* (Cambridge, Mass., 1943); Godfrey M. Lebhar, *Chain Stores in America, 1859–1950* (New York, 1952); Henry E. Resseguie, "Alexander Turney Stewart and the Development of the Department Store, 1832–1876," *Business History Review* 39 (1965); Peter Samson, "The Department Store, Its Past and Its Future: A Review Article," *Business History Review* 55 (1981).

Advertising, the media, public relations: Edward L. Bernays, *Biography of an Idea* (New York, 1965) and *Public Relations* (New York, 1952); Merle E. Curti, "The Changing Concept of Human Nature in the Literature of American Advertising," *Business History Review* 41 (1967); Douglas N. Dickson, ed., *Business and Its Public* (New York, 1984); Stewart Ewen, *Captains of Consciousness: Advertising and the Social Roots of the Consumer Culture* (New York, 1976); Morrill Heald, *The Social Responsibilities of Business: Company and Community, 1900–1960* (Cleveland, Ohio, 1970); Ralph M. Hower, *The History of an Advertising Agency: N. W. Ayer and Son at Work, 1869–1949* (Cambridge, Mass., 1949); The Roper Organization, Inc., *Public Perceptions of Television and Other Mass Media: A Twenty-Year Review, 1959–1978* (New York, 1979); John Tebbel, *The Media in America* (New York, 1974); Richard S. Tedlow, *Keeping the Corporate Image: Public Relations and Business, 1900–1950* (Greenwich, Conn., 1979).

Critics and defenders of business: Henry Adams, *The Education of Henry Adams* (New York, 1918); James Truslow Adams, *Our Business*

Civilization (New York, 1929); Irving Bernstein, *The Turbulent Years: A History of the American Worker, 1933–1941* (Boston, Mass., 1970); Harry Braverman, *Labor and Monopoly Capital: The Degradation of Work in the Twentieth Century* (New York, 1975); David Brody, *Workers in Industrial America: Essays on the Twentieth Century Struggle* (New York, 1980); John Kenneth Galbraith, *American Capitalism: The Concept of Countervailing Power* (Boston, Mass., 1952) and *The Great Crash* (Boston, Mass., 1955); C. Wright Mills, *The Power Elite* (New York, 1956); Ferdinand Pecora, *Wall Street under Oath: The Story of Our Modern Money Changers* (New York, 1939); Richard H. Pells, *Radical Visions and American Dreams: Culture and Social Thought in the Depression Years* (New York, 1974); James W. Prothro, *The Dollar Decade: Business Ideas in the 1920's* (Baton Rouge, La., 1954).

World War II, defense, and consuming success: Robert D. Cuff, "An Organizational Perspective on the Military-Industrial Complex," *Business History Review*, 52 (1978); James Fallows, *National Defense* (New York, 1982); J. Ronald Fox, *Arming America: How the U.S. Buys Weapons* (Cambridge, Mass., 1974); Jacques S. Gansler, *The Defense Industry* (Cambridge, Mass., 1980); Donald J. Mrozek, "The Truman Administration and the Enlistment of the Aviation Industry in Postwar Defense," *Business History Review* 48 (1974); David Riesman, *Abundance for What? and Other Essays* (Garden City, N.Y., 1964), and with Nathan Glazer and Reuel Denney, *The Lonely Crowd: A Study of the Changing American Character* (New Haven, Conn., 1950); Roland N. Stromberg, "American Business and the Approach of War, 1935–1941," *Journal of Economic History* 13 (1953); Francis Walton, *Miracle of World War II: How American Industry Made Victory Possible* (New York, 1956); Gerald T. White, *Billions for Defense: Government Financing by the Defense Plant Corporation During World War II* (University, Ala., 1980); Adam Yarmolinsky, *The Military Establishment: Its Impact on American Society* (New York, 1971).

Conglomerates, multinationals, and the global market: Richard J. Barnet and Ronald E. Müller, *Global Reach: The Power of the Multinational Corporations* (New York, 1974); Yale Brozen, *Concentration, Mergers, and Public Policy* (New York, 1982); Alfred D. Chandler, Jr., *Strategy and Structure: Chapters in the History of the Industrial Enterprise* (Cambridge, Mass., 1962); Rodney Clark, *The Japanese Company* (New Haven, Conn., 1979); Jon Didrichsen, "The Development of Diversified and Conglomerate Firms in the U.S., 1920–1970," *Business History Review* 46 (1972); Richard Eells, *Global Corporations: The Emerging System of World Economic Power* (New York, 1972); Henry Ford II, "Turning Points," *Quest/81*, May 1981; John Kenneth Galbraith, *The*

New Industrial State (Boston, Mass., 1967); Paul H. Giddens, "Historical Origins of the Adoption of the EXXON Name and Trademark," *Business History Review* 47 (1973); Burton I, Kaufman, "Mideast Multinational Oil, U.S. Foreign Policy, and Antitrust: The 1950's," *Journal of American History* 63 (1977); Alpheus T. Mason, "Business Organized as Power: The New Imperium in Imperio," *American Political Science Review* 44 (1950); Gerald D. Nash, *United States Oil Policy, 1890–1964: Business and Government in the Twentieth Century* (Pittsburgh, Pa., 1968); Glenn Porter, ed., *Multinational Enterprise, Business History Review* 48 (1974); Raymond Vernon, *Sovereignty at Bay: The Multinational Spread of U.S. Enterprises* (New York, 1971); Rolf H. Wild, *Management by Compulsion: The Corporate Urge to Grow* (Boston, Mass., 1978); Mira Wilkins, *The Maturing of Multinational Enterprise: American Business Abroad from 1914 to 1970* (Cambridge, Mass., 1974); Joan Hoff Wilson, *American Business and Foreign Policy, 1920–1933* (Lexington, Ky., 1971).

Consumer business people: Marilyn Bender, "Another Gamble for the Pritzkers," *The New York Times,* February 26, 1984; Jeff Blyskal, "Dr. Wang's Next Test," *Forbes,* February 15, 1982; Ann Crittenden, "The Hunt Brothers: How They Deal," *The New York Times,* January 6, 1980; Joan Didion, *Slouching Towards Bethlehem* (New York, 1979); "The Doctor's Winning Formula," *Forbes,* January 7, 1980; John Keats, *Howard Hughes* (New York, 1966); Tracy Kidder, *The Soul of a New Machine* (Boston, Mass., 1981); Stanley Klein, "Wang Labs: Head-to-Head Against I.B.M.," *The New York Times,* February 24, 1980; William Rodgers, *Think: A Biography of the Watsons and IBM* (New York, 1969); Alexander L. Taylor III, "Making a Mint Overnight," *Time,* January 23, 1984; "The Guru of Gizmos," *Time,* November 17, 1980.

Small business and entrepreneurs: Amway Corporation, "Hooray for the Yankee Peddler," *The New York Times,* September 29, 1982; Deane Carson, ed., *The Vital Majority: Small Business in the American Economy* (Washington, D.C., 1973); Ira M. Millstein and Salem M. Katsch, *The Limits of Corporate Power: Existing Constraints on the Exercise of Corporate Discretion* (New York, 1981); Joseph D. Phillips, *Little Business in the American Economy* (Urbana, Ill., 1958); Leslie Wayne, "A Pioneer Spirit Sweeps Business," *The New York Times,* March 25, 1984.

The logic of the consumer and global market: James Cook, "The Invisible Enterprise," *Forbes,* September 29, 1980; Jean C. Jester, *An Analysis of Organized Crime's Infiltration of Legitimate Business* (Huntsville, Tex., 1974); Phyllis Rose, "Hers: Shopping and Other Spiritual Adventures in America Today," *The New York Times,* April 12, 1984; Hugh Stephenson, *The Coming Clash: The Impact of the Multinational Corporation on the Nation State* (London, 1972).

Index